£5

C000143262

A HITCH OR TWO IN AFGHANISTAN

A HITCH OR TWO IN AFGHANISTAN

A Journey Behind Russian Lines

NIGEL RYAN

Weidenfeld and Nicolson
London

Patrick Cullinan, my oldest ally

My thanks are due to Miriam Gross, Antony Rouse and
my brother Peter for invaluable advice on the manuscript;
to Diana Phipps and Teddy Millington-Drake for
housing me so generously; and to Sue Pierret and Laura
Sanderson for typing round the clock.

First published in Great Britain by
George Weidenfeld & Nicolson Ltd
91 Clapham High Street, London SW4

ISBN 0 297 78363 7

Printed in Great Britain by
Butler & Tanner Ltd
Frome and London

Contents

Illustrations

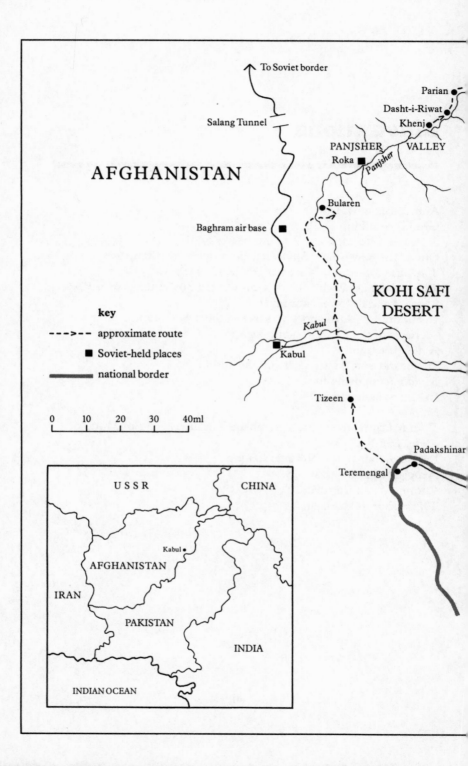

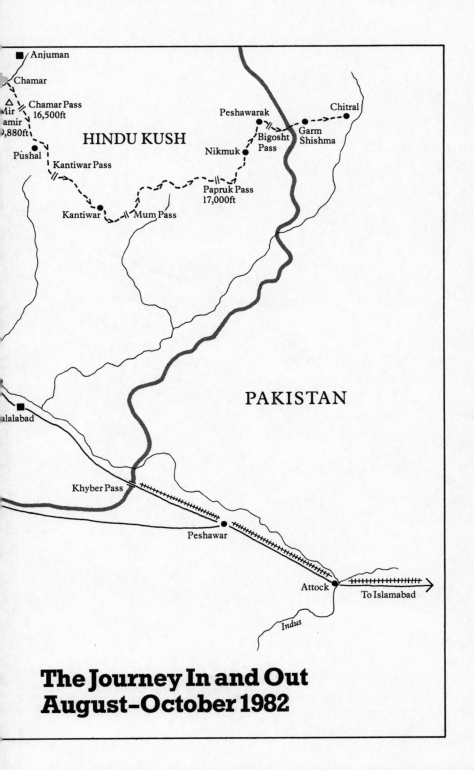

The Journey In and Out
August–October 1982

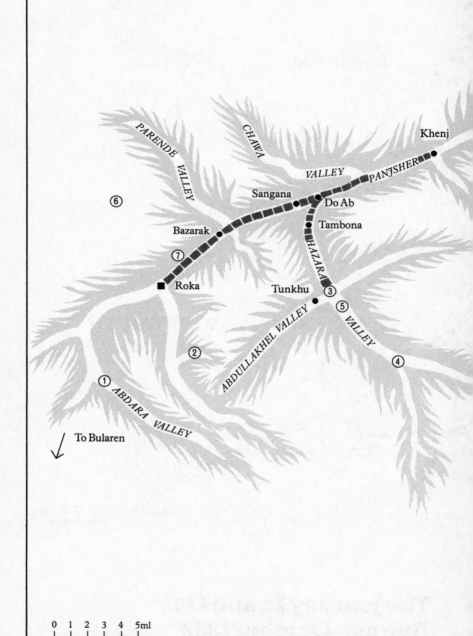

Parian

Dasht-i-Riwat

VALLEY

Astona

key

■ Soviet-held places

■■■ Soviet offensive of Aug./Sept. 1982

1 first night's camp site

2 the bus driver's cave

3 the 'confluence'

4 doctors' house

5 the school and footbridge; bombed 1 Sept.

6 guerrilla 'motorak' base

7 Soviet positions filmed from here

8 prison

The Panjsher Valley

If glory is found in the jaws of a lion
Go tear it out of his mouth.
Your prize will be honour and prestige,
If you fail, die like a man.

Khusan Khan Khattack
Pathan tribal chief, warrior and poet

Foreword

The invasion of Afghanistan in 1979 made the Soviet Union at a stroke into the biggest colonizing power in Asia. (China annexed Tibet twenty years earlier and I have deemed it history.)

During the period of European imperialism there was a constant debate between those who held that colonies were for trading purposes only, and others who believed that the mother country had a deeper Christian civilizing mission. Soviet imperialism permits no such debate. By its nature it sets out first to subvert other nations, then to destroy their culture and religion and to rewrite their history. The Soviet objective in Afghanistan logically must be to obliterate its traditional way of life and produce a new class which will accept and even support the new regime. This may take time. But for the Russians to pull out before they have subdued the resistance and established a regime acceptable to Moscow would be to lose face and authority elsewhere, for a start in Poland. With casualties running as low as 3,000 a year, they can afford to wait.

Talk of inflicting a military defeat on the Red Army must be dismissed as heady propaganda. The inequality of weaponry alone makes anything more ambitious than a stalemate unthinkable. Comparisons with Vietnam contain a central flaw: the resistance in Afghanistan has no equivalent to a North Vietnam to tilt the balance against the invaders. On the other hand, to make the resistance submit, the Soviet Union depends in the last analysis on first making it recognize that the Red Army is invincible. But the Afghans do not know the habit of submission, as invaders through the centuries have discovered. They belong to the rare group of cultures in Asia or Africa who have not succumbed to colonization by the imperialists of the nineteenth century or – so far – to the Soviet brand in the twentieth.

Since 1979 the Afghans have rejected a destiny imposed by tanks;

and increasingly the Soviet intervention is achieving one unintended effect: helping to overcome the chronic inability of the nation's anarchical tribes to unite. Out of resentment against a common enemy, a genuine national feeling is beginning to emerge.

Everything points to the long haul. That bloody prospect might change if the West, in particular the United States, took a renewed interest in Afghanistan. This, in turn, depends on public opinion, which might well demand that our leaders apply their public commitment to the right of a nation to be free to this astonishingly courageous and dignified people living in a country which, though remote, is the size of France.

Sadly, public opinion is limited by public ignorance. This book is a very personal account of a journey of discovery by someone who, shortly before setting out, would have had difficulty in quickly placing a finger on Afghanistan on the map. It is offered in the hope that a few people may be moved, as this traveller was, by the events it relates and the strength of the human spirit that they reveal, to raise their voices and try to prevent the Soviet Union from wiping Afghanistan off their maps once and for all.

Nigel Ryan
London 1983

1. A Hint in the Air of Something Special

It started lightly enough. I only began to appreciate the scale of the undertaking when I set out to buy walking boots.

Until then it had simply been an adventure to conjure with, something to look forward to, with no clear outline. There had been no weighing of arguments, no examination of details, when my friend Sandy Gall invited me to join his expedition. There was a gap in my plans, and this would fill it perfectly; the invitation had seemed to answer itself, with the blinding certainty of poetic inspiration that comes in the night but has then to survive the sobering test of a prosaic London dawn.

I explained to the assistant in Black's Camping & Leisure Shop that it was my first pair of walking boots. He led me to a wall covered from floor to ceiling with shelves of boots. 'What class of terrain had you in mind, sir?'

My troubles were not helped by Sandy's insistence that we should not mention Afghanistan. He was one of television's celebrities and we were dependent on secrecy, for a number of reasons: we did not want competitors to learn of our plans and so steal a march on us; we were anxious not to alert the Pakistani police that we planned an illegal frontier crossing from their country; and most of all we were anxious not to make an appearance on Kabul television as imperialist agents caught in an ambush by a loyal and vigilant Afghan border control.

I looked the assistant in the eye.

'Himalayas.' There was a pause. 'Sort of lower Himalayas.'

The man remained impeccable, but it was becoming clear that the eye fastened upon me was sizing up more than my feet.

'Perhaps climbing boots would be more appropriate, sir?' He pulled a selection from the shelves.

'The KSB2, for walking, running and rock approach. The

Munro has the Norwegian double-welt stitching. At the top end of the scale is the Koflach Ultra with Vibram Gold-block and hinged polyurethene upper.'

'I *was* told walking boots.' I picked a pair at random.

'Now that's the Scarpa Bonzo with special feature half-inch steel shank suitable for crampons and Yeti gaiters. Value for money.'

He laced me into a pair that enclosed the entire lower portion of my legs like a concrete clamp of the kind used in films by the Mafia for disposing of their victims in the Hudson River.

'I leave in three weeks. Will there be time to break these in?'

'Oh yes, sir. There should be no difficulty.'

'What is the normal breaking-in period?'

'Oh, about three to four hundred miles walking should be sufficient, sir.'

It was July and the air waves, filled until then with news from the Falklands, were taken up with the Israeli invasion of the Lebanon. Afghanistan earned scarcely a mention during the lull since the major Soviet offensive in June in the area to which we were heading, details of which were only beginning to filter through to us in London. The Red Army had the biggest fight on its hands since the Second World War, but because it was happening in secret, much of it within the mountain stronghold of the Hindu Kush, the world knew little of it. Again, the secrecy suited us. An hour's television documentary like the one we were planning takes many months to deliver and its topicality is fragile, especially vulnerable to the much faster reporting techniques of international news organizations. Thanks to six months of homework by Sandy, we had a long lead and there were as yet few signs of losing it. That summer our hearts were light and our hopes high.

Our expedition had established its headquarters at Bertorelli's restaurant in Charlotte Street, where in a few sunny weeks over the fried plaice it grew from a plot into a play. It was there that I met the other characters, starting with Charles Morgan, Sandy's chosen cameraman, who had been with him from the outset, and Tom the sound engineer. It was there that my role of producer of the documentary and quartermaster of the expedition gradually became defined.

Alone of the three others I knew Sandy well. He and I had been foreign correspondents together two decades earlier during the civil war in the Congo and had often worked closely in the intervening years, with myself increasingly behind a desk. I knew well, too, his gift of impregnable optimism in all circumstances, tempered with a tendency to cheerful absent-mindedness. He was a man for whom *angst* was, in all senses, a foreign word.

Sandy, the inventor and the driving force behind the expedition, was to be our leader. Six months before, he had made contact with a rebel group in the Panjsher Valley in Afghanistan in the person of Es Haq, a youthful roving liaison officer whom he had invited to London. I had not met Es Haq, who had stayed with Charles Morgan, and who briefly – more briefly than Sandy anticipated – sized up and dismissed as negligible the problem of taking the cumbersome television equipment that we would need into Afghanistan on horseback. We would travel on foot and enough horses and food would be provided – the horses at our expense, and the food along with our keep at the guerrillas'. We had only to await Es Haq's confirmation and he would meet us on 1 August in Pakistan, either in the capital or in Peshawar, where the Afghan guerrillas had their headquarters in exile. The only proviso was to keep our movements secret.

Unlike many cameramen Charles actually enjoyed being abroad, which meant that he was capable of casting his mind into a foreign mould, and would not dream exclusively of fish and chips as we wandered through the Afghan wilderness. Like myself, he was less trusting of the unknown than Sandy, and some of our similarities were to be a cause, as perhaps we both sensed, of the inevitable frictions of the ordeal that lay ahead.

My role was in the duller side of television: in planning and budgeting and organizing. I was the link with Central Television, the company putting up the money and transmitting our programme.

Sandy had once spent a night in Kabul, before the Soviet occupation of Afghanistan in 1979. The rest of us had set neither foot nor eye on Afghan soil. For me Afghanistan was little more than a passing mention in the background of something else I had learned about at school: Alexander the Great, Tamerlane, Ghengis Khan had been through it. The Great Game of intrigue, espionage and undercover war in pursuit of imperial interests had been played there by nineteenth-century Englishmen against their Tsarist Russian adversaries. Thin on my history, I had nonetheless retained

3

ever since my schooldays, by some fluke of memory, the isolated fact that Afghans had once inflicted on a British force perhaps the most devastating defeat in the history of the British army. For the rest, I had stood on elegant Afghan carpets, and admired in old photographs the flamboyant robes of Afghan leaders with fierce moustaches and hawks' faces.

Now, at the very least, my interest was aroused again in a warrior nation whose fighting spirit was still alive enough to have held back the Soviet juggernaut. After three years of war, despite internal wrangling and lack of leadership, and with little sign of effective outside support, the Afghan resistance still appeared able to deny more than 100,000 Soviet troops control of nearly 80 per cent of their country.

We knew little more than this; this and the name of Ahmed Shah Massud, a young guerrilla leader who was already something of a national hero and who was to be our host. It was not much, but it was enough to make us want to go. That summer there was a hint in the air of something special.

If our knowledge of Afghanistan was sketchy, it was compendious beside our collective wisdom on the subject of mountaineering.

'How high are the mountains?' I asked Sandy.

'Up to seven thousand.'

'Feet?'

'Metres, old man.'

'Have you ever been on a mountain?'

'Kilimanjaro, Cairngorms.'

'How high are the Cairngorms?'

'Oh, around four thousand feet. But a hundred feet in the north is like a few thousand further south. Quite a lot of people get killed on the Cairngorms.'

'I've never climbed anything except Snowdon. How high is that?'

'Not the foggiest. Never mind. Just think of it as Snowdon only higher.'

There appeared to be no chink in his armour of confidence. As August approached our roles gradually came into focus in my mind: I was to be a sort of Sancho Panza to Sandy's Don Quixote.

It was Bastille Day. I knew because at the next table in Bertorelli's some French journalists were celebrating. One of them wore a blue

English blazer with brass buttons. The radio news that morning had reported a build-up of Israeli forces near Beirut. A French woman doctor had come out of Afghanistan with a report of food shortages due to the Soviet offensive in June, but the item had been dropped in the lunchtime news.

That afternoon we were due to take our final budget for approval to the offices of Central Television on the opposite side of Charlotte Street. I had been working on Sandy's outline:

'The total is under half the minimum figure for any documentary ever made in recent history,' I told him.

'Excellent,' said Sandy.

'There are no costs for editing. Usually these would be about as much again as filming costs.'

'Now that you come to mention it I thought something was missing.'

'And no fees.'

'Fees?'

'Fees. For you, for example.'

'That's a point. We certainly must put them in.'

'What will we do in Afghanistan if we need to buy extra food?'

'We are guests of the guerrillas. My friend Es Haq assured me when he was here last month that we would have no costs – except the horses – inside Afghanistan.'

'When was he last in Afghanistan?'

'A year ago. But he knows what's going on.'

'Supposing he doesn't?'

'I'm confident he does. Everything is organized.'

'Except the budget.'

'Exactly. That's what we're fixing now.'

'I hope Central will agree when they see our new total.'

'Yes, indeed. Have another glass of wine. I think I'll have a cigar.'

From the next table the voice of the Frenchman in the blazer floated across to us: 'The Americans will have to tell Begin it's not cricket.' But already for us the Middle East was another planet.

'Was Es Haq aware of just how much baggage we would have and how many horses we would need?'

'He's very intelligent. I'm sure he knew what he was talking about.'

'Does he understand television?'

'Now that you mention it, I didn't think he was very interested

5

when he came to the studios. I wonder whether he would have preferred a night-club?'

'But did he take in what you told him about the baggage weighing two or three hundred kilogrammes?'

'Or was it pounds?'

'Kilos.'

'I may have said pounds.'

'But kilos are more than twice pounds.'

'I don't think he would want to be bothered with that sort of detail. We'll just have to get more horses if necessary.'

'That'll cost more money.'

'Absolutely right, old man. Put down more for horses.'

'I think a contingency fund is indicated.'

'For extras? Good idea. I agree.'

And so it was that over the house Chablis we more than doubled our budget. Still puffing serenely at his cigar, Sandy walked with me and Charles Morgan across the street to Central Television where, briskly and concisely, Charles Denton, the Director of Programmes, committed himself to our budget and our project with the words:

'Then that's agreed. I'm off on holiday tomorrow, and your nightmare starts before I get back. So it's good-bye and good luck.'

During the next week our affairs took shape, though by no means always the shape we had intended. I spent the days collating ever increasing lists of supplies, with the help of advice from old Afghan hands. I became immersed in a world hitherto unknown to me: of Karrymats and Kendall Mint Cake, malaria tablets, lice powder, tic repellent, hurricane-proof jackets, thermal underwear, cold water detergents and ice-picks. I became an expert on blisters and I learned that the best way to deal with them was to place the plaster without lint straight on the skin before it breaks and to wear boots tight.

As the list grew, so did my awareness of the depth of our ignorance: each item appeared to be as essential as it was incomprehensible, and I had no means of judging what was dispensable. We knew that there were two routes into Afghanistan, but not which we would be taking. The Panjsher Valley lies fifty miles to the north-east of Kabul. There was the so-called northern route through the mountains of Nuristan which would be closed in winter. The longer southern route began at a point in Pakistan directly below Kabul and ran up through the Kohi Safi Desert, leaving Kabul on the left and entering the Valley near the river mouth. The northern route would take us over a series of passes as high as Mont Blanc, well above the snow-line; the southern in August would be a Sahara. Either way was a trek of about two weeks. We were to be informed of the decision on the route only at the last minute, chiefly for reasons of security; but we had to be prepared to go in by one and out by the other, and so, in any event, be equipped for both. All in all, it was rapidly becoming clear to me that we had grossly underestimated our budget for personal equipment.

'Contingency fund, old man,' said Sandy.

'But that's for emergencies.'

'Quite right. Then we must cut back. Too much clobber. Get rid of the soup.'

Soup, to supplement our diet, was the suggestion of Sandy's French expert, Jean-José Puig, who knew Afghanistan well and who was to accompany us as guide and interpreter. Puig was a representative of one of the French voluntary aid organizations supporting the resistance. We had calculated that each packet of soup would feed four, but on Jean-José's advice we would need to share it with another half-dozen guides and bearers as well. Estimating our stay in Afghanistan at two months, by my arithmetic we would need perhaps 150 packets. Then there were the dried raisins. The French doctor who had reported food shortages had told Sandy that she always carried a packet of dried raisins for the march. Obediently I factored in sixty packets, one for each of us for every two days of the journey in and out.

So our problem was as much one of bulk as of money. Excluding Jean-José, who was to bring his own supplies, we had allowed for one kitbag and one back-pack each for personal equipment, in addition to the television gear. The signs were growing that our calculations were adrift, but just how far adrift I did not realize until the question of lavatory paper came up. Unused as I was to making estimates on the bulk use of household commodities, I consulted my cleaning lady, who undertook to make the purchase on my behalf.

At the end of the week Sandy telephoned from Rye Golf Course. He was in high spirits.

'I have a couple of essential new items. I played golf with a man today who said the Japanese make a powdered whisky. I'm told it's excellent.'

'But drink is banned by law and religion.'

'True. But this is powder. Anyway let's try it. The other item is black underwear.'

'Does your golfing partner wear black underwear?'

'This is serious. I lunched with Nick Downie. I'll explain over a drink.' I thought I heard him add: 'It's to do with the lice.'

The name of Nick Downie, a former SAS officer turned camera-man, was well known to me. He had been to Afghanistan twice to make television programmes and we had good reason to respect his advice. His first film, transmitted just before the Soviet invasion, had depicted hopeless disarray among the resistance groups opposed to the tottering pro-communist regime. His second, shot with extraordinary disregard for his own safety, showed a pitched battle between rival guerrilla forces, while Soviet helicopters flew unconcerned overhead. Above all, he knew about surviving, which at that moment most powerfully concentrated our minds. I waited with interest to learn of the role that black underwear was to play.

I had still to meet Tom Murphy, the fourth permanent member of our expedition. (Jean-José was only to be with us long enough to effect the introduction to Massud inside Afghanistan.) The four of us were due to lunch at Bertorelli's the next day to review our progress.

A part of Tom's duties was to maintain the complicated new technical equipment that we were taking with us. Traditionally, television documentaries had been shot with cine cameras, and the film was sent home to be developed and edited. Now a new system, using a portable video tape recorder, was being used increasingly. (It is known as ENG, for Electronic News Gathering. Since the system uses video tape and not film, the terms 'to film' and 'film' are technically incorrect. Both are used for the sake of clarity.) This had the great advantage over film that it could be replayed imme-diately, so that a documentary team could see its day's work on the spot and, if need be, re-shoot or supplement it on the next. More-over, with video tape we would be able to show our material to our Afghan hosts, many of whom would never have seen television. The disadvantages of the new system were its extra weight and, being new, it was relatively untried.

I was the one who had the most misgivings about adding not just to our costs but to our uncertainties as well. The deciding factor, however, was Charles Denton, who dealt with the question with his customary despatch.

'It has to come. Let's do it first.'

Suppressing my doubts, I nonetheless looked forward next day to reassurance from the key figure, Tom Murphy, who had recently completed a technical course on the new equipment.

'Unfortunately,' said Sandy when we met in my flat that evening, 'there is a small problem. The sound recordist has gone to Beirut. But there is some good news. I have a cable from my friend Es Haq to say that we're expected. So the trip is on for Sunday week.'

'I take it the sound recordist will be back in time?'

'Well, that's it.'

'That's what?'

'He might not be. He's working with an American news network and it looks as if the Israelis are going into Beirut. We may have to get a new sound man.'

'But how can he possibly be ready in time? For a start, he will never break in his boots.'

'Oh, I don't know. Timberlands break in quickly.'

'Timberlands?'

'The boots you need.'

I showed him mine.

'What are those for?'

'Afghanistan.'

'Don't be ridiculous. I said walking boots, not climbing boots.'

'You never said Timberlands.'

'Didn't I? I must have forgotten. But those are too heavy. You can't walk in them. Are they waterproof?'

'The man said all-purpose. And they take Yeti gaiters.'

'What are Yeti gaiters?'

'I didn't like to ask. I think we were supposed to know.'

'Ridiculous. Anyway they must be waterproof. There are rivers to ford.'

'You said mountains.'

'Mountains and rivers. You'll have to get Timberlands.'

The loss of the sound recordist would be a body blow. We agreed on a time limit of the following Monday – six days before our date of departure – to find a replacement; failing that, we would have to cancel the whole project. We could not delay our trip, because it was timed to end just before the winter snows would block our departure route. Tom was Charles's choice: the relationship between cameraman and sound recordist is umbilical at all times, both in technical and in human terms; on a venture of this kind its failure would be terminal.

Worse was to come.

'Nick Downie seemed dubious about our using ENG,' Sandy said. 'The camera is too heavy to carry all the time and he thinks Charles's idea of a bearer with a horse won't work, because horses and humans travel at different speeds and tend to meet up only at night. He also said that if the equipment is fragile it may be damaged by water.'

We resolved to consult Charles about the possibility of reverting to film, but in our hearts we knew it was too late. All depended now on Tom's return, or the miraculous discovery of a replacement who was fit (and therefore probably young), trained in electronic equipment, ready to face danger, congenial and available to leave in a week.

'I'm sure all will be well. I played very well at Rye today and I am in the semi-final of our competition.'

Talk of golf jogged my memory.

'What about the black underwear?'

'Ah yes,' said Sandy. 'It seems that black underwear shows up the lice better if you're looking for them.'

'Where do you buy men's black underwear?'

'That's your job. Oh, and by the way, Downie also said that if you are looking for fleas and find lice, don't stop looking. It's perfectly possible to have both at the same time. And now,' he went on, 'how about the supplies? Can we get everything into one kitbag each?'

'Have you ever seen sixty-four rolls of loo paper, sixty packets of raisins and a hundred and sixty packets of soup in one place? They fill a room, not a kitbag.' I showed him.

'We must cut back, old man.'

'We can cut back on loo paper, but you heard the French doctor's report about food shortages.'

'We'll have to live off the land. I shall be bringing one rucksack for myself and nothing more. Personally,' he added, 'I intend to live like an Afghan.'

It was impossible to have a row with this man.

'If we have the wrong equipment, and there is no one able to maintain it, and if we need more food and can't carry it and will starve without it, then I would say it's unprofessional to go ahead with the project.'

'I wouldn't put it quite that way, old man. We always knew there would be difficulties. I refuse to panic. I am confident.'

He was right, of course, about the difficulties, and his determination to override them was contagious. That week, not for the last time, it was little more than Sandy's confidence that held us together.

Quite apart from uncertainties about our organization, there were the hazards of the trip itself: the unknown guerrillas in whose hands we would be; the form another Russian offensive might take; and the risk of arrest by Pakistani police. Our equipment had to be both shock-proofed and waterproofed. One mule's slip on the way in and the camera would be out of action, the whole venture aborted and a large capital investment lost. My mind was plagued by two graphic descriptions: one in *A Short Walk in the Hindu Kush* by Eric Newby, of a horse bearing all his personal belongings rolling in an Afghan river; and another by Freya Stark in *The Minaret of Djam*, concerning the predilection of Afghan bridges for 'expiring with a lorry or a mule train in their embrace'. We had to be ready to negotiate Sahara-like desert or mountain passes in sub-zero temperatures; we had to treat with temperamental horses and famously self-willed bearers. By the week-end I was unsure whether our plot was turning into comedy or tragedy.

In the afternoon of the Sunday the telephone rang. It was Sandy's wife, Eleanor.

'I've telephoned several sound recordists.'

'Where's Sandy?'

'Playing golf. It's the final. It's an important day.'

'It is indeed. If we don't have a sound recordist by tomorrow night we'll have to cancel the project.'

'Yes. He's sure we will find one. One nearly accepted. He was quite excited until I told him there was a two-week walk each way.'

'Extraordinary how unenergetic young people seem to be.'

'This one was sixty-three.'

'What about the others?'

'One wanted to be paid overtime by the hour rather than take a lump sum. I didn't think you'd want that. It might work out rather expensive over three months.'

The telephone rang again, this time from Rye.

'I have excellent news.'

'Is Tom back?'

'No. I have won the Winter Competition at Rye.'

'Congratulations. But it's July.'

'Never mind. Things take time to organize. The sound recordist will be all right. I went round in a gross seventy-two. I'm very confident.'

'You were born confident. I was born anxious. Now I'm very anxious.'

'I always find there is no point in being anxious. It solves nothing. I usually have a whisky and soda and forget it.'

A few minutes later he rang back, this time to tell me that the American television network that had hired Tom Murphy had agreed to release him, provided they could find a replacement.

Next morning there was another good omen. Opening my cupboard to find a resting place for some of the rejected lavatory paper, I came across a pair of forgotten and unworn boots that I had bought three years before as the other half of a New York 'Toofer' ('Two for the Price of One') sale, along with a pair of shoes I had wanted. On their dusty but brand-new soles was embossed the word TIMBERLAND.

At Charles Morgan's offices we discovered a new problem. It was explained to us that the Pakistani customs might require a deposit equivalent to one and a half times the value of our television equipment – perhaps £60,000 in all – in order to discourage us from illegally selling it in Pakistan without paying import duty. Since it was our intention to risk its total loss anyway inside Afghanistan (a fact which we could not divulge to the Pakistanis), there was a real and uninsurable risk to any money we put up.

A choice open to us was to use a personal friendship between Sandy Gall and the Pakistani ruler, General Zia-ul-Haq. But the local situation was studded with complexities hard for the layman to grasp, especially at this distance.

Piece by piece we tried to put them together. Itself a group of volatile and disparate Moslem tribes held together in fragile equilibrium by an authoritarian religion and an autocratic military regime, Pakistan had always to be conscious of any threat to its stability.

The tide of Afghan war refugees flowing into Pakistani camps was approaching the three million mark, and the lessons of Lebanon and Jordan were particularly painful and clear that summer. Both countries had been willing hosts at first to the Palestine refugees, who had arrived destitute and then threatened their security. The war next door to Pakistan could be feeding a cuckoo in Zia's nest. Meanwhile the Soviet Union accused him of harbouring the rebels, as North Vietnam had harboured the Vietcong, providing them with training camps and shelter. There was talk in the air of a Soviet offer to withdraw from Afghanistan if first Pakistan would seal the border. Zia was a leader of the Moslem world. Publicly his posture was for Islam and against the infidel invader of a brother Moslem nation. But for internal reasons the Soviet proposal must have had its attractions.

There was something else Pakistan had always to bear in mind as well. After Vietnam the United States had lost the taste for military solutions. In renouncing foreign adventures it had disturbed the balance of power and created a vacuum, which the Soviets had promptly exploited in Afghanistan, calculating that they could act with impunity. And after America's experiences with a fundamentalist Moslem regime in Iran, American public opinion could not be counted on to become very indignant over the fate of a Moslem regime such as the one ousted in Afghanistan, nor another in Pakistan: the lack of media interest in Afghanistan had already shown that.

Without whole-hearted American support, Zia had to reckon with a colossus on each of his three main borders. To the east, India had recently inflicted a decisive and humiliating military defeat on Pakistan which had led to the loss of its eastern territory, now Bangladesh; and there always lurked in Pakistani minds the suspicion that its neighbour thought Pakistan was rightfully a part of India. To the north, China was an unpredictable and improbable tactical ally, drawn in, with the assistance of the United States, to a larger world game of chess against the Soviet Union. Then there was the Soviet Union itself, now next door in Afghanistan, impatient at Pakistan's support for the guerrillas and rumbling with warnings.

Long before the Soviet regime, Tsarist Russians had been ob-

sessed with their national borders. If it was unfashionable to believe that the Soviet designs any longer extended to the warm sea
ports of the Indian Ocean on the grounds that they had lost their
strategic value, nobody disputed that the Soviet Union set special store by having friendly neighbours. Afghanistan was a neighbour and the Russians would resent any attempt to turn it against
them.

For all these reasons, however much Pakistan might wish an end
to the Soviet presence in Afghanistan, it made good sense for its
government to act discreetly.

Zia was vulnerable at home; and, in the larger context of the
contest between the big powers, a mere pawn. To avoid being
sacrificed for a gain on the other side of the board, pawns have to
move with care. It was our information that in general a blind eye
was turned to the clandestine activities on Pakistan's western border, but from time to time a journalist picked up by border patrols
was turned back and even imprisoned, if only for show. An
approach to the President could embarrass him, and invite a refusal
which it would be impossible to ignore.

Sitting in Charles Morgan's offices that morning we had no other
means to test these deep and, to us, little known waters, and we
decided to devise a contingency cover story for the Pakistan im-
migration authorities that we were planning to make a documentary
film to encourage tourism in the mountain regions of Pakistan. At
Sandy's suggestion we settled on the region of Swat – legendary,
he said, as a beauty spot. My only knowledge of it was from a
Nonsense Rhyme by Edward Lear about the Akond of Swat that I
learned in childhood.

A telephone conversation that had begun behind us as we debated
came to an end.

'Tom's at Heathrow.'

'Tom Murphy?'

Our spirits soared once more.

'How is he?' I asked.

'Tom?'

'Tom.'

'Tom's fine.'

'But is he shell-shocked? Has he broken anything? Can we count
on him?'

'Oh, he'll be fine. He's off to take a driving test.'

And, indeed, Tom was fine. At Bertorelli's there appeared a powerfully built twenty-three year old, glowing with good health and cheerful directness. We asked him how he had slept after his adventures.

'Like a log.'

The accent was Hackney Irish. He said he had failed his driving test, and ate an enormous lunch. With under a week to go we set about briefing him on the ordeal ahead, the risks to limb, life and camera equipment. We explained the especial danger to the camera from the many rivers liable to floods. Waterproofing, however carefully doubled and re-doubled it might be, always left a margin of uncertainty.

'Oh, no problem,' said Tom. 'I've bought a raft, six pounds fifty, in the toy department at Woolworth's. Inflatable. It has a tow line.'

He made it sound as simple as the wheel. His resourceful demeanour extended equally to the problem of lice.

'Oh, no problem. I had them as a child. They itch a bit, but you just think of something else.'

His confidence was as infectious as it was welcome. During the preceding weeks I had increasingly had the feeling that we were like partially trained astronauts about to be launched into space. Sandy's professional credentials as a television correspondent were impeccable; Charles was a highly competent cameraman. But if we were all professionals in our own craft, we were dangerous amateurs in explorers' terms. Moreover, each fragile link in the technical chain was critical. If the new portable generator – a small petrol engine that made the electricity to charge our batteries – broke down inside Afghanistan, we would lose all: an investment of £80,000, three months of our lives, and our high hopes.

'No problem. I took it to pieces this morning,' said Tom. 'And put it together again. It works fine.'

Alone of the four I was making a journey that was not really necessary for the television programme and, indeed, my reason for going was only in part as its money minder. I was planning to write a book as well. For half my life I had been professionally involved, at various levels, with major news reporting institutions. Now I had the opportunity to test for myself what it would be like to make my own record of an event unfettered by the disciplines of news or television's constraints of format, time or budget. No expectations existed outside my own head. In so far as the phrase had meaning, I was a free man.

Not that I had resented the formal rules and informal conventions of professional reporting. I had long conspired with, and sincerely subscribed to, the attempts to exclude bias, to monitor and in some measure control the intrusion of opinion on fact. A mass audience expects its information to be presented to it fairly – whatever that might mean – as a basis for drawing its own conclusion, and I had long thrived on the fragile theology of balance and impartiality.

Moreover, as a means of communicating information, even on highly controversial matters, television could boast its successes; and when it hit home its impact was unmatched. It was through television that the Czech resistance to the Russians in 1968 caught the imagination of the world. It was television news that could claim to have turned middle America's face against war, by daily revealing a Vietnam that bore no resemblance to the myth of John Wayne movies – an unglamorous, usually inglorious and humanly diminishing affair. It was television that, during Watergate, brought Richard Nixon to us with his words telling one story, while his face, in close-up, was telling another.

Nonetheless, I had often felt intellectually bruised by the clumsy imprecision of the powerful but uneven machinery of reporting for which the institutional safeguards and guidelines, enshrined in statutes, provided the crudest of highway codes. I had become impatient with the quirks peculiar to television, in particular its way of leaving vivid but highly selective and sometimes irrelevant impressions on the mind. For every hit there are a dozen misses. All too often television edits itself, and not in a way intended: an interview conducted with a mountain in the background is liable to leave only an impression of the mountain. I was regularly exasperated by television's failure to translate on to the screen the simplest abstract idea: after all, what does inflation *look* like?

Television does not deal comfortably in nuances, and it is nuances which so often contain the heart and essential flavour of a situation. The camera needs always to be in focus: truth often is not.

But perhaps of all television's defects, communication of doubt is the most serious. Theologians tell us that by doubting we are led to enquiry, and from enquiry we perceive the truth. Yet to share feelings of doubt with a television audience is to commit professional hara-kiri. Nothing could do more to ensure the flick of the knob that consigns a programme to oblivion than a correspondent standing up before the camera to say: 'I don't know what to make of this.' And yet in truth that is more often the case than the honest reporter would care to admit.

If doubt is a virtue for the theologian, a starting point for intellectual enquiry, it is a cardinal sin in the person of action: a battle is not won by a soldier questioning orders. As a television executive perhaps I had stood too long between these two extremes: I had too often been caught by a programme deadline or a budget limit with a question that, far from answered, was not even adequately formulated. And yet the only hope of holding the attention of ordinary viewers, already muddled enough by their own lives, is to communicate simply and with clarity. To do this without distorting the facts requires quite exceptional skills, all too rarely found.

But it was not so much a falling out with television that motivated me to return to the written word as a desire for change. I knew, perhaps too well, what was expected of us. Even before we had left London I felt I knew what our documentary on Afghanistan might look like; it was fortunate that the others did not share my sense of staleness.

And then there were my own quirks. In my earliest days as a journalist I had become aware of a wayward curiosity which had little or nothing to do with the business of reporting information. Once in 1961, I had attended a press briefing for perhaps a thousand journalists all over the world, one of whom was Randolph Churchill (then working for the *Evening Standard*), which was staged as a major set piece event in the Opera House at Vienna. It was the first encounter between Nikita Khrushchev and John Kennedy, and in later years historians were to speculate that it was Khrushchev's unflattering assessment of Kennedy at this encounter that led him to make the mistakes of the Cuban missile crisis a year later. But at the time we were to know none of this. On the stroke of the appointed hour the doors of the great theatre were closed with Germanic precision, and first the American and then the Russian briefing officers read out their arid communiqués studded with clichés and statutory shafts against each other. The occasion promised to be as unmemorable as the communiqués, but for one incident. While the Russian (who had an artificial leg) was in the middle of his reading, a door burst open and there was an ear-splitting bellow. Framed in one of the entrances, face purple, contorted with an abandoned fury that called to mind a baby deprived of its bottle, stood Randolph Churchill. Clearly he had arrived late for the briefing; clearly, too, the doorman, standing beside him, had his instructions. The outcome was in no doubt. Still shouting incoherently and gesticulating, Churchill made his way to a seat in the auditorium. A minute later the incident was over, and the Russian resumed his wooden tirade. More than twenty years later as I look back on the incident, I remember nothing of the communiqué. All that remains alive in my memory is a lingering curiosity as to what the doorman told his wife when he got home that evening.

And so, at the customs I could declare not my television camera, but my own personal brand of bias. The aim of my colleagues was to report an event as objectively as they could. Mine was not: it was to record an experience – my experience. For instruments they would have the television camera's eye, with its total recall and its partial vision, whose power no pen could match. I would have the human eye, with its most imperfect recall, but much broader vision. I would be free to indulge my wayward interest in details seemingly of little or no significance; the details that catch the tail of the human eye and remain in the memory, waiting to find their place in an overall pattern. I could bring with me my doubts and quandaries; I would be free to embrace rather than eliminate subjective impressions, deal in flavour as well as content. I would be free to record, if I wished, how the doorman felt. I would write from the heart; and I would be judged by the intuitive test of whether what I wrote rang true or false.

2. A Change of Focus

Somewhere in the sky over Copenhagen a man's voice said beside us: 'You are Sandy Gall.' It was a statement, not a question.

It was inevitable, I suppose, although we had hoped it would not happen. The aeroplane was filled with Pakistanis; and there was always a chance that they had not watched British television. But it was not to be.

The voice was loud and authoritative. It went on: 'Are you coming to give us television coverage?' By now several other passengers were listening with interest.

'No. Just holidaying mainly. A little work, too,' said Sandy.

'What is the work? Trouble-shooting? I think you are a trouble-shooter. I have seen your face in Vietnam and' – the stranger seemed to relish his command of English slang – 'other trouble spots. Are you going', he continued, 'to Afghanistan? That is a trouble spot.'

There was nothing for it but to adopt our contingency plan.

'We are going', said Sandy, 'to make a film about tourist places in Pakistan. In particular, Swat.'

'And I', said the man, 'am the Ruler of Swat.'

Not given by nature to shift uncomfortably in his seat, Sandy squared his jaw and said: 'Ah.' Then, weaving another tangle into the web of deceit: 'We'll be going up there in a while. But first we will be taking a rest.'

'Where will you rest? Swat is a place to rest.'

'We thought we would see Rawalpindi first.'

'Where are you staying in Rawalpindi? I will telephone you tomorrow.'

'Yes,' said Sandy; and, nudging me: 'I think I'd like some champagne.' We had bought two bottles with us, for the airline was dry;

19

but at that moment the seat belt sign was turned on. We were coming into refuel at Copenhagen.

It was when we had taken off again, after the short stop in a limbo of tarmac, that the Ruler really set to work. He produced photographs from his wallet and passed them round: in one he stood with Leonid Brezhnev; in another an attractive woman, whom he identified as his wife, sat in a group with Prince Philip; and, as if to clinch the matter of credentials, the third showed his wife again, and in the background the crowds outside Buckingham Palace as seen from *inside* the palace.

'Very nice family, your royal family. Do you know them well?' he asked Sandy.

'Not really.'

'You should. And now let us discuss your visit.'

Seeking at any price to steer the conversation away from ourselves, I asked the first question that came to mind: who was the Akond of Swat? The Ruler explained that the Akond had been a spiritual as well as a political ruler, and that subsequently the responsibilities had been split. His own grandfather was the last of the line.

'Why do you ask?'

I cannot recall who, but someone said to me: 'You know a poem about him, don't you?'

The Ruler missed nothing. 'I have heard of it. I am told it is a very good poem by a famous English poet. Tell it to me.'

'I only know a bit.' But there was no going back. Wretchedly, I repeated the Edward Lear jingle:

> Who or why or which or what
> Is the Akond of Swat?
> Is he thin or is he fat,
> The Akond of Swat?

'That's all I know. It's very silly really. I learned it as a child. It's a sort of nonsense nursery rhyme.'

'Oh, I don't think so. I think it is a very good poem,' said the Ruler solemnly.

At about that moment the champagne cork that I had been twisting flew off with a report like a pistol shot: the bottle had been heating up slowly, and perhaps the change of pressure had something to do with it. About a third of the contents sprayed over all our neighbours. Immediately the Ruler seemed to withdraw and fade into the background. From his seat in front Jean-José Puig, our guide and interpreter, turned round and said something, but his voice was drowned in the aeroplane's engines. He came and leaned over Sandy, who turned to me and bellowed: 'He says we must be discreet. We will offend the Moslem passengers. Hide the bottle.'

'How?'

'Pour it out.'

Hastily we slopped its remaining contents into our orange juice glasses, conscious of frozenly averted gazes around us. But if inelegant, at least our gaffe bought a reprieve from the attention of the Ruler, who made no further attempt to pursue the conversation.

Jean-José had flown from Paris to London to join us for the onward flight. He was the representative of Friends of Afghanistan, one of many French voluntary organizations with interest in Afghanistan. I had lunched with him in London, and it was a source of shame to me to learn how much more, especially in medical aid, was being done by young French volunteers than by British ones. France had stronger, though much newer, cultural ties with Afghanistan, going back to a visit to Paris earlier in the century by the last Afghan monarch, who had given archaeological concessions to the French government, whereupon a Lycée Français had been opened in Kabul.

Somehow I had expected Jean-José to be a robust figure with the seasoned complexion and tell-tale stride of the long-distance walker. I had been heartened to find on my doorstep earlier that day a man of even slighter build than my own, with pale green cheeks, who walked with a stooped shuffle and smoked heavily. Jean-José spoke into a grizzled beard in low conspirator's tones, and we learned to encourage him where possible to speak his own language, since in any case it required a considerable command of French to decipher his English. Sandy had engaged his services on the strength of his familiarity with Afghanistan, and in particular the Panjsher which he had last visited a year before. He carried with him a fishing-rod, which he told us he had used on a fishing honeymoon in northern Afghanistan, and he contrived to carry it as if it were at the very least a clandestine radio aerial.

He brought us the news that we would be travelling in by the hot southern route, since, according to information he had received in

Paris the night before, the Russians had captured a key point astride the northern route. It was a consolation to reflect that in the desert Jean-José's fishing-rod would be as out of place as our thermal underwear. 'However,' he added, lowering his voice to a barely audible grating sound, 'after I have introduced you to the Panjsher I am going elsewhere. And there I shall indeed be fishing.'

'You mean, fishing?'

'Fishing.'

And there it was politely left, with myself none the wiser.

Jean-José's brief inspection of my bags had lightened our load of a foam rubber groundsheet, light but bulky, because he claimed that one rapidly became used to sleeping on rock; a picnic stool, which he dismissed without comment; and a number of individual small pots and pans bought in a camping shop on the grounds that one never ate alone in Afghanistan, since it was a rule of etiquette that food was always shared with passing strangers. I had concealed from him a frivolity in the shape of a Dundee cake in a tin, and rejected without submitting it a plastic all-purpose ice-pick that a mountaineering friend had advised. I was to remember it later. The load was, however, increased by his suggestion of boiled sweets: sixty packets, all bought that Sunday morning, and crammed with the raisins into the soup bag, which proved so heavy that when, in a fury at the quantity of our luggage, Sandy picked it up at London Airport, he ripped off the handles.

In the night, as our plane crept along the edge of the Soviet Union's borders, I awoke from a light doze to see that our interpreter was reading *Teach Yourself Farsi*, and the book was opened at page three. I turned to draw Sandy's attention to this unpromising intelligence, but Sandy was snoring benignly.

I reviewed the blur of the past few days with only a few details in focus here and there. On the advice of a friend who had been to India I had pursued from chemist to chemist, and finally hunted down, Doctor Collis Browne's Elixir for Upset Stomachs. My doctor had given me medicines for malaria and dysentery, injections against hepatitis, polio, yellow fever and cholera, and salt tablets for heat exhaustion (the modern version of sun stroke). He had given me instructions which I did not understand for treating light bullet wounds and burns, and smiled bleakly at my joke about a cure for vertigo and hypochondria. Faced at the last minute with what seemed to be a lorry load of indispensable supplies and too few kitbags to put them in, I had crept out of my house in the small hours of the morning and stolen two builders' bags filled with rubble from a site nearby; and finally I had brought not one but eight bags to the airport. With the television equipment we had weighed in at 284 kilogrammes. Eleanor Gall had brought our last-minute medical supplies from her doctor brother. They were St Christopher medals: 'He says they'll be as effective as anything else you've got.'

As the airliner with our preposterous load began to descend, I caught the first glimpse of the bare knees of mountains in the daylight, then the grey-green of Rawalpindi, bullocks and a muddy river. As a sleeper turning over to dream new dreams, letting new images emerge and old ones sink into the unconscious, I felt the sense of adventure return to chase away the fears of the night.

The hot damp Asian morning flooded the aeroplane as soon as the door swung open. Almost immediately we forgot the European priorities of elegance, and wondered if the jackets of our suits would soak through before we reached our hotel. The change of focus was beginning.

First to disembark were the Ruler and his wife: we were held back until they had been swept away in a chauffeur-driven limousine, and then led on foot to the International building, where pandemonium appeared to have broken out. 'Third World travel,' said a first-class passenger. I glimpsed the familiar faces of the Ruler and his wife for a moment, like survivors of a shipwreck swimming momentarily into view on the swell of human bodies, fighting their way like everyone else to the grille marked Health Inspector.

In an eddy of arms and legs, a face appeared: 'I am Elias of Pakistan International Airways. Welcome to Pakistan.'

And to Elias we clung, as to a lifeboat. I thought of his namesake Profit Ileas, the tiny chapel on a hill of the Greek island to which I had hiked every day that June, not for prayer (its door was Lubianka-shut against vandals), but for exercise in preparation for the great walk ahead. Elijah would perhaps protect us after all, though I still had hopes of St Christopher, on a spare bootlace round my neck, despite the inconvenient Vatican pronouncement that he probably never existed.

23

'There is a regular shimozzle today,' said our new Elias. 'A wing of Karachi airport has fallen in and planes are being diverted to us. I have a telex from London to say that you may have some extra bags.'

'About thirty-six.'

'And you have the necessary documentation to facilitate their release?'

We told him.

'Then we must go and telephone to the Ministry to apply for the necessary clearance. All you will have to do is pay the deposit of the value of your equipment and certify that you are making a tourist film in collaboration with the Ministry, giving details of where you will be going in Pakistan. Then they will give authorization.'

He added, seizing his second chance: 'There is no need for a shimozzle.' I wondered if he realized that he was using a Yiddish word.

He turned to consult a senior-looking customs officer, who ordered us to wait, and, taking Sandy with him, disappeared into the crowd.

Meanwhile, the crowd itself was slowly forming into a series of crossing lines, like trains simultaneously negotiating multiple points, before rushing two uniformed officials. Tom and Charles plunged into the flotsam and jetsam of baggage being washed up on the tarmac. As the human tide slowly ebbed through the customs, the Europeans (I could not help noticing) seemed to pass for the most part unchallenged, with heads down, saying 'tourist' as they went.

Gradually a solitary island of bags grew in the sun outside the customs building. Charles and Tom began loading them on to three enormous barrows, while I began fawning on an influential-looking youth with flowered silk shirt and Gucci belt who declared himself to be the son-in-law of the late President, Ayub Khan; he had come to meet the Ruler of Swat and was confident that for us there need be no problem. Had I, he enquired knowingly, taken the necessary precautions? Uneasily I fingered the sweaty pound notes concealed in my passport, ready to be corrupt, but with all the public-school Englishman's ineptness àt perpetrating dishonesty on a small scale.

Finally Tom and Charles were ready with the baggage. As if inspired by a single impulse, we took one barrow-load each and, crying 'tourist!', heaved the great weight unchallenged past the twin Cerberuses and into the heart of the crowd beyond the barrier. It was all over before the senior customs official had time to take in what was happening.

When Sandy and Elias returned, we told them that we had solved the problem by taking the law into our own hands. Elias at once entered into the spirit of the battle, which to him was not one of right and wrong, but of wits. He told us to wait at a spot out of sight of the barrier, where he arranged for a minibus to meet us. Our equipment filled its benches and racks, inside as well as on the roof-top. There was no time to check for anything missing.

The traffic moved at snail's pace along the uncertain dusty surface as our bus threaded its way among the tired Morris Minor taxis and past the bullock carts. Near our destination, as though suddenly remembering its capital status, the city made a half-hearted effort to be modern, but somehow only succeeded in losing all vestige of identity in a street of mediocre concrete buildings. We passed the grandest hotel, with galleries of carpet shops ready to take American Express, and turning a corner arrived at our own. It was agreeably down-at-heel in appearance, laid out in colonial barrack style; its wooden bungalows with rows of doors opening on to a verandah, designed not to impress the eye but to keep off the sun. Outside my room two men were watching a third putting the finishing Aldershot touch of whitewash to some flower pots lined up in muster parade. Better a borrowed identity, perhaps, than none at all.

It was only when attentive hands laid out all our bags on the floor of Tom's room that we noticed that the one with its handles torn off was missing. We had lost the soup.

At the reception desk the switchboard operator told us that he would try to get us a line to London 'within an hour, or perhaps two days'. We clambered in an old Morris taxi with a sticker printed DO NOT DISTRUB affixed to its back window, and set off for a rendezvous with our Afghan hosts at a doctor's house.

Our route took us past the new courthouse where Ali Bhutto, the Prime Minister overthrown by General Zia, was tried before being hanged for murder. I could just remember Bhutto as a fellow undergraduate at Oxford. Even in a nation with so violent and volatile a recent history, judicial execution seemed a chillingly brutal affair.

At the doctor's, a young man led us into a large waiting-room with cushioned benches against one wall, a brass chandelier, and a picture of the Toe of the Prophet. Rising to greet us were three Afghans in chocolate brown robes, white scarves and black beards: all of them startlingly youthful in appearance, and all of them smiling. It was my first encounter with an Afghan, and I was struck at once by an aura of physical dignity. It was a little like being introduced to three of the twelve apostles.

The leader of the group stepped forward to greet Jean-José with an embrace, then Sandy and Charles. Introducing himself to Tom and myself as Es Haq, he said: 'Welcome to Afghanistan. Welcome to the Panjsher.' As grandly as any medieval potentate, he waved us to sit down.

The servant brought in two trays, one with green and one with black tea, and placed them on tables beside us. The sugar was in a blue plastic bowl, but it might have been imperial silver for the gesture with which it was offered to us.

My first and, as I look back, most enduring impression of our Afghan hosts was of grandness – grandness of manner rather than of matter. It is often said that the hallmark of the Victorian English-man was an air of conscious superiority, and one of the most widespread exports of colonial days the inferiority complex. It was easy to see that any such phenomenon had bypassed Afghanistan. These were people who had never been part of anyone's colony. Indeed the boot seemed to be on the other foot. Throughout our contact with Afghans I experienced the sense of being treated with the condescending courtesy of a securely based and unquestionably superior race according a rare privilege to one who, after all, was no more than an infidel. Here in a modest doctor's waiting-room in the suburb of a foreign city, I sensed that I was making contact with a people who, whatever catastrophes had overtaken them, had still not lost their personal glory. Whatever else lay ahead to test and try us, here was a hint of style.

In English that was both fluent and elegant, Es Haq outlined our programme. We were to wait in Rawalpindi where our presence would not attract attention, while he went ahead that evening to Peshawar with Jean-José to make the final arrangements. As soon as a date was set, Jean-José would summon us by telephone. Finally, and most welcome of all in view of the apparent level of Jean-José's Farsi, came the news that Es Haq hoped to lead our convoy into the Panjsher personally.

★   ★   ★

Islamabad is a new political capital laid out on a grid of squares with a logical system of numbering for both streets and houses that is not, however, uniformly translated into practice; we spent much of the next two days in our ancient Morris wandering in the damp heat of its suburban wilderness in search of embassies, as we waited for the call.

During our wanderings, I discovered that for the equivalent of £6 I could have a new pair of spectacles made within the hour, but that there was no question of replacing our Swiss soup: in the Third World hard work is more readily available than hard currency. At one embassy a plumpish diplomat shrugged hopelessly in the sticky air and told us that all the West could hope for in Afghanistan was to embarrass the Russians. It was all part of another game for higher stakes elsewhere in the world, over which he had no control. These people – did he mean Pakistanis or Afghans, I wondered – had no chance of deliverance on their own. He spoke of them as if they were without rights, inconsequential; indeed, as if his own government must have undergone a moment of mental aberration to have consigned him to so irrelevant a post.

On the second evening we were still without our soup bag and we had been unable to trace Elias, our friendly airline official. When Tom rang his office he was told that he had been posted to Oslo, three years ago. But there was a message from Jean-José summoning us to Peshawar the next day; our crossing into Afghanistan was imminent, and we must still keep our movements quiet. We arranged for a minibus to take us at eleven o'clock the next morning.

I rose early in a last bid to retrieve the soup. At the airport an agent of Pakistan Airways accompanied me to the lost property office where, in the hope of cutting some corners, I told a clerk that we were making an important film for television and emphasized the urgency of my mission. The clerk rose at once to the occasion. He assembled three sheets of paper, placed carbons between each, and the completed file in a typewriter. The more important the task, the more elaborate the ceremony.

'In order to expedite the matter of your bag, it will be necessary to seek the required certification,' he said. He typed with relish for several minutes. Then, leading the way and escorted now by a group of hangers-on, he took me to a great hangar in the corner of the airport inside which was a thriving industry devoted wholly to baggage, arranged in groups of little tents, occupied by uniformed officials who communicated with each other by means of runners.

'Take a seat, please.'

'Thank you.'

'Passport please.'

'I've already given it to the man in the next tent.'

Perfectly satisfied, the official then explained the procedure. I needed to present my case, properly authenticated, to an official who would then agree that it could go forward to the next stage. Then I would have to pay a fee which would depend on the outcome of a hearing. When this was complete, it would be possible, subject to correct description and satisfactory identification, to hand over to me my missing bag.

By now it was a quarter to ten. Accompanied by the Pakistan Airways' agent, I was escorted by runner to the next tent.

'Take a seat, please.'

'Thank you.'

'It is hot.'

'And getting late.'

The official roared with laughter. 'Good!' He set to work at his typewriter, and with triplication triplicated a runner set off again. I was accumulating a dossier.

While we were waiting I asked the official if he thought the customs actually had my bag. The man appeared taken aback, as if the question were out of place: it was as though an opponent at bridge had asked to see his hand.

'That we will see in the due course of events.'

Instead, he explained the fine points of my case. I lacked, it seemed, the essential document: the customs 'A' form for baggage not accompanied by a passenger. Without this a minimum fine was automatically imposed of 250 rupees – equivalent to £25 – unless there were special circumstances to be brought into consideration.

'But it was accompanied. I have the ticket to show I was travelling with it.'

'But it is no longer accompanied.' He spread his hands with finality. 'You have arrived. Until it passes the customs, the baggage has not.'

The runner returned. On our short walk to the next tent, I suggested to the Pakistan Airways' agent, who was still at my elbow, that I should simply pay the fine and have done with it.

The agent appeared horrified. 'You want to pay?'

'No. But I want to go.'

'We have a saying in Urdu: the mother will not give milk until the baby cries. You must protest.' I was threatening to spoil a promising morning's entertainment.

'Take a seat, please.'

This time I remained standing. 'I am the guilty party,' I said. 'Guilty, but ignorant of the law I have broken. I trust there are mitigating circumstances.'

The speech was a huge and instant success. Behind the desk the officials in uniform put their heads together. Finally their leader turned to me:

'Can you pay thirty-seven rupees fifty?'

I calculated the sum as a little under £2. 'I believe I can.'

'Then,' said the official, 'we have cracked the case.'

Grasping my hand the airline agent smiled in triumph and asked me to give him my address so that he could visit me in London. Then he led me back to the point where I had entered the maze.

'Can I have the bag now?'

'Yes, as soon as the procedure for payment is complete.' A runner would take my money to the cashier. The cashier would give him a stamp. Then another official would authenticate the stamp. I could then exchange the authenticated stamp for my bag.

In the land of trade unions that I knew, the conflict of priorities between providing service and providing jobs often resulted in an attitude of truculent indifference to the mere customer. Here the basically British model had been taken a step further. All pretence at common sense had been abandoned, and in its place had been set up a shrine to Procedure, at which seemingly limitless adherents worshipped with cheerful zeal.

While we waited, I asked the customs official to check that he actually had my bag.

'Oh yes, it's waiting.'

To him it was a detail, a by-product of the grander process. He waved to a pile of orphaned possessions on top of which I saw the bag with no handles.

The runner returned, my bag and passport were handed over, and, after shaking hands with several officials who rose to their feet as if in congratulations, I left by a side door to the street, where the loyal Morris, with its DO NOT DISTRUB sign, was waiting. Clasping the bag as if it were a lost child, I climbed in and we set off to the hotel at 15 miles an hour. The change of focus was almost complete.

3. The Land of the Great Game

It was a happy journey to Peshawar as, with minor obstacles overcome, we headed across the great fertile plain towards the land of the Great Game and Kipling's Kim, set in a ring of mountains that separate the Indian sub-continent from Afghanistan.

We came to the yellow-green waters of the Indus at Attock, where it is joined by the Kabul River and where Alexander the Great and Tamerlane had passed by on their way to conquer India. To our left stood a handsome fort of polished stone erected four centuries earlier by a Mogul emperor to impress his rivals. We crossed the 200-yard stretch of water by an imposing iron bridge carrying both the road and the old North-West Railway to Peshawar and the Khyber Pass beyond. In the distance we could see mountains starting out of the flatness.

Two hours later we were in Peshawar. The town seemed more alive although hotter than the one we had left, and, in keeping with its long and devious history, less ready to give up its secrets. If Islamabad was laid out in open plan as a political capital, Peshawar, weaned on conspiracy, was more closed. Its streets were less uniform; its trees seemed higher and more leafy, as though to offer better protection; and the open storm drains in its pavements, into which one could easily fall at night, were larger and deeper. Hidden, too, somewhere behind its walls, was reputedly the best bazaar in all Asia (though travellers from Kabul disputed its claim).

Dean's – named after the British governor Harold Dean – was like our last hotel, a collection of verandahed bungalows, only hotter. Everything mechanical was old but somehow kept going beyond its intended working life: large fans blew the August air around our rooms with an agreeable whirr, while ageing air-conditioners cooled it slightly with a deafening roar; the light switches looked as though they did not or could not work, but they did.

The ceiling of the windowless dining-room had been lowered to ease the task of the air-conditioners, and was covered with dark red squares that concealed dim lighting, so that even at lunch-time it took on the half-hearted look of a night-club behind the Iron Curtain. Despondent groups of lunchers waiting for food huddled like conspirators in islands of light in a sea of gloom. In one of these we found Jean-José, who told us that Es Haq would be coming to the hotel to see us at four o'clock that afternoon.

The menu was wartime English and fixed for all time: for breakfast, tinned fruit juice (fresh mangoes, growing on the trees around, were out of the question), porridge, cornflakes, eggs, and Nescafé or powerful black tea with condensed milk; lunch and dinner were tinned soup and mutton or chicken, spiced and grilled rock dry, followed by nursery jelly with artificial whipped cream. The single variation was that Mondays and Tuesdays were meatless days, which translated to mean chicken only.

We spent the afternoon as we were to spend many others: waiting for Es Haq and learning to withstand the August heat.

I closed the door of my bedroom, and the bed became a temporary respite; temporary because body heat soon defeated the air-conditioner, and in any case the noise of the machinery was insupportable. I tried not to drink so as to slow up the body's cycle of sweating and dehydration. But every twenty minutes I would have to leave the writing desk in my little sitting-room for a shower or a spell in the bedroom. To step outside, even on to the little corrugated iron porch, near which the room-boys hovered waiting to bring fresh drinking water, was to soak one's clothes in the space of moments.

Between sleeping and the business of trying to stay cool there was little to do but read, and during our short stay in Peshawar I became conscious, not for the last time, of the chasm separating the contemporary English from their immediate forbears. It was almost within living memory that Lord Curzon was Viceroy of India and modern Afghanistan was created as a buffer state – the product of a compromise between Tsarist Russia and the British Empire. In the process the imperial architects had carved up tribal areas including the land of the Pathans, giving one piece to Afghanistan and the other, with Peshawar as its capital, to British India, which left to administrators of exceptional stature the unrewarding task of governing the discontented fragments. This they accomplished with a relatively small number of civil servants, without cholera vaccine, air-conditioning and other comforts that their children would take for granted, and, despite fashionable misconceptions, relying for the most part on political acumen rather than force. It was little more than half a century before that the governor of the North-West Province, Harold Dean, used to invite Pathan dignitaries with whom he wished to negotiate to go for a walk with him, having first taken the precaution of presenting them with a pair of patent leather shoes, which were then in vogue. After a mile or so the shoes would pinch so terribly that they would be all too ready to agree to any terms Dean might care to propose.

These men, only a generation or so older than ourselves, appeared to be of a different clay. Dividing us from them, others such as Lenin, Gandhi and Freud had unleashed forces that undermined the confidence of British leaders in absolute Victorian values and the unquestionable superiority of their way of life. Or was the dividing line perhaps the First World War, which so gruesomely demonstrated that the human will, trained by public-school discipline, was no match for the machine-gun? In an age of technology, stout hearts and sharp swords would no longer be enough.

During my stay in the hotel that bore Harold Dean's name I sensed the presence around me of the household gods that had once presided over the Great Game in this region of the world. At the reception desk there hung an old photograph of a polo team. The players looked proudly out from under the brims of their white colonial topees (that imposing symbol of British rule now superseded by the salt tablet), as if to challenge me as I passed through: 'Are you on for a first-class show?'

As I thought of my soft urban way of life, I doubted whether I would do them much honour in the Game ahead.

Es Haq did not appear at four o'clock; no more did Jean-José. It was not until nightfall that we found them, sitting in a pool of light in the dining-room over dried-up chicken and lemonade, heads together and surrounded by a group of Europeans, speaking French. They took no notice of us and, containing our curiosity as best we could, we made our way through the perpetual twilight to our own table.

'French doctors,' said Sandy. 'I was talking to them earlier. One of them has been waiting for two months to go in. He seemed rather worked up.'

'Let's hope he wins the argument for all of us.'

As he spoke one of the group, with black beard, spectacles and high-domed head that sat oddly on his short and slight schoolboy's frame, rose and stalked out of the room, an angry owl disappearing into the night. Es Haq came over to our table with Jean-José and sat, unsmiling, reading the question our eyes could not conceal.

'Westerners are always in a hurry. Time is very important. It's always when, when? Well, soon we go. You must understand that there are one or two things that have to be done.'

And so began another lesson. We knew already that we had to do without warm water, soft beds and alcohol; now we were learning too that we would have to manage without the psychic comfort of a set plan. Small wonder that so few American journalists had ventured into Afghanistan: if the act of walking was close to being an unAmerican activity, to do so without a schedule was unthinkable.

Es Haq told us that his chief of convoys would be calling next morning at nine o'clock to survey 'our minimum requirements' of baggage, in order to estimate the number of horses and the amount of money that we would need.

That night we unpacked and repacked once more, separating our needs for the next few days (we dared not ask how many) from the television equipment that was to go on ahead of us with the convoy's other supplies. A third pile was for our needs for the journey which we would carry with us.

We had gleaned that we would definitely be travelling in by the southern route, and that there was an acute shortage of available horses, so that we would certainly be walking: any spare animals would be used to carry guns and ammunition, not footsore travellers. A delay in our departure date appeared to stem from a hitch with the other equipment. We had allowed for a wait of up to two weeks in Peshawar, which would give us a month of filming inside Afghanistan. We were impatient and curious, but not unduly worried.

Understandably Charles was concerned to have a horse especially to carry the television camera, so that it could be at hand at all times. Of all our European needs this one proved the hardest to convey.

'I hope', said Es Haq, 'that everything will be possible.'

34

Next morning he reappeared, this time punctual to the minute, accompanied by an eagle of a man whom he introduced as Akha Ghul. Akha Ghul's reputation had reached us ahead of him: he was a former police official from Kabul and Massud's most trusted convoy leader. He had dark commanding eyes, deeply cut features and a surprisingly high-pitched voice. Somehow it surprised me, too, that he was a heavy smoker.

Es Haq appeared aghast at our 'minimum requirements', laid out in Charles's sitting-room. Against advice, I had smuggled in the soup bag (but removed, from fear of derision, the Dundee cake). At this point Charles had the happy inspiration of showing off the saddle with panniers at either side, made specially for him in London, to carry the camera and sensitive electronic equipment. Akha Ghul, horseman at heart, was delighted with it. Then, walking among the twenty-six or so pieces, he picked up several at random to test their weight and, after a moment, said a few words to Es Haq.

'He says you have about fifty *sers*. That's about three hundred and fifty kilos. You will need to bring about fifty thousand *afghanis* in cash. Akha Ghul will send the Toyota this evening to collect everything. You must personally carry as little as possible in order not to attract attention when you pass the Pakistani police points.'

Emboldened by his earlier success Charles asked Es Haq how long we would have to wait before starting out.

'A little time, not a long time.'

We were learning, slowly.

We waited that afternoon in Charles's room, watching through the open door for the Toyota to come and drinking tea until the sweat poured from our bodies. Es Haq had fostered the spy fever in us with his parting words: 'Many people in this hotel are not just waiters. THEY know all about you, but it is best to be quiet. The Pakistani police are the police of the closed eye. It is best not to open it.'

A hotel waiter staring curiously at us through the open door at once became an enemy agent, until I realized he was the nephew of our taxi driver, whom we had omitted to pay; while Jean-José, mumbling mysteriously into his beard, defeating us every bit as much as any bugging device within earshot, remained as ever the very embodiment of conspiracy.

As the heat reached its zenith the Toyota arrived; it was a three-wheel affair with a canvas covering. A few minutes later it had left again, fully loaded. With our bags it also removed the burden of decision. The dye was cast: we had shed the dubious Western luxury of choice and were entering a world of simpler needs. We were now in the hands of Allah and Massud's Jamayat-i-Islami Party.

The temperature had reached 100 degrees fahrenheit with 90 degrees of humidity as we drove to the bazaar in a three-wheel motorized rickshaw taxi.

Until now I had associated all bazaars with the clichés of film travelogues, but Peshawar deserved the highest accolade of guide-book language. Set in finely carved wooden arcades and cubicles, in a fantastic and different world of its own, it was an emporium on a scale I had never seen before. It appeared to offer for sale every-thing on earth that could be made by hand, if only you knew how to find it. Street after street opened into mysterious side corridors that in turn led into little squares composed of larder-sized shops on three or four storeys. Every square foot of space was taken up with business. Here, for centuries, Afghan travelling merchants had brought their caravans each autumn from Bokhara, Kabul and Samarkand, loaded with wool, silks, dyes, gold thread, precious stones and carpets; and there were no signs that the war had slowed the pace of business. Near a mosque, canvas flat-topped Pakistani tents in bright green and red designs covered a crooked street, which curled away like a cornucopia crammed with offerings of spices and yoghurt, fresh fruit and painted eggs. In another side street a row of shops set several steps above the level of the tho-roughfare was devoted to making gunbelts for Afghan guerrillas. Opposite it was an arcade of guns for sale, mainly Pakistani-made copies of Russian Kalashnikovs costing $2,000 each. The impres-sion of industry was overpowering. There were no signs of those two hallmarks of Western civilization: laziness and compassion. Here to fail was to starve.

Jean-José piloted us to the money changers where, following the ritual minuet of bargaining, we settled on a rate with a man squat-ting on a step beside his suitcase. Having done his sums with a pocket calculator, he counted our notes with bank teller's dexterity and, asking us to wait, disappeared into the crowd for three heart-stopping minutes with all our money. He returned with a dozen bundles of notes so worn that it was hard to make out either their face value or the features of Babrak Karmal, the Afghan communist leader. 'One hundred and seventy-six thousand *afghanis*,' said the man.

The first of the bundles contained notes of 50 and 20 *afghanis*. After counting 100 of them, we gave up and, with our haul of approximately £2,000 worth wrapped in a scarf, set off on foot into the human jungle. It was impossible at that moment not to feel a guilty twinge of relief that we were protected by a legal system which enforced the ancient Moslem punishment of amputating a hand for stealing.

In another street we found the local attire we had been instructed to buy, as much for comfort as for disguise: loose fitting cotton trousers with pyjama cord and shirt to match hanging outside to below the knee, in dark colours for crossing the frontier at night. With Es Haq as guide, Tom bought us strangely rolled khaki serge berets, known as Chitrali hats and worn by Massud's followers; scarves that at first seemed an encumbrance, but which we soon found to be an essential all-purpose item for the traveller in Afghanistan; and *patous*, blankets used against the wind, as prayer mats, for sleeping and, in their role as cape, for fine mysterious gestures.

We assembled in our new attire in the hotel's Permit Room, where, after signing two solemn forms declaring ourselves to be neither of Moslem faith nor of Pakistani nationality, we were allowed to buy a local beer that tasted of soap suds.

Over our drinks I wondered whether an Afghan in a suit would be as diminished as we looked in our borrowed robes. Charles, though sheepish like myself, was by far the most presentable. Tom, a powerfully built man, looked frankly bulky; but it was Sandy who stole the show: with scarf slung over his shoulder like a towel, he resembled most of all himself unaccountably wearing someone else's pyjamas and a pair of gardening boots, stopping for a quick one on his way to taking a bath.

Like molten lead the days flowed sluggishly by as we waited for the final summons. In the dining-room we sat in our little groups, always hoping for scraps of information – French at one table, ourselves at another, Afghans at a third – frozen in everlasting discussion.

Now and then we picked up hints. A pass for the lorries to take

us into the tribal lands adjoining the border had been signed by the
Pakistani authorities: another obstacle overcome, and one not to be
taken for granted. There was an ever-present concern among the
guerrilla groups lest the Zia regime would lose its nerve under
Soviet pressure: there was fear of a clampdown on their border
activities in order to slow down the tide of incoming refugees
threatening unrest in the border province, already unsettled enough
by another rivalry, between Sunni and Shi'ite sects. Worse still was
the spectre of a deal with Kabul, bringing a sealing of the border
and terrible and terminal consequences for the resistance movement.

The niceties of local politics made our minds reel. But with
centuries of political intrigue in their blood, our Afghan mentors
seemed well able to follow the twists and turns; and they were not
slow to appreciate the dilemma of their host country.

Overshadowing everything was the rivalry between the Pathans,
who lived on both sides of the Durand Line marking the border
with Afghanistan, and the Tajiks of the Hindu Kush led by Massud,
dedicated single-mindedly to a fundamentalist Moslem Afghanistan under the banner of the Jamayat-i-Islami Party.

The Pathans were the biggest single tribe in Afghanistan,
accounting for almost half the population. Even under successive
pro-communist regimes they had tended to enjoy the plum jobs
in Kabul. They now regarded the Hisb-i-Islami Party, in which
Pathans predominated, as the only one that counted.

But there was suspicion among their rivals that other loyalties
tugged at them as well: that certain Pathans had been beguiled by
Russian overtures, perhaps even the lure of a measure of autonomy
for a Pathan nation, in exchange for turning against the guerrilla
movement. Already there had been clashes with the Jamayat
forces.

Since their territory lay across the supply lines from Pakistan, a
Pathan deal with the communists would be a devastating blow to
the resistance. To complicate matters further, it would also be
devastating for Pakistan, since Pathans spread across the North-
West Frontier Province, including Peshawar and the Khyber Pass,
which historically was the key to control of the vast flat land mass
of the Indian sub-continent.

The local Pakistani authorities, themselves largely Pathans,
tended to favour the Hisb-i-Islami in their dealings, and it was said

38

that supplies destined for the Panjsher would often find their way into Hisb-i-Islami hands.

Eventually, it was Jean-José who brought news that we would be starting out in two days, but that Es Haq would not now be coming with us. Some visas for Saudi Arabia had come through and he was being sent to raise funds for the resistance. It was a bitter blow, for he was at once interpreter, host and direct link with Massud.

However, we now had a new travelling companion in Tony Davis, an Australian journalist from *Asiaweek* magazine, who had been to the Panjsher the year before and spoke good Farsi. He had sought to introduce himself by telephone the night before, but schooled in secrecy, we had stuck to our story of tourism in Swat. We mended our fences over a cup of Nescafé on the hotel's front lawn, where beside us a plump lady Maoist from Basle, wearing a Chitrali hat, was addressing a group of silent Afghans sitting in a ring around her. Jean-José glowered at her: 'There are idiots and amateurs everywhere. First the French, now the Swiss!'

After we had explained our misunderstanding, Tony raised his cup of Nescafé and said: 'Cheers!' We were to be more than glad of him in the days ahead.

That night the weather broke. I was woken by rain drilling on the corrugated iron roof of my porch, and walking through my little sitting-room I looked out on to an entirely new view: where flowers had grown in regimented pots by day a river now swept by. The vertical downpour glistened and danced in the porch lights. Opposite me, under the light of number sixteen, a man's face peered, like my own, into the darkness – a fellow passenger aboard a storm-bound liner. For an instant our eyes met, drawn together by a common experience. The face was steel cold in the light. In the town the storm drains in the pavements would be swamped.

There was no sign of the rain next day when we made a final excursion to the Khyber Pass to reconnoitre the Afghan border. The road on the Pakistani side was excellent. It swept, pencil straight and dry, past a camp of 35,000 Afghan refugees, a fraction of the total of nearly three million that had poured across the border so far since 1979. Inside the semi-autonomous tribal frontier area we came across fortified mud compounds with watch-towers and prison-high walls; through iron grilles we had an occasional glimpse of a lorry or a car. 'Smugglers,' said our taxi driver.

These were the Pathan warriors of old, now turned lorry drivers with commercial links all over the Asian continent, but principally involved in local frontier traffic. To judge by the heroin and hashish offered to us in the bazaars, the problem of negotiating customs caused no one too much loss of sleep. We stopped in a town where, squatting beside our car, boys offered us 'brown sugar', the partly refined heroin of Afghanistan.

Further west, the hot flat plain came suddenly to an end and, rising steeply, the road split into two parallel strips of ribbon twisting in and out of the bare grey mountains. Beside us the line of the North-West Railway, itself a major feat of engineering, followed a separate course up the formidable gradient of the pass. On the roadside, freshly painted and whitewashed signs proclaimed the British military presence in the early part of the century. We stopped by a plaque reading 'Royal Sussex Regiment 1932' to visit a bleak little cemetery containing graves of a dozen English soldiers. Most of them had died of cholera in 1920 or 1921. One had drowned. All of them were under twenty-one years old. Several of the graves were defaced, their stones pillaged to make meagre dwellings for the living fated to share these desolate surroundings with them.

Higher up the pass pride of place was reserved for the Shagan Fort, headquarters of the Khyber Rifles, a huge prison-palace reminiscent of the Escorial. 'Number One fort,' said our driver. Built in the 1920s, it dominated the stretch of the pass where it stood – the most magnificent of the many hilltop fortifications that for two millennia had marked the passage of armies between Asia and the Western world.

Nearer the border we came upon the ugly pillboxes and 'dragon's teeth' tank traps of the kind I had seen as a child on the drive of my preparatory school in wartime England. They had been built by the British in 1940 to hold up a German invasion, at a time when it was thought that Hitler might defeat the Russians.

Short of the frontier we were stopped by police. Ahead, and below us now, the stones of a barren river bed followed a cleft in the hills. In the distance a patch of green marked the Afghan border post; from there the stony unmade road wound into the distance towards Jalalabad and Kabul, passing on its way through a series of tunnels over which we would have to make a clandestine crossing. It was thereabouts that in 1842 Pathan tribes had annihilated a

British convoy 15,000 strong, all but for one doctor who limped home to Jalalabad to tell the story of one of the most humiliating episodes in British military history. We found, to mark the event, a tactfully worded tablet: 'Here the Pathan nation looked their British counterpart in the eye.'

At this point we were turned back. Only a few lorries, with bodies intricately painted like travelling shrines, were plying their local trade (or smuggling, as our driver preferred to put it). There were no buses that day; we were told that they were on strike against Russian interference.

'Perhaps the Russians have tried to stop the smuggling?' we asked.

Our driver bellowed with laughter. 'Perhaps they try to turn back the rivers?'

On our return the dining-room was alive with a new excitement. A guest had been found dead in room sixteen that morning: outside the door, across the courtyard from my room, an ambulance was standing, watched by the room-boys. I remembered the face in the night and tried hard to recollect the features, but could only remember the look of curiosity without warmth.

By evening, increasingly extravagant rumours were circulating. The dead man was said to be an Englishman, a painter called Paul Daniels. According to another story he was an oil company executive. He had arrived three days before and was twenty-seven years old; by another account he was forty-five. There was said to be blood; it was a heart attack, just a routine death in the heat.

At the reception desk a Pakistani guest was cross-questioning the clerk.

'I could not sleep all afternoon. The police are next to my room.'

'The police?' said the clerk, who had earlier told us of their arrival.

'Is it a murder case?'

'It is nothing,' said the clerk.

All the same more police came back that night. There was formaldehyde, suitcases being taken away, people standing about. We never knew the true story.

For us it was time to go: we had been long enough in the pressure chamber of Peshawar and were as ready as we ever would be for the adventure ahead.

4. Teremengal

We were ready to leave at 7.30 sharp next morning. The four of us gathered in Jean-José's room together with Tony Davis, an Afghan student of Grenoble University who was hoping to visit his parents in Kabul, and Jean-Phillipe, the owl-like doctor from Bordeaux. Jean-José had laid particular emphasis on punctuality so that we could make our departure before the hotel was fully awake.

Two hours later the guerrilla transport arrived. It was a Toyota ambulance, a little larger, though not by much, than the three-wheeler that had come for our bags a few days earlier. We piled on to the two benches facing each other in the back, together with our kitbags and back-packs. Once inside there was no question of move-ment. The floor space was too small for our sixteen boots and the last arrivals had to sit with knees hugged to chins. Four *mujahideen*, including Akha Ghul the convoy leader, climbed in the front and the Toyota set off past the railway station, with its Upper-Class and Lower-Class waiting-rooms, and, turning west, picked up speed along a tarmac road towards the Afghan border.

Our destination, we learned, was Teremengal, 150 miles away, deep inside the tribal frontier area where it was technically illegal for us to go. As we began to climb, still heading due west along the Afghan border running parallel to our right, the tarmac ran out. The ambulance, hard sprung for rough terrain, crashed and lurched through the potholes, scarcely dropping speed. For most of the journey, to our left, there was open country and for some time a railway line followed us; at one point we passed an open rail-car propelled by six men in flowing robes sitting in two ranks facing each other, pushing a lever to and fro like oarsmen.

At the first police checkpoint there was a prolonged discussion, followed by laughter. At another our ambulance siren sounded and we roared straight through, waving. At a third we were told to hide our faces and draw the curtain across the windows in the back.

We stopped in a village for a lunch of lamb stew and rice, where we were joined by an excitable man, much given to waving his hands, which served to draw attention to the absence of both his thumbs. This was Jamir, who appeared to have some seniority in rank as well as age, under the overall authority of Akha Ghul. We learned that he had been overtaken by his misfortune when illegally dynamiting fish; and the story, which we were to hear more than once, was an unfailing source of mirth with our company, including Jamir himself.

We pressed on through the heat of the day over ever-rising ground, and late in the afternoon, legs and feet numb, spines jarred, soaked in sweat, we climbed out of the Toyota inside the courtyard of a house belonging to the Jamayat Party. We were now just short of the last but, we were told, most formidable of the checkpoints: Afghans could pass without trouble, but foreigners and baggage were another matter, and subject to negotiation. On the first floor of the house, we stretched our grateful bodies on *charpoys* (couches) and drank sweet tea. Already the last hot bath I had had that morning was a hundred years away, and Dean's was the Ritz.

As we clambered into the ambulance to continue our journey, our kitbags were taken from us and loaded into a second lorry which had been waiting at the Jamayat house with the other equipment, and which was to follow us through the checkpoint. This greatly eased our aching bodies but not my mind: we were now separated from the red plastic bag carrying the bulk of our money.

The two vehicles stopped at the checkpoint – two wooden posts and a barrier. Inside, curtains were drawn and heads lowered into *patous*. I was conscious of a pair of eyes peering into the darkness in the back of the ambulance, scrutinizing us. After a full minute we started off again; out of the back I could see the second lorry draw up at the barrier. It was still standing there as we rounded a bend in the road and lost it from view.

We reached Teremengal at five; we had been doubled up for almost eight hours when we were decanted into a dusty, sloping street of uneven stones, with houses of mud and wood, one of which was ours.

Around us a Hollywood movie version of a frontier town seemed to have been put on for our benefit. Knots of armed men roamed among tethered horses, or squatted on the flat roof-tops, opening and closing their rifle bolts. Every now and then a shot would ring out and echo back from the steep mountainside on the top of which, out of sight, was the Durand Line marking the border with Afghanistan. On the fringes of the settlement cedar wood, dragged in by camel from the forests across the border, lay in stacks waiting to be taken to Peshawar where it would be sold. The fresher air told us that we had gained height, and to prove it we could see, behind and below us in the distance, the great plain stretching back towards Peshawar.

Some young *mujahideen* directed us to climb a wooden outside stairway, to which a donkey was tethered, leading to a first-floor room: this was to be our home, and we were enjoined not to leave it in daylight. We were given varying reasons: 'Many bad people ... they shoot everybody ... some of them don't like Europeans ... they think you are Russians ...' and, as effective to us as any, 'the Pakistani police will take you back to Peshawar'. The mere thought of the journey back was deterrent enough, but we were aware, too, that there was force to their other arguments. Until a week before the route through this territory to the Panjsher Valley had been closed by a dispute in which fighting had broken out between Pathan and Panjsheri guerrillas. Here in Pathan territory the writ of the Pakistani police ran shakily and our hosts had reason to be apprehensive.

Our room occupied a whole floor, perhaps 20 feet by 15, with a single wooden supporting pillar in the middle. When we peered out of the windows we were ordered to stay out of sight. Pasted to the walls were dramatic posters of the resistance: doves rose like spirits over inky photographs of dead patriots. One, in colour, depicted a blood-stained martyr kneeling with his severed head in his hands.

At nightfall there was still no sign of the second lorry. We took mattresses from a pile in the corner and arranged ourselves as best we could in rows and waited. A *mujahideen* came in with a long cloth which he laid on the floor, signalling us to sit in a line beside it; then he poured water on our hands from a brass jug. A moment later the *nan* arrived (fresh cooked unleavened bread), followed by boiled rice, more mutton stew and a huge melon without taste which, however, provided much-needed liquid; and sweet green tea to which we were so quickly to become addicted. We ate three to a bowl; Akha Ghul, and a bearded man in his forties who was proud of his English, ate with us. The Afghans showed us how to break our bread into the stew so that it became a sodden pulp that we could then scoop into our mouths by hand, and laughed at us when the hot rice scalded our delicate fingers.

Through the bearded man we asked about our missing belongings.

'They have been held up at a checkpoint. Sometimes it is the formality. Sometimes it is the money.' He paused, and added what sounded like: 'It is really bad.'

'Really bad?' we asked.

'Ah,' he said, beaming. 'There is "really" and there is "rarely". This is a distinction I have learned at school.'

'But which is it?'

'Most certainly,' replied the bearded man, after which he could be drawn no further.

Our medicines had been transferred to the missing lorry with our kitbags, but since Jean-José's had been overlooked, it was he who now dispensed to us our new set of nightly needs: insect repellent, tic powder, malaria tablets and, not least, a ration of lavatory paper, on receipt of which Tony said: 'Cheers'.

We were permitted to venture out under the stars in search of a stream and privacy, where the knot of onlookers that followed us everywhere demonstrated that far from being incompatible, prudery and curiosity appear to be opposite sides of the same coin.

As I fell asleep I had the sensation of an army of insects marching across my body exploring and setting up bivouacs for the season ahead. Around me the floor began to shake with the rhythm of snoring. Sandy, at least, was not troubled.

We woke at daybreak to the sound of rifle shots, followed by shouts, and from the foot of the stairway came the prehistoric sound of our donkey braying. Breakfast followed with the same routine of table-cloth, water and bread, and sweet tea. We were by now dishevelled and unshaven, our clothing crumpled with sleep; by contrast our hosts, who had fared no better, appeared immaculate.

At mid-morning the bearded interpreter came in and squatted beside us.

'What news?'

'I have come to say good-bye. I go to Peshawar. I hope you will have a good journey.'

'Have you, by chance, news of –'

'I hear one truck.'

'Where?'

'Not here. At Padakshinar. Not far.'

'Is it ours?'

'Ours?'

'Yes.'

'Yes, it is ours. I don't know. I hope.'

At noon the lorry arrived. From it the *mujahideen* unloaded a consignment of machine-guns, Chinese mines, rocket-propelled grenades, Pakistani- and Russian-made Kalashnikovs, ammunition boxes; finally, with the relief of air travellers spotting their own luggage on the conveyor belt, we recognized our camera cases and kitbags.

The day gathered pace. Advised by Akha Ghul that we should not try to carry even back-packs on the first part of our journey up the forbidding cliff awaiting us, we rearranged our belongings yet again so as to carry as little as possible, and despatched a *mujahideen* to buy waistcoats with ample poacher's pockets.

Tom, the sound recordist, still cheerful, had made friends with the cook, who shared a tiny alcove on our balcony with a bucket and stove. He had even begun to converse in self-taught Farsi. When we asked him the menu for dinner, there was a lengthy exchange, then a pause. 'Coupladogs,' said Tom.

In the afternoon Akha Ghul arrived to discuss payment for the horses; this, he explained, was calculated not on the number of horses needed, but on the weight carried. The Pathan horsemen who were responsible for hiring out, loading and feeding the animals on the journey would decide how the weight was to be distributed. A huge antique weighing scale had been set up in the little square below us and half a dozen roughly hewn boulders of different sizes acted as weights. Business was conducted in *sers* (the equivalent of 7 kilos); during the process Akha Ghul perched like an eagle on a nearby roof-top, shouting directions, and even with the Pathans his voice carried authority. With all our hand baggage now included, we turned the scales at 55 *sers* and, together with Charles, I set to counting out 55,000 *afghanis* from our collection of small blackened notes.

Then the horsemen took our bags and pooling them with the ammunition bags made up individual loads for each horse. These were put into wicker nets and roped so tight that once on the horse there was no question of putting a hand into a case to retrieve so much as a pencil, far less a spare battery for the camera.

The final loading of the horses was to take place in the early morning before daylight. In the meantime Akha Ghul undertook to try to negotiate for a separate horse for the camera.

Our convoy of about sixty horses was due to set off before daybreak. Akha Ghul would lead a second and larger one, to follow on once the bulk of the supplies, held up by trouble at checkpoints, had reached Teremengal. Our convoy would be led by Ghul Bas, a slight and mild man who wore the Pakistani derivative of a British service dress tunic in light khaki material, which, with his baggy cotton trousers, gave him the faintly disreputable air of a cashiered army officer. I noted that, like so many Afghans we had met, he was a chain-smoker. Under Ghul Bas a young Kabul university student turned guerrilla would have special responsibility for the seven Europeans.

At sundown Ghul Bas produced an incongruously modern-looking compass from his pocket and, lining up his *patou* so that he faced in the direction of Mecca, began to say his prayers. While he did so I went out to survey for the last time this extraordinary encampment of mud houses, sheds, timber stacks and tents, animals and armed men by the hundred, stretching up into the heavy layer of mist that was now descending from the mountain cleft above, perhaps to cloak us during our critical frontier crossing in a few hours' time. On the way back from my walk I paused at the bottom of the staircase to pat our tethered donkey.

We were woken at 1.30 in the morning with a cry we were to learn as a soldier learns the reveille trumpet.

'*Arakat!*' – 'Let's go!'

Ghul Bas stood there in his beret, torch in hand. Hastily and clumsily we gathered our unfamilar belongings and assembled ourselves as best we could. We were to leave in an hour. In the square horses were being loaded by torchlight.

There was no sign of our donkey as we went down the stairway. Then, across the square, we saw our camera in its case with the London saddler's panniers at either side, bearing the dead-weight of its two power units. Between them projected a familiar pair of ears: all but buried under the load was our humble donkey.

At first Akha Ghul was nowhere to be seen; but Sandy and Charles made clear to Ghul Bas that we would not leave until he was found. They explained that the donkey was inadequate, and that in a crisis we could not even ride it. It was explained to them in turn that weight was the governing factor, and the camera did not warrant a whole horse. We said we would pay the extra. Finally Akha Ghul emerged, and, with Sandy stabbing the air with a finger to emphasize, if not to clarify, his argument (Akha Ghul had no English), an arrangement was struck and a horse found.

As the last of the animals was being loaded, there was a cry of alarm from one of the horsemen. From within a bag there issued a strange buzzing sound. Tom was summoned to make a technical diagnosis. The prime suspect was a box of his electrical equipment. He shook his head and, placing his ear to the load, pointed to my bag. Listening carefully, we finally identified the sound of a battery-operated razor that I had bought at London Airport and that had somehow switched itself on.

'Too much clobber,' said Sandy. 'Ridiculous.'

It was still dark as we set off up the mountainside. Horses and humans together, we resembled something between the start of a marathon and a scene from *Macbeth*. To either side the moon silhouetted hurrying ghostly figures; below us the lights of the strange and lawless outpost flickered in the mist. Ahead, high above us, was the border. Unleashed at last, spurred by excitement, each of us anxious above all not to be the one to fall behind, we sped straight up the incline. At the top our student guide made us walk in single file past an abandoned fort where the semblance of a barrier told us that we were entering Afghanistan.

5. Baptism of Fire

With the relief that it was too late now for the Pakistani police to send us back, I was not aware until we took our first rest how exhausting the climb had been. We lay flat on the ground, our bodies and clothes soaked with sweat, panting and almost unable to breathe. Our guide signalled that we should sit up rather than stretch out, and not to drink too much water from our bottles. We were past paying attention.

Pleased enough to have survived this first test, we set off again, this time downhill for perhaps half a mile. Another cruel ascent awaited. More slowly this time, planting one foot laboriously in front of the other, we tackled the second of the lengthy calvaries that was to make up our journey through Afghanistan. Following Sandy's footprints that endlessly spelt TIMBERLAND backwards in the dust in front of me, breathing in time with each step, I slogged my way with the others to the saddle of the mountain.

At our second resting place, an old man gave me an apple and showed me his swollen hand: evidently he thought that I was a doctor and, unwilling to accept that I was not, insisted that I accept his offering. A craving for liquid in any form overcame any inhibition that I might otherwise have had.

By now we had crossed the first range of hills and faced a second: Pakistan was lost from view. We were emerging from a lightly wooded area into a bare high wilderness. Nearby some armed nomads were coaxing a camel, unreal as a dinosaur, which was hauling huge cedar trunks back the way we had come. Soon we would see no more of them or of the frontier trade in timber which carried on with no concern for a line drawn on the map by a foreigner some ninety years before.

Trees grew more sparse as we marched, and then stopped altogether except for clusters marking an occasional hut or village.

49

There was no road through the mountains, not even a regular path: we simply followed the traces of previous convoys which were often too faint for my urban eyes to spot.

On the next big climb a barefoot youth with a sack of apples many times the weight of our loads overtook us, conducting a conversation at the top of his lungs with an unseen travelling companion, and I experienced for a moment the feelings of the bad skier when a party of children skims past on the nursery slopes; but dignity was beginning to lose its hold as we puffed and strained in silence, dragging the burden of our unhealthy living laboriously upwards and onwards.

Already the faster walkers had pulled ahead. The horses, which moved more quickly than humans uphill but more slowly down and on the flat, were far behind, and the convoy straggled over more than a mile. Now and then our student guide would fire his captured Russian Kalashnikov in the air and shout, apparently to muster his little flock, but to no effect. Already Jean-José and Tom were nowhere to be seen.

At the bottom of a steep sandy descent that blistered our tender booted feet was our first serious resting place: a tea-house, the famous *chaie khana* of Afghanistan. We had been walking for five hours. Inside its single smoke-filled room we cast ourselves on the ground around a fire, where we were served sweet green tea in cups: first a spoonful of sugar, then, from a china pot made in the Soviet Union, the tea. At that moment it tasted indescribably delicious.

News of early casualties began to come in. Most serious for us was the report that Tom, who had been up with the leaders at the start, had succumbed to cramp in both thighs and was having to be pushed up the hills. Jean-José was still unsighted; meanwhile our guide was chiding us for our slowness. Jean-Phillipe advised me that cramp could be caused by heat exhaustion and prescribed salt tablets. As I searched for them in my transparent plastic bag of medicines, an Afghan beside me asked for a pill and insisted that I peer into his eye. I obliged and gave him a salt tablet, which perfectly satisfied him. Not so Jean-Phillipe.

'Medicine is as important as ammunition. You should not waste it,' he said. 'What is needed here is planning and organization not useless gestures inspired by compassion.'

But of planning and organization there was very little. Most Afghans never see a doctor in their lifetimes. There was just over

1,000 of them for a population of nearly twenty million, most of them practising in the towns, when the Left took over in 1978. Since then there had been virtually none in rebel areas, other than visiting French doctors and the Afghans they had trained.

Afghanistan is one of the most economically backward nations on earth; only one in two babies survives until the age of five (compared with 96 per cent in most European countries); most adults have intestinal parasites from the water; the average life expectation is fifty, which means the mid-thirties in many rural areas; and on average only one in twenty Afghans can read. In these circumstances for Afghans to see a doctor was as important for prestige as for health, and they did not always listen to what he told them.

It was Jean-Phillipe who taught us not to give antibiotics away. He explained that in most cases Afghans would not take a complete six-day course and therefore the cure would be ineffective, the natural immunity of the body might be broken down and the pills wasted. Shamefacedly we learned to hide and hoard our stocks of medicine for our own pampered bodies, softened by our infinitely less savage environment.

Retracing our steps up the sandy hill I came across Tom, hobbling between two *mujahideen*, his distress due as much to fury as to pain. His cramp seemed to come and go. After giving him a salt tablet, I was fit enough that first day to hurry to the head of the convoy where I found Jamir, our excitable acquaintance from the Toyota, on horseback. Not for the last time I regretted my lack of even elementary Farsi. In vain I gestured and signalled our predicament, indicating as best I could that we needed a horse. But Jamir only waved his thumbless hands in the air, shouted at me and cantered off towards the bare hills ahead.

By now our disarray seemed beyond control. We were scattered over the wilderness, separated from the horses and our bags. It was quickly becoming apparent that Ghul Bas was unused to exercising authority. This was his first command of a convoy, and he had the air of a man who was more concerned to avoid being disliked than to instil obedience. By contrast, we were buoyed up by the cheerful enthusiasm of our young escorts and still, above all, by the excitement of the adventure.

In the afternoon we came on the first sign of the Soviet presence. We had planned to stop at a second *chaie khana*, only to find a gutted and empty shack. It had been bombed or rocketed – we could not tell which – by Soviet jets and helicopters attempting to cut off the supply line to the Panjsher Valley. This was our first evidence, too, that Es Haq's information that there was plenty of food was out of date, a portent of worse conditions to come.

We stopped for our evening meal at a cluster of houses, where we watched bread being baked in a clay oven scooped out of the ground. Inside a house Tom was stretched on a mattress while two *mujahideen* massaged his limbs with surprising skill.

Just before sunset Ghul Bas produced his improbable compass and the convoy knelt to say its prayers. While their chants went up in unison a figure approaching from the distance gradually resolved itself into Jean-José. He had been suffering from toothache, but had been delayed not so much by indisposition as by a spectacle which had absorbed his attention for over an hour.

'Have you ever watched lizards copulating?' he asked. 'It takes longer than you'd expect.'

After the evening meal we agreed to split forces. While Charles stayed with Tom, Sandy and I were to go ahead with Ghul Bas and an escort to the encampment where the horses, which did not stop to rest on the march, had gone on for the night. There we would try to negotiate for a mount for Tom.

'Is it far?'

'Not far.'

'How far?'

'About half an hour.'

We walked in silence, single file, stumbling to keep up with the torchlight ahead. We were still in unfriendly country, dependent on local truces or Jamayat-controlled houses for our safe passage; and the Panjsheri *mujahideen* treated all locals as potential enemies, not to be trusted, unless arrangements had been made in advance.

After forty minutes we came to a fortified village that had been recently bombed. We could make out a line of shattered settlements against the night sky. There was a hasty exchange of handshakes by torchlight, and a young man gave Ghul Bas some fresh batteries. As we left the town, dogs began to howl. Over a wall to our left a large mastiff ran up and down and then, leaping the wall, danced towards us, snarling. Two *mujahideen* turned, cocked and aimed their guns, while Ghul Bas flashed his torch in the animal's face, which reminded me unpleasantly of the hound of the Baskervilles. I recalled reading that Afghan nomads keep fierce mastiffs expressly to attack strangers and reflected that this would be less than the ideal place to contract rabies. After two more sallies the brute slunk away, mercifully content to have seen us off its territory.

An hour later we heard a horse's whinny and saw lights in the distance. In a few minutes we were fumbling among the baggage in the dark. Finding our sleeping bags we climbed by means of a broken wall on to a roof-top, where we slept soundly under the stars.

We were woken at four. On the flat roof all round us a dozen *mujahideen* were preparing to depart. With our complex paraphernalia of sleeping bags to be folded (the *mujahideen* slept under *patous*), boots to be laced, malaria and salt pills to be stealthily swallowed, unfamiliar items of clothing to find and put on without offending Moslem modesty with a naked limb (the *mujahideen* slept fully clothed), blistered toes to tape, we were as painfully slow as new boys on their first morning at school.

As Sandy went to open negotiations for a horse, I took my wash-bag and set off in the vain search for privacy. Once again I had occasion to appreciate the validity of one of Jean-José's conspirator's warnings, though not issued in this particular context: 'In Afghanistan one is never free from the watching eye.' In desperation I finally climbed a wall which seemed to offer relative sanctuary from human curiosity, only to find myself confronted by another mastiff, every bit as large and seemingly more savage than the one of the night before. From a tactical point of view my situation was not a good one. In my squatting undress, the only weapons to hand were stones. I picked one up. The dog stopped barking and, baring its fangs, advanced snarling quietly. I hurled the stone, missed, and picked up a second one. The animal hesitated, then came forward again, flecks of foam starting from its molars. This time the stone, heavier than the first, struck it amidships, and I gained enough time to gather my possessions and retreat to where a group of *mujahideen* sat thoroughly enjoying the spectator sport.

The horses were being loaded. Sandy, helping to put the unfamiliar saddle on our camera horse, shouted over his shoulder to me: 'Where have you been? Get two more horses quickly.'

I could read the signs. People behave differently under pressure. Sandy gave orders. I asked him what had happened. Then as I

53

caught sight of Charles, supported between two *mujahideen*, it became all too apparent: we had a second case of cramp.

There was no question of finding two extra horses. Ghul Bas had with the greatest possible difficulty secured one after bargaining with a villager: as it turned out, there was no room for a rider on our camera horse. Charles could still manage to walk, although particularly on the downward slopes his muscles were liable to seize up. Apparently the combination of dehydration and unaccustomed exertion was too much even for the younger and stronger bodies which had not been prepared for the trip. For Sandy, fit from his golf, the exertion was not such a shock to the system, and I looked back gratefully to my comparatively gentle but regular walks in Greece.

With both Jean-José and Tony as go-betweens we negotiated with Jamir that at the top of the next mountain range he would surrender his horse so that Charles could ride on the downhill slope.

We helped Tom on to the bare back of the other horse, a mangy animal which he shared with a pair of ammunition boxes. There were no stirrups. It was the first time he had sat on a horse in his life.

Ghul Bas watched while we laboriously laced up our boots and then, pointing to the river that flowed beside the encampment, signalled the convoy leaders to wade across. As we sat down again to unlace our boots, he called out: '*Arakat!*'

The problem of communication was growing. We were seldom told what to expect, but even when we were, as often as not we did not understand. Gradually we were forming ourselves into groups round the Farsi speakers: Tony, the more fluent by far, and Jean-José, whom I had yet to hear utter more than odd phrases. The rest of us knew only single words.

Tony, compact and muscular, strode steadily ahead in his black Australian army boots, wasting few words and carrying all his possessions, including two cameras, perhaps 50 pounds weight in all, on his back. Jean-Phillipe, an owl in gym shoes, seemed quite untouched by hardship.

The rest of us were sorrily down-at-heel. Jean-José's toothache had grown worse, we had two walking wounded with one horse between them and ten days at least to go, and even Sandy complained that morning: 'Some bloody fool's given me a cold.' As we climbed the bleak mountainside that sloped away from the river, with more and still more mountains ahead, I asked myself how I, who had an aversion to walking and communal living, and suffered from vertigo as well as hypochondria, could have let myself in for such an expedition. But to my own surprise I was the one at that early stage who, blistered but unbowed, was the fittest of the four.

There was little time to dwell for long on any but our immediate problems. We were embarked upon a great sea change and were already beyond the point of no return. A continent away and seemingly an age ago our cares had been with London's malfunctioning telephones, with draughts, what curtains to choose, noise from a neighbour's record player, the cost of holidays. Now our first concern was with food; the Afghans with us seemed able to eat a few pounds of rice at a sitting. We were quite unable, despite the increasingly savage demands from our stomachs, to swallow more than a few handfuls at a time. In our minds the humble cup of tea stood close to the very summit of human happiness. We were living at the edge of our experience, crossing a frontier not just on the map, but into an unknown and untried part of ourselves. And in this new terrain our animal appetites for sustenance to deal with the dangers in hand were so acute that the future seemed to lose its meaning; and where everything was uncertain, uncertainty itself held less fear.

Our Afghan guides were perfectly content without any known time-table, such as whether and where we would eat or stop the night; and without such planning, anxiety ceased. All our concentration, sinews, will and thoughts were invested in immediate survival: food for going uphill, plaster for feet blistered going down the other side (Who had I lent my plaster to? Who would give me some? Where were my folding scissors, made in China and bought in the Peshawar bazaar, with which to cut the plaster?). There was no question of finding replacements, even for a piece of string. We had to carry everything on our backs, and with every ounce of weight counting there were no spares. I kept my soap in a little airline bag together with razor and mirror. The bag's dye had run over the soap and when I washed, my hands turned purple. That morning the soap had broken in two and I had wrapped the fragments in a piece of paper, the part of my map that showed India, which I would not be needing. Another victim of the disintegrating bag was the mirror, also made in China. (Gradually its backing wore off, so that daily my face grew smaller until eventually it

vanished altogether and, unable to replace it, I gave up shaving.)
In my poacher's pocket I carried a torch (at night a prize, but a
problem as well since, owing to a muddle, we had no spare batteries); for immediate energy a handful of raisins, glucose tablets and
some boiled sweets, and money for cigarettes or an apple in case
the chance arose.

In my back-pack was a sleeping bag, which rolled miraculously
into a little sack no bigger than a baby's pillow and boasted on its
label that it could resist temperatures well below freezing (so far it
could not have fallen much below the eighties, even at night); a
plastic bag for medicines – aspirins, malaria pills, salt and water
purifying tablets, antibiotics (one kind for mild, another kind for
acute diarrhoea, the more powerful doubling for chest infections as
well); sterilized dressings and powders for afflictions ranging from
athlete's foot to napalm, sunburn cream (two kinds for different
altitudes), cold water detergent, note-books, spare socks and,
strangest of all our belongings to inquisitive Afghan eyes, a roll of
lavatory paper. Finally, round my neck supporting St Christopher
was a spare bootlace. Already our hands were filthy and our bodies
caked with sweat, yet we could not undress to wash for fear of
offending Moslem modesty. Lazarus stank after the fourth day. We
achieved it in two.

At the top of the first line of hills, the appointed place for Jamir
to yield his horse to Charles, the thumbless horseman was nowhere
to be seen; and there was no further sign of him that day. By now
in only slightly less distress than Tom, Charles took turns with him
to sit astride the bare and bony back of the ill-fed ammunition
horse.

At noon we came to a village where we had our first taste of the
magic that from time to time Afghanistan bestows upon its visitors,
invariably when least expected, just as with equal capriciousness it
withholds the reliefs and comforts that they may have been unwary
enough to count on.

Ghul Bas had attached himself to us, having apparently lost the
rest of the convoy. Uneasily at first, he approached the village, a
cluster of stone cottages with outside ladders for staircases, windows without glass, and set in an intricate patchwork of terraces on
which we could see vines growing. The little settlement had an air
of rustic prosperity.

While Ghul Bas went ahead to negotiate for food, we sat in the shade spread on our path by a mulberry tree, its fruit out of our reach, and waited. Our student guide called to two boys with catapults who had been studying us from afar, whereupon, grinning and tucking their weapons into their trousers, they clambered up the tree. A minute later mulberries were raining upon us. We fell upon them, still pale pink and not fully ripe, but sweet enough to eat.

Another resident, a youngish man with turban, approached and addressed our guide, who signalled us to withdraw to another tree, this time in a grove beside a river. It seemed that the villagers were nervous of being seen to befriend us for fear of retribution, not from the Afghan authorities nor from the Russians, but from the Hisb-i-Islami in whose heartland we were trespassing.

The youngish man turned out to be the local *mullah* through whose priestly control most of the village's business was conducted. It was the 250,000 local *mullahs* all over Afghanistan whose opposition to change and modernization had done so much to thwart a succession of right- and then left-wing Afghan governments in the two decades leading up to the Soviet invasion; and it was the *mullahs* that Massud in the Panjsher was reported to be shrewdly courting. It was the local *mullah* who now held the key to our lunch.

A tray of tea appeared, with heavy but welcome biscuits, followed shortly by a beaming Ghul Bas, bearing a basket with twenty-seven eggs. The *mullah* joined in and, between the ten of us, we ate our first outdoor Afghan tomato omelette, with freshly baked bread and more tea.

After our picnic we sat under the sun with a sense of well-being, surveying the little terraced village stretching below us to one side. In the distance, here and there, heavily veiled figures worked in a field: these were the first Afghan women we had seen. For a moment as I contemplated this rural scene I had an atavistic sense that it was the rest of the world and not Afghanistan that had lost its way. Somewhere here the individually worked and carefully tended little patches of soil, each with its neat vines, a goat or two and a tree, had a message of comfort. Or perhaps it was the eggs.

Our moment of contentment was brought to its end with the now familiar '*Arakat!*' And on we trudged, in ever rising terrain, on the northward journey towards the Hindu Kush, still more than 100 miles away.

We caught up with the horses that night beside another river; as light began to fail we found a stretch of deep water where with no prying eyes we could take off our clothes and bathe. I had never before experienced total immersion as total pleasure, but indeed it was. I washed my hair in Boots' Lice Lotion, brushed my nails with a hat brush bought in the Peshawar bazaar, and sprayed my feet with Dr Scholl's Foot Refresher, and then covered myself with insect repellent. For the first time our bodies were comfortable, and comfort itself had become the highest of luxuries. Our pleasures were simple but total.

We returned to the camp to find more mulberries, and a supper of boiled goat and tea awaiting us.

Sandy, his cold now on his chest, sneezed and snored through that night but awoke, as ever, at peace in a secure world of cloudless skies and declared that he had never felt better. He looked awful.

We left at dawn, fording the river; then climbing by a series of false crests, each as cruel as a broken promise, we reached a mountain saddle, perhaps 10,000 feet high, from which we had a bleak but awe-inspiring view of the land ahead. This was the terrain of which I had heard a former British prime minister say: 'It is a little like Scotland without the trees, majestic but bare, if you like that sort of thing.' He had paused, and added: 'Personally, I don't.'

That third day, 30 miles or more inside Afghanistan (no one was much concerned any longer with measuring time, let alone distance), there was still no sign apart from a few gutted *chaie khanas* of the biggest threat to us of all – the Russians. Nor had we encountered the troubles that held up earlier convoys, and in one case led to a shoot-out between Hisb-i-Islami and Jamayat forces which left a score of dead and wounded. Our column had skirted a hostile village here, a tea-house there, but mainly as a precautionary measure. Now word was passed back that the valley ahead might be hostile: there had been fighting in it only a week before, and we would need to cross the saddle with care not to be seen.

The problem was to provide our first practical illustration of the difficulties facing an Afghan guerrilla commander.

Ghul Bas ordered a young *mujahideen* to go ahead and scout out the land. The young man refused, whereupon an argument broke out that we could not follow. In the end Ghul Bas went ahead himself, while, as perfectly silhouetted against the skyline as any sniper could wish, the rest of the company stood watching him. But there was no enemy waiting for us that day. As if in celebration several of the young guerrillas fired their weapons into the air.

Increasingly I was bewildered by the human contradictions in the *mujahideen*. Sustained on an unbalanced diet of rice with insufficient protein, they seemed nonetheless to possess demoniacal stamina, so that for them walking was no more tiring than breathing was for us. They combined extraordinary strengths and weaknesses: a wild indiscipline with an exacting self-restraint demanded by a code of hospitality by which at all times they were ready to share their last scrap of food; the childish need to give orders combined with an inability to obey them; great personal pride, physical courage and panache, but without the smallest sense of strategy or military efficiency. Increasingly I wondered what manner of man it was that we were going to meet who had welded this anarchic group into a unified fighting force effective enough to have held back the Red Army.

Our own spirits were recovering: we were growing stronger, and the night in the mulberry grove, where sleep had followed two meals and a bathe, had encouraged us to hope for more such treats.

Our reward was the stiffest climb yet, but by now we were able to measure gains. Although thigh muscles still ached from the unaccustomed demand of going uphill, the blisters from going down were slightly better. We had survived; and a few days' march away, there was the prospect of another horse.

We paused at Tizeen, the largest place we had yet seen inside Afghanistan. In its little square was a charming mosque and an even more charming elaborate wrought iron water-pump. Tizeen boasted three shops, two of which were closed because it was a Moslem holiday. In the third we bought apples and Pakistani cigarettes, and rested in a courtyard where we were asked to put out our cigarettes because it was a part of the mosque; (curiously, everywhere else that we visited smoking in the mosque was considered normal).

Our midday meal was a bowl of oil and yoghurt into which we dipped our bread with fingers ceremoniously washed in the all-purpose canal that flowed through the middle of the village, just below some watering goats; yet however open to question its hygienic value, the washing ritual manifestly served a separate purpose of bestowing a sense of order and form on the act of daily living.

Tizeen had sheltered Englishmen before. It was here that the remnants of the British column of 15,000 had passed on their retreat to Jalalabad in January 1842 after a sixty-five-day siege at Kabul.

Then, as now, the Pathans were apt to take the law into their own hands; and with their old enemy at their mercy, they chose to ignore the treaty signed at the end of the siege, guaranteeing the British safe passage through their territory. By the time it had reached Tizeen the retreat had turned into a death march, described by the sole European survivor, Dr William Brydon, an assistant surgeon of the East India Company.

Brydon's official despatch tells of the progress of the column towards Tizeen from Huft Kotul in the hills towards which we were heading:

The heights were in possession of the Enemy who poured down an incessant fire upon our Column. Lieutenant Sturt of the Engineers was killed by a shot in the Groin. Captain Troup was wounded and Captain Anderson's eldest child was missing when we arrived at our ground at Khurd Kabul....

On the morning of the 12th we resumed our march near the Huft Kotul toward Tizeen. So terrible had been the effects of the cold and exposure upon the Sepoys that they were totally unable to resist the attacks of the Enemy who pressed upon our flanks and rear: and on arriving at Tizeen, towards Evening, a mere handful remained of all the Native Regiments which had left Kabul.

We halted a few hours at Tizeen and found that Major Swayne, Captain Miles, Lieutenants Deas, Alexander and Warren of the 5th NI, Lieutenant St George of the 57th NI, Major Ewart of the 54th NI and Doctors Duff, McGrath, Bryce were killed or missing and that three European women and one or two soldiers of the 44th had been carried off by the Enemy....

During all this march we had been fired upon by the Enemy from the heights, and as we moved on to Jug Dulluk they pressed still harder upon us.

One hundred and forty years later we were following the same stony-hearted route in the opposite direction to our Victorian forebears; and although they had made the journey in a cold that killed, while we were travelling in August in a heat that was merely trying, the closeness of the parallel left little room for comfort.

Jean-José had been missing again for the midday meal. Two *mujahideen* went off in search for him, and discovered him asleep under a wall. After that the waiting continued, without any apparent reason. But as I observed to Jean-José, I was beginning not to care. For me, Western *angst* was receding. '*C'est le début du début,*' said Jean-José.

When finally we moved off, there was a sound like distant thunder.

'Rockets.' The voice belonged to Tony, our unchallenged authority on all military matters. The *mujahideen* had heard it too, and split us into two groups. One went ahead, while the two Frenchmen, Tony and the four of us followed our armed escort over a wall where we crouched in a field of clover and speculated whether the combatants were Russian planes or our local rivals. If Tony was right and the sound we had heard was rocket-fire, then it was almost certainly Russians. Though potentially more devastating, air attacks only occurred in daylight, leaving us free to move under cover of darkness, whereas the Hisb-i-Islami, operating on the ground, could bar our progress at any hour. The sound of a jet high overhead resolved the question. Tony produced a manual of Soviet weapons from his back-pack and showed us silhouettes of MiG and Sukoy jets.

It was our first taste of fear, and suddenly we felt very naked. If spotted we would be at the mercy of Soviet helicopter gunships, only a few minutes' flying time away from the Soviet air base at Baghram, near Kabul. We had no means of retaliating. *Angst* was back.

The heat was becoming unbearable, and a sneeze told me that I had caught Sandy's cold.

It was growing late when we moved on to join the rest of the convoy at a tea-house where the horses and their drivers were sheltering under a copse of poplars; but there was no tea.

While we stood about uncertainly awaiting instructions, a cry of rage went up from a knot of horsemen. It came from Jamir, and he appeared to have gone berserk. Waving his fingers he advanced, shouting, on a young *mujahideen* who stood his ground with an insolent grin. Infuriated, Jamir hurled himself on the youth; whereupon two others joined in and, pinioning Jamir's arms, led him struggling and wild-eyed to a corner of the copse where they attempted to reason with him. We turned our backs and pretended not to see. Apparently of like mind, our guides hurried us away to spend the night in a place 'ten minutes away'.

Half an hour later we heard a second jet. Exposed in a sea of stones stretching several hundred yards to gully walls either side of us, we crouched as best we could among them. Our instructions were to cover ourselves with our khaki *patous* for camouflage. I had left mine behind with the horses which were supposed to bring our equipment on later. The plane was flying too high and in any event too fast to see us, but it was pointless to explain to Afghans who had never been in an aeroplane that a human being is impossible to spot from the air at 500 miles an hour and I accepted my scolding in silence, conscious that had it been a helicopter the outcome could have been very different.

We stopped for the night in another grove of poplars planted around a flat patch of earth, with the comforting knowledge that beside us a thick copse with undergrowth offered some sort of cover from the air.

As if from nowhere a man appeared and sold us apples at a cost equivalent of eight pence a pound. We passed the time concocting a lemonade drink with river water, chlorine tablets, lemonade powder and glucose. It was curiously disgusting.

Two guerrillas had found an abandoned Russian jeep and managed to start its engine. A group of local boys began chasing each other in a mock air raid, arms extended for wings, roaring at the top of their voices, like schoolchildren in wartime England pretending to be Spitfires. As the sun set behind the bare hot hills the Russian jeep returned with six shouting *mujahideen* aboard, covering us with dust as it passed.

I woke to a sore throat and the sound of Soviet jets, now becoming almost a commonplace, but still unseen. There was no sign, either, of the horses; and Sandy and I resolved to walk back to the copse, where we found Jamir doing sums with pencil and paper under a tree. He greeted us warmly, having apparently forgotten the indignities of the day before.

We had since learned that his role in the fracas had been an honourable one: a group of the young *mujahideen*, not Panjsheris, had questioned his orders and, unlike Ghul Bas, he had not been ready to tolerate mutiny. In spite of his unreliability over the horse I found I was becoming attached to his volatile Dickensian figure. We left him engrossed in the business of counting his load of weapons and ammunition, and, having retrieved our back-packs so as to be independent of the horses in future, sat down under a tree.

We could feel the heat rising as we waited, listening to the dry rasp of leaves in the motionless air. A boy came over and showed me how to tie my scarf into a *burnous*, a lighter alternative to the Chitrali hat. As a reward I offered him a sweet: whereupon he clutched his stomach and began to groan, pointing to the back-pack from which he had seen me take a salt tablet. Without Jean-Phillipe to reprimand me I gave him one, and he appeared to be delighted as well as instantly cured.

Tired of waiting we returned to the grove where we had spent the night. Ahead of us was a seven-hour walk to the Kabul River: the plan was for us to move off in the day, then lie up beside the river in order to make the crossing in the dark without alerting the Soviet army outpost nearby.

Early in the afternoon there was the sound of yet another jet overhead, louder than the ones we had grown used to. It was followed by explosions that shook the ground, then more jets. We scurried into the copse and squatted or lay in the mud. We could now hear a new sound, more persistent than the jets, the rotor blades of helicopter gunships. Peering out I counted eight mosquito outlines high in the sky. Somewhere up the valley in the direction from which we had come, rockets or bombs were hitting the earth; we thought of the horses waiting with Jamir. It was the first of many times that we were to regret being separated from the television equipment. Through a gap in the branches over my head I watched a lone helicopter, lower than the others, hovering in the air, its stillness somehow more frightening for being against nature. A jet of smoke shot from it, followed by a noise like the trumpeting of a bull elephant. This, I learned afterwards, was its heavy machine-gun capable of firing 1,000 rounds a minute, or approximately seventeen every second. It was an unearthly sound and it instilled the fear of God in us. Then the jets came over again, and, after what seemed a long lull like the pause between lightning and thunder, the distant explosion of rockets.

Inside the copse the *mujahideen* shouted orders to us and to each other to stay under cover. It was hardly necessary. Beside me one of the children pointed to the sky and said: 'Boom!'

It was all over in ten minutes. We learned that the strike had been at a point behind us a few miles higher up the valley, and that six people had been killed. As I thought of Tizeen and its pretty water-pump and finely proportioned mosque, fear mixed with anger.

The raid had disrupted our plans. Instead of setting off for the river, we were sent to wait in some caves in the valley wall nearby. There we found the local population assembling, together with a number from our own convoy. I sat next to a youth of sixteen in a bright blue waistcoat, who was introduced to us as the son of a *mullah* from the Panjsher. In his hands was a Kalashnikov AK-74, the latest Soviet infantry combat weapon, which he cocked and un-cocked with its barrel pointing at Sandy's stomach.

The atmosphere in the cave called to mind London Underground stations during the Blitz, waiting for the all clear siren; eager *mujahideen* told us how they had shot down thirteen (or perhaps it was thirty) Soviet jets. As the afternoon dragged on I remembered the soldier's definition of war as 5 per cent terror and 95 per cent boredom. In a corner of the cave Jean-Phillipe whiled away the time with a miniature Rubik Cube.

Between ourselves we speculated, for want of anything else to discuss, on the chances of the Russians knowing, or caring, that a party of Western journalists was in Afghanistan.

The more interesting question, which we could not answer either, was why the Russians did not fly their helicopters lower, and why they had not succeeded in closing the ammunition supply lines from Pakistan. The MI-24 was the deadliest Soviet weapon in Afghanistan and probably the world's most lethal helicopter gunship, capable of annihilating all life within its range in a matter of moments. According to Tony's manual, it carried rockets, a rapid-fire rotary cannon and four 1,000-pound napalm or high-explosive bombs. It had a titanium bullet-proof cockpit and heavily protected underbelly, so that it could only be shot down by a missile, a well-aimed rocket-propelled grenade or a fluke shot from a heavy machine-gun at its rotor blades. Whatever their reasons, the actions of the Soviets seemed to us mercifully timid.

One answer could be fear of ground-to-air missiles; we certainly had none with us, but photographs of guerrillas standing beside SAM-7 missiles had been published in the world press. Another answer might be that they did not want their weapons to fall into Western hands for scrutiny. Yet another was simple incompetence: according to this theory, the Russians had sent in second- or third-rank commanders to Afghanistan in 1979 when they thought it would be a quick police operation, and now these commanders did not want to draw attention to their shortcomings by having to ask Moscow for replacements. Already it was widely rumoured that a senior Soviet general responsible for bungling the last *coup d'état* in Kabul had committed suicide.

The *mujahideen* had their own explanation. It was that the Hisb-i-Islami were negotiating a sell-out to the Russians in exchange for political advantages for themselves and, therefore, the Soviet forces were holding back their firing in Pathan areas. They predicted that Russian activity would intensify as we approached the Panjsher, the true centre of resistance.

The sun was low in the hills when we resumed our journey along the valley floor. We spread out, walking in single file, this time with *patous* at the ready, ears cocked for the sound of aircraft, eyes marking down points for shelter, as we picked our way among the stones. Twice we heard jets and lay flat, but each time they passed high overhead. There was nothing to be done about the horses, which once again had gone on ahead, except to hold them still and hope that they would look as innocent from the air as the groups of camels tended by nomads that we passed from time to time. We ignored the third jet altogether.

The setting sun turned the stones of the valley to honey and gold as we left it to cross the line of mountains to the north.

Just before light failed there was another alert. We paused, and high above the jagged crests a line of mosquito shapes could be seen heading north-west towards the air base at Baghram. But the crests themselves were bare, and there were no Pathans, as there had been in 1842, to fire down upon us.

As I walked I went over in my mind our recent baptism of fire. We had all been rattled by it in varying degrees. It is said that healthy human beings relive danger in their dreams until fear has been exorcised; while those who do not dream, disturbed children for whom an experience has been too overwhelming, often store trouble for themselves in later life – a characteristic of the trauma being that its victims are fated to be punished twice.

Sandy, and to a lesser extent myself, had been under fire before. An Israeli jet had demolished Tom's hotel room in Beirut. I did not know whether Charles had any experience of action.

It was not a question of physical courage. That they had shown in full by volunteering for the expedition. Courage may be the grandest of virtues, but for working under war conditions experience is every bit as important, both to control fear and to help in anticipating the enemy's behaviour, as a pedestrian crossing the street gauges the speed and direction of the traffic. The difference of course was that, unlike those Soviet aircraft, traffic is not intended to kill.

What we had experienced had only been a dummy run; next time we would – so we hoped – have television cameras with us, but we would not be able to use them lying face down in a copse. But our initiation had rendered one important service towards overcoming fear: it had established in our minds the possibility of survival. From my own previous experience I knew that next time it would be less frightening.

At that stage we kept our darker thoughts to ourselves. As it turned out, I need not have been worried.

Our next obstacle was the Afghan army post at the top of the pass ahead. We had been told that our passage had been 'arranged'. But in the middle of a war an assurance that the enemy had been successfully bribed was something that even our Afghan guides treated with circumspection. We were warned to proceed with caution and in silence.

The moon had risen by the time we reached our midnight tryst. As we came up the saddle of the mountain near the limits of Pathan territory, the convoy leaders called a halt. Our student guide put his fingers to his lips and signalled us to sit. Ahead we could make out silhouettes of the ammunition horses, the dim line of pylons carrying electricity to Kabul, 30 miles west of us, and the shapes of the Afghan army outposts, old forts probably built by the British army in the nineteenth century. Somewhere beneath us in the bowels of the mountain was the tunnel taking the main road from Kabul to the Khyber Pass.

We held our breath as torchlight threw a human shadow against the wall of one of the forts. There was a smell of thyme under the waxing moon.

Then, quite loud in the darkness, there was a cry of '*Arakat!*'

Nobody ever said so, but I suspected that the forts were deserted.

Scrambling to our feet we headed at breakneck speed in the direction of the Kabul River since this, too, had to be crossed under cover of darkness, and with even greater care for, unlike the forts, it was guarded not by Afghans, but by Russians.

Yet another dry river bed followed the reverse slope of the mountain down to join the Kabul River. We had been warned of deep water and fierce currents awaiting us, but not of the ordeal by

stones on the approaches. The path beneath our feet descended like
a Scottish scree, except that instead of pebbles it was made up of
boulders, large loose footballs ready to twist an ankle or hurl one to
the ground. We headed down this at '*mujahideen* speed', twice our
normal pace. We were not allowed to use torches, nor to speak. In
the course of a penitential descent, I discovered that my eyesight
was unusually poor in the dark: mistaking the black patch of a small
but dense thorn bush for a gap between the stones, I tripped and
somersaulted over it. My watch and note-book shot from a pocket,
and a bag of boiled sweets flew from my hand. By a miracle the
note-book and watch were found but the sweets were lost, and such
was the change in our values that I regretted the loss of this source
of quick energy more than I would have the watch.

I fell twice more in the dark, painfully and headlong, once blundering into Sandy ahead of me, but the pain scarcely mattered and
the humiliation not at all: the fear I shared with all my companions
was for a twisted ankle or a broken limb, the consequences of which
were unthinkable.

As we stumbled on blinded and bewildered by fatigue, I became
aware of a searchlight sweeping the ground ahead of us; then quite
suddenly we were at the water's edge. The *mujahideen* told us not
to talk (we weren't) and then began to shout amongst themselves.
We were told to head straight across the river, and at once cannoned
into a group which had stopped just ahead of us. Instead of waiting
under cover to catch our breath and then proceeding in silent
groups, we finally advanced on the river together in a frontal rush,
sounding exactly like the herd of animals and humans that we were.

But if the *mujahideen* were displaying a lamentable lack of professional competence, the Russians and Afghan government forces
were happily matching it. With advance warning, or even a rudimentary network of patrols, we would have been all too easy meat
as, boots hung about our necks, we entered the river water. As it
was, we took the absence of activity as confirmation that Soviet
tactics had remained to keep a permanent hold only on the towns,
and attempt to subdue the remaining 80 per cent of the land they
had invaded by a system of selective air strikes and hit-and-run
ground offensives.

We were accustomed by now to inaccurate information, so it was
no surprise to find that where we had been warned of a flood we
found a trickle. It was August, and the waters that would carry

away a horse in December lapped refreshingly about our ankles on this summer's night.

Thirst being sharper than fear of the Soviet tanks reported to be guarding a bridge nearby, I paused to fill the plastic bottle hung about my waist. As I did so I saw with relief that Charles and Tom had somehow managed the descent in spite of their cramp. Sandy, rock-like as ever, was just ahead of me, and Tony, the Australian, waited impassively on the opposite shore.

The searchlight was too far away and revolving too fast to do more than frighten us. Otherwise there was no detectable sign of an enemy. The entire convoy crossed the Kabul River undisturbed.

I was all but sleep-walking as we wound our way up the far bank towards a settlement half an hour away, where we finally laid our heads in the dust to sleep.

I opened my eyes after three hours to find myself staring at a white horse standing rock-still on a flat roof nearby, apparently asleep. I wondered idly how it had got there. Beside it two young goats were playing at butting one another. Otherwise there were no inhabitants to be seen, and as the sun rose over the run-down and blackened mud and stone houses it gradually dawned on me that they were derelict.

We had not eaten for twenty-four hours and were beginning to be seriously concerned for our bodies' failing strength. We watched the bare landscape turn from grey back to yesterday evening's gold and hoped for tea.

But there was to be no tea, nor anything to eat. The village had been abandoned a month before after an air attack; a reprisal, we were informed, for helping the resistance. Behind the euphemisms of war, the human face: in the dictionary of military jargon selective air strikes mean homeless families, gutted villages, and to pacify means to frighten, starve and kill – the lot of any conqueror, whether American, Russian or Israeli, committed to occupying a country against the will of its inhabitants. The question here, given that the Russians had failed to cut off the vital supplies reaching the resistance, was what would they try next? More of the same, only more intense? More troops for more ground offensives? The only certainty was that if it came to an escalation of ruthlessness the Kremlin would not be inhibited by the inconvenient pressure of public opinion. The Russians were free to turn the screw until it suited them to stop.

6. Some Early Hitches

The disappointments were beginning to pile one upon the other. We were critically short of water. Our student guide, saying he was not feeling well, had drunk most of the bottle that I had filled the night before. To be able to sit in a lice-ridden room sipping cup on cup of tea, the first loaded with a thick sediment of sugar to last through the refills, had become a prize beyond compare. But as we trudged across the increasingly dry land at the edge of the Kohi Safi Desert to the north-east of Kabul, we found first one closed *chaie khana* then another.

If we were thirsty and tired, we were also more hungry than I had believed it possible to be. We were nowhere near to the stage of weakness, when craving for food gives way to hallucination and then euphoria: we still had the resources of protest whereby yesterday's sustenance was converted into the energy to clamour for more today. We were, quite simply, ravenous.

As an undergraduate extremely short of money I had once spent a week in a Paris attic following in the steps of my hero, the poet Arthur Rimbaud. I was only too eager to put up with the pangs of hunger and turn my mind, as Rimbaud had, to the problem of solving the universe. But far from the great thoughts I planned, all that I could think of during that week was food. Now, three decades later, it was not the web of geopolitical strategy in which we were caught up that filled our minds: it was menus. Lovingly Sandy and I discussed a meal we had shared in a three-star French restaurant as young correspondents: *gratin* of shrimps' tails in cream and champagne sauce, roast lamb, raspberries in a strawberry sauce.

'I think I'll have chicken for dinner tonight,' said Sandy.

'Where will you get it?'

'I'm confident we'll get chicken in the next village. Or lamb.'

'Lamb yesterday, lamb tomorrow, but never lamb today. It'll be boiled goat or nothing.'

'Oh, I don't know. We should get lamb. I would be quite happy with it, or chicken. Or goat,' he added. 'Delicious.'

There are times when nothing is more lowering than optimism.

We paused in mid-morning in one of the now rare patches of trees and vegetation that formed oases in the increasingly sandy scrubland. Our guide lay down and instantly fell asleep. This was the birthplace of Mohammed Daoud, the last king's cousin and usurper, credited with opening the door to Soviet penetration. Daoud had conducted an aid auction between East and West, and committed the twin blunders of imagining that he could have aid without influence and of trying to buy out the political aspirations of ordinary Afghans with social and economic advancement; then, after a series of repressive measures, he lost out to the progressive forces he had unleashed, and paid with his life. He was liquidated in 1978 in the course of a *coup d'état* almost certainly stage-managed in Moscow. There followed a series of experiments in instant socialism, each of them more brutal and ham-fisted than the one before, each ending in bloodshed, the last to the accompaniment of the Red Army. Here in the countryside the point the reformers missed was that peasants owned their own plots: what they desperately wanted was not redistribution of their land, but irrigation. Backed by the *mullahs*, who also had a stake in the status quo, they vigorously rejected the ungodly visitors in city suits.

On the heels of our hunger came a thirst so fierce that we tried some unripe pomegranates growing in the little oasis, but we could not swallow more than a single mouthful of the acid liquid that exploded from their seeds. Instead we took a supply with us for the stretch of desert to come.

It was now clear that our guide was ill. Yesterday's young lion, strutting in his camouflage uniform with matching Kalashnikov and deriding us for our sloth, was now a sorry figure as he awoke and sat holding his head in his hands. Someone suggested that it might be the fault of the pomegranates. His student English did little to aid the diagnosis.

'What's the matter?'

'I have a headache. Here,' he said, clutching his stomach.

'How long have you had it?'

'Five years,' he replied.

We now started crossing the Kohi Safi, a desert with grey dust for sand. All at once the sun seemed to redouble its intensity, as if challenging us by raising the stakes. As we trudged, still in single file, I thought of the characters in *Beau Geste* scanning the horizon for Touareg, seeing oases that were not there. I followed, always just ahead of me, the endless sequence of reversed TIMBER-LANDs mirrored now in grey. In an equally endless repetition of split-second impressions I felt sure I heard the sound of spring water; each time the sound resolved itself into the dry chink of stones under our feet.

At the top of a slope, beyond which we could see another identical in every way, we came to a square rusting metal plate beside which, waiting like a mirage, was a bucket with rope attached. A *mujahideen* pulled at the plate and it moved, uncovering a well, too deep and too dark against the glare for us to see whether it had water. We gathered around while someone threw a stone. A moment later the hollow echo of a splash came back to us. The *mujahideen* picked up the bucket and, before we had time to stop him, threw it into the well without, however, taking the precaution of holding on to the rope, which thereupon vanished with the bucket into the darkness. For a moment there was murder in our hearts.

There was said to be a village fifteen minutes away. We allowed for half an hour, and when we reached it an hour later it was deserted. Petty irritations broke out like flash fires: Charles and Sandy had a dispute over a water bottle. Soon even the compact and solid figure of Tony began to falter. Three of us – Sandy, Tony and I – had become separated from the others in the dazzling grey waste. Near the top of another rise, Tony sat down and would not be coaxed to his feet.

'Join you in ten minutes.'

I shook the last half inch of water in my bottle.

'You can have two sips.' Tony took it: 'Cheers.' Later I asked him, out of curiosity, whether he would have taken the rest as well. He paused for only a moment and looked at me: 'You mean, if it had been life or death? If it's a question of you or me, I'd choose me.'

I thought then that I would too. The difference was that Tony could say it without guilt. It was an initiation; or rather the beginning of an initiation: *le début du début*.

But for the moment there was no life and death drama. On the other side of the rise we came to a line of abandoned shacks. In a gully to the side we saw a field of maize, and near it some villagers were threshing corn by hand. We also heard – and then saw – a real waterfall; beyond it trees and more houses. Resting in the shade were out horses, with bags unloaded. Beside them, his eyebrows – like his beret – slightly raised, a magician waiting for applause after a specially surprising trick, was Ghul Bas.

We sat down to lunch sixteen strong on the floor of the mosque in our village tucked in a cleft in the hills. The menu that day was rice, which we made more interesting with a sprinkling of Sainsbury's raisins; and fresh yoghurt with a light crust, incomparably more delicious than any I had tasted before. Our single, unanimous complaint was that there simply was not enough. The meal aroused rather than satisfied our appetites: after it we were like very hungry dogs given a single lump of sugar.

We were allocated the first-floor room of a house as sleeping quarters where we spent a disgruntled afternoon trying to blunt the sabre's tooth of hunger in our different ways, and getting on each other's nerves. Even Sandy's obstinate optimism, as he confidently awaited an inexplicably delayed but imminent banquet, became an irritant; unfairly, since his buoyancy was the mainspring of our survival. I stood accused of sowing the seeds of pessimism and panic. Charles took refuge in racing driver's slang: 'Fantastic ... Smashing ... Terrific ... Actually ...' ('I thought Englishmen only talked like that in films,' said Tony.) Tom escaped from reality in long bouts of sleep.

Matters did not improve next morning. We had planned a late lie-in, since we would not be leaving until the afternoon. Apparently eager to demonstrate his authority, the village *malik* (head man) woke us noisily at five for tea; there was no tea. We went to wash in the waterfall cascading down the cleft at the top of the village only to be turned back because women were drawing water and we must not set eyes on them, let alone ourselves be seen bare-limbed. We were led back to the mosque where there was still no tea, and thence to the first-floor room where we had slept. Then after more shouting from the *malik* we returned to the mosque feeling like bad-tempered package tourists deprived of a breakfast they had paid for in advance. The third time we struck lucky.

The sweet tea galvanized us. Sandy and the camera team went to work checking the cameras, and began to film the *mujahideen* cleaning their weapons. For myself, the horizon of thought narrowed to devising a way to achieve a meal of soup. The need to charge our batteries was now imperative: our little army was no longer marching on its stomach, but on will-power, and it was not enough.

The trouble was that it is an absolute rule of Afghan hospitality that food is shared with strangers. If we obeyed the rule, we would use up half our entire stock of soup in one improvident gesture of the kind I was perfectly aware that our hosts would not hesitate to make. On the other hand if we could exclude those who could survive on a diet of pure rice, we would have enough to keep feeding the seven Europeans and one or two guides at least for a while. Still I hesitated, fearing to give mortal offence with the implication that the hospitality was less than adequate; then, on learning that lunch that day was to be boiled rice on its own, I hardened my heart, determined that we would have enough to eat at least once before reaching the Panjsher.

Clearly there was no question of cooking a meal undetected: we would need a full-scale fire, and the villagers, many getting their first sight of infidel, were as interested in us as any other Afghans we had met. However, I congratulated myself on discovering an L-shaped wall, admittedly in the blazing sun, where there were remarkably few people about and which would suit our purposes.

I began to build a small house of stones on which to prop the camping pots I had smuggled past Es Haq's kit inspection, when a small boy came up, shook hands solemnly and squatted beside me. After studying me for a while he rose to walk off. I detected a rattle and called him back, whereupon he pulled my box of matches from his pocket and handed it back to me. Unabashed, he helped me build a fire with gorse and sticks for fuel. The combined heat from sun, flames and steam was almost intolerable as the water began to boil.

The soup bag, which I had found among the television equipment, was unnaturally flattened, like a Mercator's Projection map of the world, from being repeatedly roped tight and unroped on its journey from Pakistan. Inside it the packets of raisins, boiled sweets and soup powder appeared to have begun to undergo a chemical change in the heat. The labels were by now only partly legible, and there was the warm smell of active compost.

I laid the soup packets into three piles to choose from – meats, vegetable and fish – and began with a first round of Tomato, Leek and Chicken, and Lentil; finding there was not enough, I added a packet of French Onion with Cheese Croutons, hoping at least to disguise the chlorine of the water purifying tablet, and another, with the title of Hackbraten Fix, described as beef rissoles; to this my young assistant now added, before I could intervene, two packets of Bouillabaisse with Garlic Flavouring.

The result was a culinary triumph. Sandy raised the concoction to his lips and drank my health. Tony said: 'Cheers.' In all, the seven of us drank twelve pints. I have seldom felt more flattered in my life; but I decided to keep the recipe to myself.

Some rice arrived and spirits, raised by the soup, now soared. A goat, which had been grazing nearby, began to eat the rice from one of our bowls. We shooed it away and ate the rest ourselves: in the reshuffle of priorities hygiene was the first casualty.

High above our heads as we ate our fill, two helicopters flew by, but no one took any notice.

On the ground, however, we had begun to attract attention. I had attributed our relative privacy to my skill in choosing a place in the sun. Now a knot of men gathered at a little distance; one of them called to us and Tony translated. 'They want us to move. It seems we are sitting in the middle of the village lavatory.'

We lay on a bank beside the pond in our leafy resting place, comfortable enough by our new standards. Around us were the amenities of the village - water, mulberries, shelter - all the desert traveller could ask for. Our bodies were rested and above all, for the first time since we had been inside Afghanistan, our stomachs were full. My three companions had broken the ice of all film making: they had got some film in the can. Three small girls in bright red cotton dresses settled beside us to watch every movement we made. Overhead a magnificent mulberry tree stretched out its elegant branches to offer us fruit and shade.

The pond served as the village swimming-pool, and Charles photographed some boys bathing. After wading in to retrieve a tin of film that floated away he came out with slime on his legs. One of the boys offered to trade his catapult for the video camera.

We had gone back in time. For almost a week we had not seen a road, an electric light, a chair, a fork or a window pane. Apart from the abandoned jeep and a line of pylons, everything on the ground that we had not brought with us belonged to somewhere in the Middle Ages. Meanwhile we were two minutes' flying time from

74

one of the largest Soviet bases in Afghanistan and in the air over
our heads flew millions of pounds' worth of the very last word in
the machinery of destruction, some of it so new that it had never
been seen in the West.

Once there was a report like thunder in the distance, followed by
a jet that streaked across the deep blue August sky: the sound
barrier? Or was it a bomb?

The village had sustained casualties. Several of the children had
had limbs blown off by plastic mines disguised as bottles that had
been dropped from the sky. It still seemed incomprehensible that
our convoy had not been attacked; and though the mud roofs might
be hard to see from the air, it was unthinkable that the Russians did
not know of this link in the supply route. (Just in case, I have not
given it a name.)

I was watching a donkey being shod, blindfolded by the all-
purpose *patou*, when there was a commotion, and we became aware
of new arrivals in our midst. Horses and donkeys fully loaded with
arms, mines and ammunition began to pour into the village. A
moment later, like a conquering eagle, Akha Ghul appeared and
shook hands with each of us in turn. The main body of the convoy
had arrived.

I had no preconceived idea of what a master gun-runner should
look like, but it was engraved on my mind at that moment, as Akha
Ghul strode among us, all smiles and confidence. His presence
imparted fresh vigour and authority to our leadership. The pace
quickened: horses were loaded and again we split into groups. Ours,
still with Ghul Bas, who would personally accompany the Europeans now that the student guide was sick, was to set off second.

For once we had the semblance of a briefing. We had two obstacles to negotiate: the first, the Soviet base at Baghram, which we
would have to skirt in the dark, passing within a few hundred yards
of its perimeter, and the second, the Panjsher River, which at the
point of crossing we were told spread into a delta: in winter, it was
a single fast-moving body of water; in summer, usually no more
than the fingers of a hand forming several streams. I wondered
about 'usually'.

We were to carry with us as little as possible, and no torches. We
would lie up near to the base and move quickly and silently, after
dark.

After two hours' march we sat down to wait for the night in

grassy ease on a hillside, amazingly lush by our rocky standards. We had grown used in the desert to the idea that our greatest threats were from hunger and drought, but now within our gaze was a truly tangible enemy. Below us, less than 10 miles away, in the huge fertile plain that runs to the edge of the Hindu Kush, we could clearly see the Soviet air base at Baghram. Every few minutes a flight of jets would take off and roar overhead, or disappear soundlessly in the direction of the Soviet Union to the north. A lone Antonov spotter plane, which we had learned to distinguish by the old-fashioned sound of its propellers, landed, seemingly in slow motion. To our left, 25 miles south, Kabul lay out of sight.

The landing lights came on long before dark, and in the twilight the mysterious base seemed to hum, as if it had itself just arrived from another planet.

Our little party of gun-runners, donkeys, doctors, television men, with rockets, water bottles, Chinese mines, cameras and notebooks, passed the time posing for family-style photographs. We smiled for the cameras and listened to the jets coming back perhaps from a strike on the Panjsher Valley. Some we could see with extraordinary clarity in the empty sky. We ourselves would have been as hard to see with the naked eye from the air as it is to spot any human activity on the ground a mile away, unless of course the Russians had been looking for us; or unless the infra-red equipment in the Antonovs, that is reputed to be able to detect the presence of life on the ground several miles away by a heat-seeking process, was switched on and directed towards us. These were contingencies for which we had made no provision, and events so far suggested that the Russians were not devoting that high degree of precision to their operations, nor that much attention to ours. Once more we had reason to be grateful for the gap between capacity and performance.

We were again a hundred or so strong, as Indian file, horses and donkeys head to tail, we climbed down the hill. At the bottom we sensed rather than saw the great wall of the Hindu Kush in the darkness to our right, still four days away: the sheer scale of its bulk, even in the darkness, dwarfed all my previous conceptions.

In silence we approached Baghram. Then, when it was no more than a mile to our left, we turned north. Every two minutes flares fired into the air exploded soundlessly into half a dozen fairy lights and slowly descended on to the airport's perimeter wire. Now and then, to our dismay, watch-dogs howled at the night as our little army passed by. But there was still no sign from the base except the humming of a generator – perhaps simply the illusion of sound suggested by the eerie silence and the shimmering lights on the runway.

We walked for several hours in the unfamiliar flatness of scrubland, but seemed to make no headway as the lights to our left appeared to advance in step with us. We had no means of judging our progress.

Discipline, never strong, began to break down again. Our little group took a wrong turning in the dark and became lost. The convoy stopped and Ghul Bas went forward to find out what had happened. We heard voices raised recklessly in the night, a weapon being hurled to the ground. We sat helpless as lost luggage waiting to be redirected, and with no idea what the quarrel was about.

The tinkle of tinny piano music reached my disbelieving ears. It was Jean-José's wristwatch alarm, which played the first few bars of a French cafe tune I recognized but never identified. He switched it off with a muffled curse.

A moment later Ghul Bas reappeared, all caution forsaken, shouting over his shoulder at his unseen adversary, and we retraced our steps. Eventually we caught up with the main body of the convoy, from which loud cries in Farsi of 'Silence!' floated across the darkness to us.

By the time we reached the Panjsher delta, we were exhausted; once again we blundered into groups of *mujahideen* in the dark: once again we were given conflicting orders to take our boots off, not to take them off, to cross the river now, to cross further on. The first four fingers of the Panjsher were like the Kabul River, the merest trickles. Not knowing what to expect, we crossed them bootless, and I was grateful to a Greek friend who on my holiday had insisted that to walk barefoot was good for the liver; regardless of its abdominal benefits the practice had certainly hardened the soles of my feet, so that I was able to hobble in the blackness across the stony river bed with relative ease.

For the *mujahideen* nothing seemed to be a hardship. Heavier laden than we, with their Kalashnikovs and bandoleers of ammunition as much for decoration as for use, they sped on into the night with the excitement of schoolchildren breaking grounds. Most of them wore no socks, and their footwear ranged from old gym shoes

77

to boots captured from Russian soldiers, usually with no laces, so that to take them off and put them on again was the work of a second. Our laborious process, involving heavy socks (two pairs in my case) and laces from toe to ankle, was a constant source of amazement and occasionally impatience to them.

After the fourth shallow crossing several of the Europeans were limping. Conspiring in whispers we agreed to stage a sitdown while we put our socks and boots on again. It was an ill-judged act. Hurrying to catch up with the convoy we came upon our guide standing on the edge of a torrent, urging us impatiently across. Fully dressed we entered the icy water and at once sank to our knees. Ahead of me a donkey had almost submerged. There were cries from both banks for us to turn back. A few hundred yards further along the bank we tried again, and again waded first up to our knees and then to our thighs in the fast-moving water. This time a human chain stretched hand to hand from the far bank towards us. In the middle of the stream the current became so strong that at thigh level it was almost impossible to keep balance. Grasping the nearest hand I managed, but only just, to remain upright while I was hauled exhausted to the shore. With cheerful voices still ringing in my ears, I fell panting in the mud of the opposite shore, aware to my shame that the *mujahideen* had thoroughly enjoyed the incident: perhaps the smack of the witches' ducking stool appealed to their medieval sense of humour. Just then the centuries seemed to yawn between us.

We lay strewn under the stars, flat on our backs, oblivious to fleas, dust, dirt and the real danger of being trampled on by passing horses' hooves. In memory I cannot recall whether the lights of Baghram were still in view, but certainly I no longer cared.

Wondering how the others had fared, particularly Charles, now with upset stomach, and Tom with his cramp, I sat up and looked around me. Tom was lying beside me, mouth open, staring vacantly at the sky above. For a moment I thought he was dying.

'Tom. Are you all right?'

'Oh yes. I was just thinking that there aren't any shooting stars. The sky is fine. But I did expect shooting stars, and I can't see any. Not one.'

The Panjsher River flowed through territory held by Afghan government and Soviet forces, notably the town of Roka which blocks the natural entrance to the valley; so we could not simply follow its banks to our destination. Instead we would be obliged to make a detour, climbing and crossing the main barrier of the Hindu Kush itself, rejoining the valley higher up at Bazarak, which we had been informed was the largest town still not in Russian hands.

The obstacles we had met already had been so many and so varied, the advance information so spasmodic and unreliable, that we were beginning to lose our capacity for surprise. But the slope of the mountain that rose from the river bank, leading towards the outer wall of the Panjsher Valley, was so inhospitable and above all so strange as to baffle the senses. If the river had been a medieval test this next trial belonged to an obscure chapter of mythological punishments. The ascent was steep and straight enough, but it ran along an uplifted corkscrew of rocky ribs between which, unheralded, lay a fine white sand soft and deep enough to engulf feet and ankles. In the dark it was not possible to tell the ribs on which to find a foothold from the powder in which there was none. It was like wading blindfold uphill in glucose, but with the added twist that to fall meant the risk of cracking one's skull. We forced our eyes, closing with sleep, wide open in the vain effort to distinguish sand from rock. Even the sure-footed horses fell every so often, rolling over on their loads. Beside me Sandy went down with a cry like Don Giovanni's last, but with rich Anglo-Saxon *libretto*. Once I somersaulted; and, on looking up at the stars, heard myself proclaiming aloud that I wished I had never set foot in Afghanistan. It was three o'clock in the morning.

Half an hour on, a group of horses silhouetted on the skyline beside some buildings told us that we were stopping for the night. The Europeans, together with Ghul Bas, were mustered on a flat enclosure of stones, cold by night at this altitude, that served as entrance to the village mosque. There we lay, without our sleeping bags under blankets on the stone floor, the way Afghans did every night, except that while they thought nothing of it, we felt we would die. Too cold even to consider removing our water-logged boots, we huddled together for body warmth.

Three hours later we awoke to our first full view of the great wall of the Hindu Kush. It stretched along the whole northern horizon, rising greyer and higher than the lesser range guarding it on our side. Its uneven spine of crags and razor edges undulated in and out of the clouds just above it. Round this great natural fortress that presided forbiddingly over a surrounding barren world, the armies of Alexander, Tamerlane and Genghis Khan had fought and forced their way. When he first set eyes on these mountains Alexander is said to have been seized with *pothos* – a powerful yearning, in his case for spectacular deeds. Here the Moghul conqueror Babu spent a night in a frozen pass crouching for warmth in the disembowelled corpse of a camel.

Today the Russian-built road through the Salang Pass over to the west, linking Kabul to the Soviet Union, bypassed the core of the Hindu Kush. Aeroplanes flew over it. But still the bastion of rock itself remained unconquered due to the stoutness of heart of a small, not very well-armed guerrilla force and the strength of will of one young man who for three years, virtually unknown and unaided, had defied the Soviet army. It was a brave sight.

As we watched, the high mountain sun warmed our frozen limbs and began to reach the damp in our boots.

We had been warned that as we approached the Panjsher the attention from Russian planes would intensify. As a precaution a pattern had now been established for our convoy to make the bulk of its progress by night, leaving after a midday meal. That noon, with the heat of the day as intense as the cold had been at night, we ate in the mosque, a humble enough dwelling no different from the farmhouse buildings which we had grown used to.

The meal was a strangely formal affair. We sat in four separate groups of about twenty each, lined round the long table mats on which were set bowls of yoghurt or aubergine. Servers came round with towel and jug and we washed hands in silence as the *mullah* took his place. To my surprise this was not on the floor with one of the groups, but in a niche in the wall, 6 feet above the floor, where he lay on a nest of cushions, placed a pair of horn-rimmed spectacles on his nose and surveyed us as we ate. I observed that the lenses appeared to be entirely misted over, giving him the appearance of a carved stone figure on a medieval tombstone wearing goggles. On the other walls of the little mosque were frescoes of flowers and aeroplanes being shot down by cheering guerrillas.

Bularen was to be our last stop before we crossed the final barrier of the Hindu Kush into the Panjsher. It lay in the upward slope of the mountain wall, and we were told that it was a journey of two hours. We adjusted this in our minds to four, to allow for the twin weaknesses of Western flesh and *mujahideen* arithmetic. But we did not allow for getting lost.

Soon after we set out, Charles and Tom unpacked the camera to record the convoy's passage: donkeys laden with Chinese mines, rocket-propelled grenades, the dark shapes of canvas-covered ammunition boxes and, in the background, magnificent mountains in the unfiltered afternoon light.

We had been unable to predict Afghan reaction to the television camera. In the event, far from being camera shy, or fearful of losing their image and with it their passport to the next world, the young *mujahideen* posed quite another problem. They grinned and postured and demanded, shouting, to be filmed with their weapons. Told to take no notice of the camera, they walked up to it, stopped dead and stared into the lens. As I watched Tom and Charles linked by wires, wrestling with exhaustion and irritation on top of the technical difficulties of operating in these conditions, I thought, as I had often thought before, how little I envied the cameraman's lot.

What the camera could not record, being no better able to see in the dark than I was, were the details of night travel in Afghanistan. This particular night was not very different from the others, except in my case, in one respect. It began to play tricks on me.

We had been walking for perhaps two hours when it grew dark; several sorties of jets had passed over us, but too high to cause alarm. The sun set in glory while we walked across the bare plateau separating the final ridge from the wall of the Hindu Kush itself.

Then we took a wrong turning. Instead of forking to the left of a bluff in the wall, Ghul Bas led us along a cleft to the right. The track ran out, and we turned and clambered down the mountain again to the foot of the bluff. In the dusk we met another group, as lost as we were.

After four more hours of climbing we were once again tired and thirsty. Believing – I cannot think why – that it would be a short walk, I had not filled my water bottle. We began to rage again against our guides, their improvidence, disorganization and inability to understand our simple need to anticipate the obstacles ahead of us; but as the hours passed, anger yielded to exhaustion, and in my case an overpowering need for sleep.

Then, strange things began to happen.

It started with *Aida*. To my right it became clear that a rock I had been gazing at was in reality a building; and not a simple building, but a palace. Could it, I asked myself, be the Pharaoh's

Palace, or was it the Temple with the Dungeon beneath? The question did not strike me at the time as odd.

A few moments later invisible scene shifters appeared to have been at work, and what had been a building melted into a shadow. I remember then thinking that I could not possibly have mistaken Afghanistan for the banks of the Nile at night, for the two were continents apart; and these robed figures could not be Ethiopian slaves, because I could clearly see Sandy among them, and Charles on the horse. Was this a new kind of sleep-walking, where you fall asleep while walking, rather than wake up walking? Had Dante been asleep in Hades? Was I sleep-walking in hell? I stumbled on a stone, not for nothing the symbol of heartlessness: at least stumbling kept one awake.

Then in the distance I saw another phenomenon. Two swinging lanterns threw their light on the portico of an inn. Figures in starched uniforms stood in the courtyard to greet us. Clearly we were expected. I wondered if they would have food for us at this late hour. Once, in France, I had arrived by car late in the night at a hotel outside Aix-en-Provence and had been welcomed by the hotel staff like a long-lost family guest. I had never forgotten the warmth of the hospitality, and I recalled reflecting that English hotel keepers had long lost the art, along with that of cooking. But Afghans were famous for their hospitality and, given the raw materials, for their cooking. The difference here was that the figures waving their lanterns would be men, not women. I hastened forward.

But the scene shifters had been at work again. As I arrived, the building turned to rock, the lanterns to torches and the innkeepers' servants to *mujahideen* signalling to us the way ahead: up, always up, along another gully of stones, Afghan stones stretching into the darkness.

That night I had my first lift. Tom, not yet fully recovered from his cramp but wanting to get back into walking stride, offered me a ride on his horse. If nature were left to make its own selection for survival, I knew that night that it would not choose me; and I was all too happy to accept an outside helping hand. For half an hour I sat on the beast's bony spine, legs numb and dangling, slumped against the sharp corner of an ammunition box.

Then in the dark the voice of Charles asked: 'Do you think two can sit on this horse?'

Ahmed Shah Massud

Ghul Bas sulking

A Soviet T-62 tank knocked
out near Khenj

One of the new Soviet
Su-25 jets bombing in
the Panjsher. They had
never been seen in the
West, nor for that
matter been photographed
before.

The little footbridge, over which we scuttled between the bombing runs, lay with one end in the water

The camera crew, with Sandy Gall, filming Soviet tanks near Roka

Massud and followers at prayer. He never let them forget they were fighting a *Jehad*, a holy war.

In children, hidden shock was one of the most common after-effects of the Russian bombing

The old man looked as if he had been got up for the part of a holy warrior by a theatrical outfitter

Down and out: Sandy Gall and the author taking a break during the walk
in to the Panjsher

The moment the *mujahideen* caught sight of a camera they would strike
heroic poses, weapon in hand

Rahman, the tempera-
mental horseman

Stephane. His presence came
about by chance; it was soon to
prove essential.

Left to right: Tom Murphy, the author, Stephane Thiollier, Charles
Morgan, Sandy Gall; *mujahideen* in background

Rahman, Sandy and a Nuristani guide

A mosque in Nuristan: Afghan hospitality provides free
lodging for travellers

Coming down from Papruk, the highest of the passes on the way home

The author in Nuristan

We both knew the answer. I slid to the ground, and found myself not more but less able to walk after the rest in the saddle.

Near me another voice said: 'You very slow!' I recognized our student leader in his camouflage uniform. His five-year-old headache appeared to have vanished, and he was laughing heartily.

Ungraciously I asked: 'Where the hell are we going?'

The student pointed vaguely into the night: '*Bolo!* Up!' He had no more idea than I.

A French torturer is said to have consoled his victims by telling them: 'The day is long but it will come to an end.' I tried to find comfort in Gallic logic and failed. The end would only come if I stopped expecting it. We kept going only because there was nothing else to do. And it was long after I had stopped thinking of anything at all that I found myself sitting among the unloaded horses propped against a wall next to Tom and smoking my first cigarette for two years.

Bularen was a terminus for the horses. We woke under a walnut tree on a neatly terraced hillside. Below us in layers on the terraces were groups of guerrillas handling and caressing their weapons, then horses and donkeys and their drivers. Women's voices, in a half-shouted, half-chanted rhythm that I knew from Africa – up and down, as if telling a long plaintive story – floated up to us from an unseen river. We could hear the sound of the rushing water that was seldom to leave our ears during the rest of our stay in Afghanistan.

All day jets flew overhead, lower now, and we were told not to cross the open space to the river. Soon the guerrillas were breaking their own rules and going down to the river for their own brand of ablutions: one half of the body at a time – though not over-frequently – gravel or dust for soap, scarf for towel, *patou* for screen (the *patou* had to be kept clinically clean for praying). We followed with our washing-bags. By now India had disintegrated, and I learned to use a leaf instead to wrap my soap. With my life I looked after my small hat brush for nails, my comb, toothbrush and collapsible scissors for plaster (blisters were better but still going strong). Our need to wash had more to do with holding on to a familiar routine than with cleaning our bodies, for we stank as much afterwards as before.

Through Tony we learned that we would be travelling onwards separately from our bags. Our consternation at being parted from the cameras was blandly set aside: 'Ghul Bas says that a team of bearers will take everything, arms, ammunition, as well as cameras and meet up with us in Bazarak tomorrow.' He permitted a momentary twinkle to illuminate his dour Australian countenance: 'Or maybe next day.'

In retrospect I cannot be sure how we came to make up our minds what to do. Perhaps it was more a process of erosion than of decision. Two of our number were far from well: all four were exhausted. The horses could not manage what even the guides had referred to as the 'steeper' climb ahead. We could not carry our own material – even the money bag was too heavy – and our guides were refusing to allow us to stay behind. Had we taken a stand we would have had to wait without any means of communication. To keep going and reach Massud as quickly as possible was a gamble, but we decided to take it.

We had a last meal of mutton stew, yoghurt, fresh onions, potatoes and fruit. An old man, smiling puckishly, presided over us as we ate. Fatefully we set off, with rucksacks containing sleeping bag and needs for two or three nights, and, in my case, a camera as well.

The 'steeper' hill did not fail to live up to its promise. But we were prepared for it and, although it took us exactly twice the announced time (which we had also anticipated), we arrived at the crest of the wall of the Hindu Kush with a surge of excitement. Stretched before us was a grand view of the territory of Ahmed Shah Massud. It was exactly ten days since we had crossed the border into Afghanistan.

Our plan was to travel down the Manjour Valley, a range away, and stop the night at Bazarak in the main valley. There, a year ago, Jean-Phillipe and Jean-José had stayed in the house of Siddiqi, an Afghan who had been a chef in France and had given them every manner of Afghan meal.

We set off briskly. We had broken the back of the mountain. The descent ahead should only take us the rest of that day; with good luck we might even dine at Siddiqi's.

The landscape was little changed from what we had grown used to: the eye, yearning for green, lighted here and there upon a patch of trees, where neat terraces huddled round a small holding – islands in a sea of stones.

By mid-afternoon we had reached our first resting place: a group of farmhouses among which the river ran before diving under a cover of trees. We sat by its bank at an intricately built junction of stones, where an irrigation channel siphoned off water for the tiny cultivated area before rejoining the river further down at the edge of the shade. I again became conscious of the insistent sound of water washing stone.

There, too, we were initiated directly into the Panjsher war. A boy came up to us as we rested, asking for a doctor. It seemed that two men had been hit in an air raid that morning, and one of them was lying on the ground outside a nearby house. While Jean-Phillipe went off with the boy, Ghul Bas sent a runner ahead to scout our path.

Jean-Phillipe came back in need of a scarf to act as sling: the injured man had wounds in his neck and head.

'Will he live?'

The young doctor appeared taken aback by the question. 'Given proper care, yes. Left on his own, possibly. If he is moved he will probably die. It depends. *On fait ce qu'on peut.*'

One does what one can. And after that, speculation is not healthy. If the Russians or Afghan government troops came they would probably kill the wounded man. Adult males in the Panjsher were assumed to be guerrillas – wanted bandits to be tortured for information and them summarily executed. We fell silent and listened to the earthy sound of water, a reminder of forgotten sanity.

Perhaps forty minutes later the runner came back with news of our first real set-back: Bazarak was in Soviet hands.

Suddenly all our plans, so precious to our Western psyches, were in the air again. At risk were our rendezvous with Massud, our cameras and, hardly less important, our evening meal. The capture of the second biggest town in the Panjsher meant the likelihood that another Soviet ground offensive was being prepared for the main valley, and possibly even some of the side valleys, such as the one we were in. This was the pattern of five previous offensives, when, with model guerrilla tactics, Massud's forces had withdrawn to high ground and waited, harassing the extended enemy lines of communication at night, until finally they had pulled back to Roka. If this was a second offensive in one year, from our point of view it was a few days premature. We urgently needed Massud and our cameras.

For Ghul Bas the problem was simple and he seemed puzzled by our concern. If we could not meet Massud at Bazarak, we would meet him elsewhere: he would get in touch. We had only to walk back up the valley, cross two ranges and join the main valley above Bazarak, walking by night to make up for lost time. In all this he was, of course, right: we were unfamiliar with the extraordinarily efficient if primitive system of runners that linked every corner of the Panjsher operation with Massud. Where Ghul Bas was wrong was in his assumption that without food we were capable of the physical effort of accomplishing two days' journey in one.

About an hour after nightfall we decided we could go on no longer. Poor Ghul Bas, looking crushed in his bogus service dress uniform, appeared utterly confounded by our lack of stamina and our persistent interest in our fate – How long would it take? When would we eat? Where were we going? – all of which he took as an act of infidel distrust in Allah, Massud and himself.

In the past I had often been embarrassed by the poor manners of my fellow countrymen abroad and appalled at the demands made by camera crews on people who, like our Afghan hosts, had put themselves out to look after us. Now all of us, myself included, lost all pretence of behaving as guests in Afghanistan are expected to behave. By that evening Ghul Bas had a strike on his hands.

'Where are we going?'

'*Bolo*. Up.'

'We stop here.'

'There are robbers.'

'You will protect us, Ghul Bas.'

'And wolves.'

No answer.

'There is no food.'

'We have soup.'

Ghul Bas's conversation with us was conducted through Tony in the manner of eleventh-hour negotiations through a mediator with a sullen but resolute workforce. But it was too late for orders, threats or appeals. We were dead beat.

Almost as an afterthought, I had brought half a dozen packets of soup with me. We chose a camping place beside the river and, seeking kindling by torchlight, found only dung. Somehow we got a wretched fire going, and began to heat water in a pan. Ghul Bas had disappeared. As we were about to share two cups of watery soup between ourselves, half a dozen more *mujahideen* appeared from the darkness and squatted beside us. Damnable though it was, we knew we had to share our rations, as they would have done in our place. There was scarcely enough for two sips each.

That night I felt the zest ebb from my limbs, as much from weakness through lack of food as from a sense of helplessness in chaos. I lay awake on the bare rock, my stomach even less tutored than my head in the ways of fatalism, too hungry to sleep.

After about half an hour we heard someone approaching: it was Ghul Bas and on his face was his magician's smile, while in his arms was a steaming bowl of boiled goat.

Greedily as beggars we gathered round. There were ten of us, and enough meat for four. Even before the bowl was set down each eater had measured his share with an eye quickened by hunger, then dipped a right hand in, taking not too much to reveal the ravenous beast within, but enough to be sure of not being cheated.

An ugly little incident marred the meal. It was over in a moment but it was to linger in my memory like a splinter.

I drew a bone with some of the grey unsalted meat on it; another bone, with more, clung to it. As I raised it to my lips, Charles, sitting next to me, stretched out a hand to take the second bone from my grasp.

I took the whole portion and set it down before him, a counter-challenge to his challenge.

'Oh no. I didn't mean it like that,' he said, in a voice of distress. 'Not like that.'

And perhaps he didn't. As quickly as lightning it had come to us and gone again, the moment of naked aggression; but for a pinprick in time the beast was let loose, then barred and caged again. Thinking back on that instant I found the story of Captain Oates the more extraordinary. When survival is at risk survival is all that comes into the mind: honour and shame come a poor second. Perhaps hope brings out the worst in us all, including a mean streak in the will to survive; and it is only when hope has gone that there is room for the noble deeds that distinguish men from animals. Or perhaps Captain Oates and the Astor who gave up his place in the *Titanic's* lifeboat were not noble after all, but only afraid to live with the shame of surviving at another man's expense.

But our meagre supper that night provided no uplifting insights: only the lesson that hunger is a diminishing experience. We ate like hungry rats.

'What I aspired to be, and was not, comforts me.' Browning's words mocked me now. It was not the aspiration but the falling short that filled my mind; and as we climbed into our sleeping bags the goat tasted bitter in my mouth.

Not so in Sandy's. 'Perfectly delicious,' he said. All his geese were swans: now even his goat was chicken.

7. Our First Panjsheri Acquaintances

The first jet of the morning came over just before seven o'clock. To our surprise it was a commercial airliner, passing by like a parody of normality, presumably carrying passengers between the Soviet Union and Kabul. It did not seem to be flying particularly high; if the Russians believed their own propaganda that Western mercenaries were running the resistance, they surely would not have exposed a civilian aeroplane to a ground-to-air missile.

We were three-quarters of the way up a side gully, having retraced our steps of the day before but then turned off at a divide in the mountains to a route that would lead us to the next side valley called Abdullakhel. We had been walking for two hours. Tom was suffering again from cramp, Charles from upset stomach. Even Sandy was irritable, but there was something reassuring about the two figures ahead of me, looking like a pair of eccentric sportsmen: Jean-José with his fishing-rod, and Sandy with the air of a testy golfer who had been misinformed about the whereabouts of the nineteenth hole. Every now and then he would pause as if to say 'Bloody fools!' to the world at large.

At noon we stopped at the home of a Kabul bus driver. His plot of land in the main valley had been destroyed in the June offensive, and he had moved his family to a cave, the opening of which was shut off by a tarpaulin. Inside, everything was as neat as a pin. An empty Johnnie Walker bottle stood unexplained in the entrance beside a silver snuff-box. We sat cross-legged for our meal of tea, fresh *nan* and mulberries.

Our host, whose patrician manners matched his features, wore a shirt with blue and white stripes that might have come from Jermyn Street. He appeared to be in his late fifties, elderly by Afghan standards.

When funds were low he would walk over the mountains to

Kabul and drive his bus. His age protected him from being press-ganged into the regular Afghan army, to which extended compulsory conscription for all males between nineteen and thirty-nine had been introduced as a result of mass desertions to the guerrillas. Many Panjsheris commuted in this way across the frontiers of war, as the Vietcong had done in Vietnam, providing Massud with a courier service to resistance cells in Kabul, bringing him money to buy arms; but above all giving him access to an excellent intelligence network with reliable advance information of Soviet intentions.

The news that a doctor had arrived spread quickly. Outside our tented cave a little queue had formed. While we ate the leader of the local guerrilla cell came to greet us. Once again I was struck by an indefinable air of authority. There was something that commanded respect in his very youthfulness. The little crowd, seeming to sense it too, parted as he approached. He was well turned out in black Soviet boots, captured or bought, cavalry breeches and tunic shirt as elegant as ours were filthy. But it was to his head, the apostle's beard and eyes, that one's eyes were drawn, as he greeted each of us formally in turn, kissing twice on both cheeks, and thanked us for being there to tell the world what was happening.

Another dignitary appeared, shouldering his way towards us, with wilder eyes and blacker beard, a John the Baptist among lesser believers. This was the village *malik*, pulling rank to get to the doctor. Jean-Phillipe examined him under the respectful gaze of the other patients. There was an exchange in French and Farsi (which Jean-Phillipe scarcely spoke); questions from Jean-Phillipe: 'Ask him if he has diarrhoea.' Gestures of acute agony from the patient; finally, to the spectators at large: 'Tell him he has worms.' And for our benefit, in English, triumphantly: 'Ee 'ass vermss.'

But any loss of prestige the *malik* may have suffered from the diagnosis was adequately compensated for by the course of six capsules attached to a card which appeared from nowhere in Jean-Phillipe's palm and which he gave to the *malik*, who went away greatly satisfied.

After the *malik* came the children, suffering in the main from diseases related to malnutrition. For most of them there was nothing Jean-Phillipe could do.

We decided to separate that afternoon for the first time, Tom staying behind to rest his cramped legs and Charles with him, while the rest of us went ahead to make contact with the main guerrilla network, and get word of Massud.

Taking leave of our elegant host we confused courtesy with accuracy and believed his grave assurance that, allowing for our slow speed, the journey onwards would take us three and a half hours. After six we reached the top of the grassy climb.

There was a moment of elation at the crest of the ridge, perhaps 12,000 feet above sea level, as we gazed at the valley of Abdullakhel. Before our feet there now stretched a frozen cascade of rock, reaching to a settlement 3 or 4 miles away, but almost as many thousands of feet below us.

We were learning to ignore pain, take will-power for granted and treat our bodies as machines. One critical factor was the equation between food and energy – and we had eaten enough to manage the journey. The other critical factor was striking the right balance between the danger from air attack by day and the more immediate one of falling and breaking a bone in the dark. What made sense for an ammunition train of horses at night over relatively open territory was dangerous nonsense for amateurs on foot in the dark over mountains.

As night fell it became clear that Ghul Bas had once more grossly underestimated the time the journey would take us. He had let us linger too long over lunch.

We started to pick our way without torches (Ghul Bas had commandeered mine), but soon I, who seemed to see least well in the dark, had had enough. At my instigation we gathered in a little knot, all but Sandy who had disappeared, and settled for another mutiny.

'Tell Ghul Bas', I said to Tony, 'that I refuse to break an ankle in the dark. We stop here. We should have left earlier.'

This time Ghul Bas met our protest by hurling his torch to the ground with a shrill cry of fury. A moment of shocked silence followed, broken by a sound in the darkness. It was Sandy, who was taking advantage of the natural opportunity afforded by the pause. A moment later he reappeared.

'We stay here,' said Sandy, stoutly.

Ghul Bas picked up the torch and threw it to the ground again, still chattering with rage like a monkey.

'Hey,' said Sandy.

'What's the Farsi for "Hey"?' I asked Tony. But Tony, fitter and stronger than we were, did not have his heart in another night on the mountainside, and in the end, whether out of concern for Ghul Bas, or self-interest, or because we were too tired to resist, the mutiny collapsed. Muttering futile threats, playing blind man's buff with the rocks, we blundered and stumbled and cursed our way down the mountain until all of a sudden our path straightened and ran along the edge of a cultivated field; it was not until the following morning that I discovered a 10-foot drop on one side formed by the terracing.

Below the field was a village. We continued round and down a theatrical maze of twisting steps, using solid overhead timber cross-bars between the houses to steady ourselves in the dark, until we came to a little square where Ghul Bas called a halt.

At the first door his knocking yielded only a wail of protest from a sleeping woman, followed by utter silence. Then from somewhere an old man with a lantern appeared and ushered us indoors to an enchanting room with balcony, giving on to unseen rushing water, where on the carpeted floor we crept once more into our sleeping bags, the only wholly private place left to us.

Daylight brought the sounds of Afghanistan to my ear: a young goat's cry, frail as a baby's; rushing water; then six separate distant ominous thumps, not accompanied by aeroplane engines and therefore presumably artillery fire (if so, the first we had heard); and finally, closer to me and strangest of all, human grunts, neither pleasure nor pain. I sat up to see a young *mujahideen* standing on Ghul Bas's back, giving him a foot massage.

The room was as fine as I remembered it the night before, a prosperous farmhouse room with cross beams on its ceiling: the heavy carved balcony gave on to a hillside falling away to the irrigation canal and finally the river. Quicker now with practice, we gathered our belongings, and performed the routine morning miracle of cramming our sleeping bags into their tiny nylon sacks.

The new plan was for us to meet Massud that day. News had arrived in the night by unseen messenger that he would see us in a village at the entrance of our valley and the Panjsher itself: a point near Do Ab (meaning 'two rivers') where the stream we could hear met the Panjsher River. We quickly discovered that the strange and seemingly haphazard system of communication by couriers was an effective substitute for a daily news service throughout the

Panjsher. Wherever we went we would find the locals up to date with the latest development which passing messengers would trade with them; and since the valley was small enough for most faces to be known, the danger of sensitive information reaching enemy hands in time for counter-measures was apparently considered acceptable.

In recollection a day's march is hard to recapture: an inch on a map, a minute in a MiG, a half-hour car ride – had there been a car, or indeed a road. For us it was an obstacle course of stepping-stones on an endless sea of rocks, paths down and nearly vertically up; and between the islands of green, always bare grey and ochre horizontal cliffs on all sides under the angry eye of the sun. Perhaps we could average a mile or two an hour, but we had long ceased using such measurements; our preoccupations were with meeting Massud and getting to our cameras before the Russians chased us out, and when we had no more practical matters to occupy our minds, the void was filled instantly by insistent, banal and repetitive thoughts of food.

That day it was downhill, and pain moved from thighs to blistered feet, as we walked through leafier, more civilized land that made me think of Austrian or Swiss Alps, probably because it was beguiling to imagine the meal that would have been awaiting us at the end of the hike.

Our path followed a neatly sculpted irrigation channel round the curve of the hillside high above the river which it would rejoin a mile or so further down the valley. At the fullest point of the bluff its built-up side became a precipice, with our skinny path running along the edge outside the water. It may only have been a 50-foot fall, but as one for whom vertigo begins at knee height I was unable even to consider looking down to measure it. Arms stretched out in front of me, I advanced like a sleep-walker, eyes fixed on a point in space straight ahead. It was at the narrowest point, with room for one person only to pass, that I became aware of a man in a pin-striped suit standing and waiting to give each of us in turn the full Afghan greeting. This would normally mean a vigorous handshake, formal exchange; then gestures on our side to insist that we were not doctors (or Russians); and parting formula, usually the same, trusting that our journey would not be tiring (as far as I was concerned the equivalent of wishing a drowning man a good swim).

As I approached fear eclipsed shame and I stepped, boots and

93

all, into the irrigation canal and stood up to my calves in the flowing water while we completed the formalities. The unhurried elegance of the other man's gestures was in no way impaired by my posture, at which he betrayed not the least sign of surprise.

'*Salaam aleikom.*'

'*Mandeh nabashi.* May you never grow tired.'

'*Khub hasti*? Are you well?'

'*Jur hasti*? Are you in harmony?'

The ritual incantation would sometimes take on a life of its own, but my own repertoire was limited to a few stock responses. Also, I was getting cold feet.

The pin-striped stranger brought news that Bazarak had been destroyed by the Russians, but that thanks to advance information it had first been evacuated. Massud would be at a place called Tambona, near Do Ab, late that night.

We paused to rest under some trees bearing apricots and green-gages that tasted of wool, beside a carved farmhouse door. When I tried to photograph it Ghul Bas stopped me. It appeared that there were some women in the background. Massud was progressive, he explained, but there were people who did not yet understand. Here it was 'difficult'. If we wanted to film women it would be 'easy' if we asked Massud. Massud was the key to everything.

Soon we came across scars left by the June offensive. Tucked into the mountainside, above a lake where naked village children were swimming, stood shells of houses, their windows eyeless sockets, scored with black smudges. We bought apples in a shop where shelves lay in a heap beside a charred hole in the wall made by a rocket. We crossed a half-mended wooden footbridge where our stream became a river as it gathered its waters to meet the Panjsher proper. Here and there our path skirted a bomb crater.

We stopped again in an orchard where we were greeted by the local *mullah*, and boys spread a big cloth beneath a mulberry tree and shook its pale purple fruit down into it for us to eat. We rubbed our sore feet while the *mullah* led Ghul Bas and the other *mujahideen* in midday prayers.

Early in the afternoon we reached Tambona, where three of a family of eight brothers greeted us at their prosperous-looking farmhouse, which was a cut above the others we had seen before. Two more of the brothers worked in Kabul, and one was in France. There were smiles to welcome us to carpets laid out under a tree while we waited for Massud, sitting eagerly forward on our haunches so as not to miss the first sugared cup of tea.

We now heard more news of the damage: the most serious was that the French hospital a little further down the main valley had been gutted. The hospital was to have been the centrepiece of Jean-Phillipe's plan to set up a system eventually to be administered by Afghans whom he would train. Based on the main hospital but with mobile units as well, it was originally intended, in addition to nursing war wounded, to provide a service to eliminate the diseases associated with childbirth. In due course mothers, themselves properly nourished, would provide milk that would be both adequate and healthy: pre- and post-natal care would help to reduce one of the world's most catastrophic mortality rates (around 50 per cent). The service would be carefully co-ordinated with neighbouring areas so that travellers did not reinfect places where diseases were eliminated. High on the list were malaria, worms, tuberculosis. Drugs would be properly administered, also in a co-ordinated drive against specific diseases.

Now at a stroke Jean-Phillipe's plans were set at nought. Far from there being a hospital at his service, he was separated, as were we, from the main body of his supplies, and could only administer what he carried about his person: which under the circumstances was no small accomplishment. He seemed to have medicines in every pocket; somehow he managed to keep his hands clean.

On the march into Afghanistan I grew to respect both Jean-Phillipe's intelligence and his character. He hated to waste words or time. He professed to despise compassion, and showed no patience with it, preferring practical help to the refuge of make-believe or pity. And at only twenty-eight years old, he seemed ready to suffer the consequences of his own philosophy. When he complained it was of stupidity, not of hardship. He appeared to resent the separation from his supplies, which he attributed to incompetence, more than the bombing of the hospital, which had to be accepted as a hazard of war. He begrudged five minutes of his time telling a patient the same thing for the third time, but he would walk for hours, sometimes during the night while we slept, to attend a sick person, even though his journey might be fruitless. I picture him, usually at the front of our marches, in his wholly unsuitable canvas tennis shoes; or else sitting waiting for us perched like an owl on a rock, cleaning his nails or busying himself with his Rubik Cube.

While we were sitting under the tree a woman brought a listless child to the brothers' house. It was perhaps fifteen months old, too weak to move its matchstick limbs; the will to live was ebbing from its eyes. With surprising gentleness Jean-Phillipe took the tiny creature in his doctor's hands, and after the deftest inspection reached his diagnosis: chronic malaria, worms and malnutrition. He told us in a level voice that the child would almost certainly die. I never found out if it was a boy or a girl.

What use are human feelings? Perhaps pity, like fear, is no more than a warning signal, not a guide to behaviour, and useful only if it leads to help. Doctors do what they can to save life: when they can do no more, there are others they must save. I looked in the dark submitting eyes of the child and tried to say, there's no point in my pity, so I will forget you. But it seemed like saying, you don't matter because I cannot help you.

8. Ahmed Shah Massud

While we waited for Massud we rehearsed our needs.

Our mechanical ones were easily stated. We needed the camera, an operating base, and if possible transport on the rough road along the floor of the main valley, for which we had been vaguely promised use of a captured Russian jeep.

Massud would also want to know what material we were hoping to film, and what our story-line was. The background to it was too complex to do more than outline.

The Soviet Union, an alien power, had committed an act of aggression on the threadbare moral grounds that it was invited in by a regime it had virtually imported, and against which the country was in open rebellion. The irony was that in blundering into Afghanistan on the miscalculation that it was engaged in a quick policing operation, Russia was now faced with the choice between failure and staying on as the biggest colonial power in Asia.

On the other side was a fragmented patchwork of rival resistance groups, most of them tribally based, some with pretensions to nationalism, others religious fundamentalist groups on the lines of Ayatollah Khomeini's supporters in Iran, with a history of violent internecine dissension and a robust culture that belonged to a limbo between the Middle Ages and the twentieth century.

Es Haq and our Afghan hosts clearly hoped that the effects of our report would be to martial world opinion on the side of the resistance. Forced to choose, the West traditionally supported freedom even at the price of disorder, in preference to order at the price of tyranny. But a third option existed: given the isolationist mood in America with the scars of Vietnam and Iran scarcely healed, continued indifference seemed more likely, with political leaders continuing to treat Afghanistan as a bargaining counter in the struggle between the super-powers to be traded in for gains elsewhere.

97

Jean-José took a longer and more thoughtful view. Whatever the outcome of a Soviet invasion, he argued that Afghan society would now change for all time. Before consenting to leave, the Russians would obliterate the politics, culture and traditions of Afghanistan and rewrite its history. With the revolution came the unique opportunity either for a permanent communist solution or for an alternative. His business was to explore the alternative. It would entail persuading the Pathans, with their traditional dominance, that in the long run it was not in their interests to deny the minority a share of power; that a tribal approach in a detribalized society would deprive them of an opportunity to make a leap into the twentieth century. Jean-José expressed his regrets that the French government that had called itself socialist should turn its back on a relatively long cultural link with Afghanistan and show so little interest in its fate today. But his French intellectual training rebelled against the crudeness of violence: he was happy in an ordered world of concepts, and he railed against the short-term military objective of one exalté diplomat who, misunderstanding his mission, had been pressing him to assist in organizing the dynamiting of the Soviet-built Salang Tunnel that took the high road from the Soviet border to Kabul. 'They explained to me explosion and implosion and angles,' he said with the contemptuous gestures of his race. 'The non-communist Left has a wonderful opportunity and they cannot see it.'

In Farsi we asked one of the brothers who had sat working the bolt of his Kalashnikov to tell us what sort of a country he wanted for himself. 'Don't ask me. Ask Massud. I just kill Russians,' he replied.

Jean-José had a busy programme ahead of him.

Massud did not come that night; but next morning Ghul Bas shook Tony awake at five o'clock. 'Kassim,' he called, using the Afghan name the *mujahideen* had given the Australian. 'Kassim!' No further explanation was needed; the awed urgency in his voice conveyed the imminent arrival of his leader.

A knot of *mujahideen* had formed itself into a reception party at the end of the dried up field on the rocky path that ran by the river. The air of expectation recalled memories of other grand occasions: my first sight as a new boy of prefects at school, an impossibly remote élite in special striped ties; officers glimpsed as a recruit; crowds on television waiting for the President of the United States, with every now and then hushes followed by relieved murmurs as a new arrival turned out to be a false alarm, a press car or another bodyguard. Despite the bizarre circumstances the build-up was the same. Three more *mujahideen*, better turned out than ours, joined the knot at the edge of our humble field and at first we mistook them for the real thing. There were some more waiting, and then, unmistakably, he had arrived.

Massud strode confidently, alone and ahead of the little group that escorted him, unarmed amongst the glinting gun barrels, a striking, energetic, youthful figure. He seemed to know exactly who we were, as he seemed to know exactly who he was himself. He greeted us, in a hurry, and made us sit down. At once tea arrived, this time with milk – an unheard of privilege – as well as sugar. He turned and talked in Farsi first to Ghul Bas and to the brothers. I studied the strangely semitic features with hawk nose and the penetrating decisive gaze of a man who has his world at his fingertips: he seemed at once unassuming and confident, did not waste a gesture to demonstrate his authority, which thereby gained all the more; he had the manner of a man with inner strength of character rather than flamboyant personality. There was an uncommon stillness of the head, as all other heads bent to catch what he was saying. From time to time he would take aside someone with whom he wished to speak, and sit with them out of earshot in our dusty field; throughout there was never any question of who was in charge. His face was grey with fatigue and lined beyond his reputed twenty-eight years, and I could not help wondering whether this was simply his publicly stated age, or whether his strangely spectacular yet isolated career had prematurely lent him extra years. He could have been anything up to forty.

To the Russians, Massud was officially a 'bandit' to be wiped out; but they had not been able to do it. By other standards he was a small-time leader of a minority sect in a remote and puzzling country. Just then he was the absolute monarch of the 80,000 people in the Panjsher and had an almost mesmeric power over them; and besides them a growing adherence from over three and a half million Tajiks, a quarter of the nation, in other areas of the north-east. But most important of all he was the single most successful military leader in the field against the Red Army, and what he lacked in the traditional Afghan extravagance of gesture he had made up for in achievement. In consequence he was perhaps the most wanted man on the list kept by the Khad, the Afghan government secret service trained in East Germany.

There was a speed and concentration about his movements, as if he needed to despatch his business before his enemies could catch up with him. He never announced his whereabouts in advance or if he did he changed them; seldom stopped more than an hour in one place; and only the tiny élite that guarded, cosseted and worshipped him knew where he slept, which was rarely more than two nights running in the same house.

And so it was with us. After perhaps half an hour he turned to Tony and told him, in his surprisingly high metallic voice, that he would see us in a little while; we were to wait and he would send for us.

In the event, this meant in the house of the brothers. We began to learn his method of conducting business. He would arrive, greet everybody, and over tea establish his time-table and tell us the latest news, but matters for decision were for discussion privately at meetings that he would organize. In due course we were summoned to a room with a coloured photograph of the Taj Mahal on the wall, where he addressed us in French.

'What can I do for you?' Also in French, Sandy listed our needs: a base, transport, access to Massud himself, some film of the *mujahideen* preferably in action, film of women if that was possible, an interpreter and, of course, our cameras.

'*Oui. C'est tout?*'

It was already a lot. At first we thought he had not understood. He turned to Ghul Bas and told him in Farsi to send for the cameras. Ghul Bas went out at once.

Apparently losing interest in us, Massud consulted a surprisingly elaborate gold digital watch, presumably a present, which contrasted with his otherwise puritanical demeanour. He also had with him the latest model of a portable Sony short-wave radio which he now switched on to the BBC News in Farsi. He listened intently for a moment or two, and then switched it off. There had been no mention of Afghanistan.

'There will be a Russian offensive on the ground in three or four days' time. It will probably last two weeks. There will be a softening up process, mainly bombing. We will retreat and then counter-attack. Everything is ready. As soon as you have your cameras, you can come with us and film the counter-attack. Meanwhile I am going to send you to Khenj further up the valley.'

He smiled while we digested the information, and turned back to the radio. It was over a series of meetings like this that we were able to piece together the broad outline of Massud's military strategy; and increasingly we were to be impressed with the clear and single-minded grasp that he had of the problem confronting him.

If he became involved with every detail and seemed to take every decision himself, he was able as well to sit back, above the battle, and train his sights on horizons beyond the visions of his lieutenants. At our very first meeting he told us that Afghanistan was fighting a war for the West, and that the West seemed not to understand. But there was a mysterious self-confidence that seemed to spring from within, which he spread to all those with whom he came in touch. The *mujahideen* explained it easily: this was a holy war and Allah was on their side. Whatever the explanation, I felt myself to be in the presence of a man with a quite exceptional talent for leadership.

Later that day, when we saw him again, he told us that he would have made a pre-emptive attack on Roka before the Soviet offensive, but for a shortage of ammunition. Now it would have to wait.

'There are twelve hundred Afghan government soldiers on the way to Roka at this moment, with Soviet supervisors. By the time they arrive a lot of them will have defected to us,' he said with finality. 'Then we will counter-attack – in a week, maybe.'

Just then it seemed as unreal as Hitler's talk of a counter-offensive from the Berlin bunker. But Massud had done it before, and the eyes showed that he meant to do it again.

Statistics were hard to come by, and harder to believe, partly because of the Afghan tendency to confuse hope and faith. The official figure given to us by Massud was of 300 Russians and 200 Afghans killed so far that year, mainly in the May and June offensives, with 350 wounded in all. The strange proportions of more dead than wounded, even allowing that it is always hard to estimate enemy wounded, supported the view that neither side in this undeclared war paid much attention to the Geneva Convention. Wounded *mujahideen* were wanted bandits and wounded Russians or Afghan government troops more mouths to feed. Mindful of stories of atrocities on both sides (in the town of Herat Pathan guerrillas had flayed alive a group of Soviet advisers in front of their families), we asked the delicate question of what had become of the Soviet prisoners of war. Massud told us that we would be able to film inside the prison. We accepted the invitation.

Massud also claimed twenty-five tanks and one Soviet plane to the credit of the *mujahideen* in the May and June offensives, in addition to another thirty-six planes destroyed on the ground in a daring attack on Baghram.

Collated figures from all sources suggested that the Russians were suffering about 3,000 casualties a year from a total force of 105,000, a small percentage by accepted military standards. The biggest losses sustained by their ally, the official Afghan army, were from desertions to the guerrillas: government forces were said to have dwindled from 80,000 to about 30,000 in the three years since the Soviet invasion.

On the other side, Massud claimed to have lost about 150 dead and wounded from a force now numbering 1,000 inside the Panjsher alone. By far the most serious losses in the Panjsher were the refugees: of a total population of approximately 80,000 when the Russians invaded it was by now down to about half. These represented the water which the fish needed to survive.

In all Afghanistan, it was reckoned that about 150,000 guerrillas were lined up against the Russian and Afghan army – a parity in numbers but a gap of centuries in training and weaponry. By far the biggest group among the freedom fighters were the Pathans of the Hisb-i-Islami, but, by Massud's account, the least reliable. It was the Hisb, he claimed, which had let him down when as a younger man he had staged a *coup* in the Panjsher designed to coincide with a Hisb uprising, only to find that the Pathans had changed their mind at the last minute. He had fled to Pakistan, from where, after being trained in guerrilla warfare, he returned to the Panjsher, the land of his birth, which he had not left since.

9. The Softening Up Process

Before leaving to show the damaged hospital to the two Frenchmen, Massud promised us hot water for that evening. There was a curious price to pay for this happy prospect: since we were destined for hot rather than cold water, we were not allowed to leave the house to wash in the river in the meantime. All manner of pretexts arose: women were drawing water; we might be spotted from the air. To avoid giving offence we did not insist, and accordingly lay all that afternoon in our own filth on the dusty floor of the brothers' house.

Mutton stew and rest had taken the edge off hunger and exhaustion, and soon we were once again a prey to our ungrateful Western ways, complaining of boredom and discomfort. (I was never to hear an Afghan mention either.) I passed the time speculating whether a man who took on his shoulders the strategic response to the first direct Soviet military action outside the Iron Curtain since the Second World War should also be preoccupied with the minutiae of our washing arrangements. Was this another Alexander, with a genius embracing fine detail as well as the grand vision – the stuff of a great national resistance leader? Or was he an efficient but limited field commander without the power of delegating responsibility? Was there anybody to whom he could delegate? There was a surprising lack of show in his manner. Massud was a Tajik, traditionally despised as small-time businessmen and peasant farmers by the Pathans. But it was the Tajiks who had displayed the tactical and strategic skills of modern warfare, and welded themselves into a serious fighting force that had inflicted real casualties on the Russians. The Pathans swaggered in magnificent turbans; the Tajiks wore less glamorous but genuinely captured Russian uniforms and carried captured Russian-made AK-74s, the very latest Kalashnikovs not available on the market in Pakistan.

Meanwhile, amid my other preoccupations, I now had a new one: I was beginning to have reason to regret eating unripe grapes the night before.

At nightfall we left. After a mile we came to the main valley, where we crossed the Panjsher River by a new bridge that carried the only stretch of even road – 100 feet or so of concrete – that we came across in all our wanderings inside Afghanistan.

There we piled into Massud's personal car, a captured Russian jeep with bullet holes in its windscreen, and drove the twenty minutes or so to the village of Sangana where Sandy and I were allocated a room together in a private house. By now I was conscious that my trouble was more serious than a question of unripe grapes: I was becoming ill. As I climbed into my sleeping bag my head was hot. At one o'clock in the morning by my watch Sandy shook me awake to tell me that hot water was ready. There were two large bowls of it beside a hole in the floor; it was indeed hot, but now fever on top of sleep made it seem as unreal as a dream.

The main road, no more than a stony path, ran like an unmade bed through the Panjsher Valley for 30 miles, twisting round the bomb craters and rock slides between Roka at the bottom and up as far as Khenj, by way of Sangana; beyond Khenj a bigger landslip made it impassable even to tanks, before it resumed its journey northwards.

The jeep had come for us early. In it was one of Massud's aides, a man with bright light-blue staring eyes who spoke in orator's tones, as if reciting a speech he had by heart; he shared a common conviction that the problem of language could be overcome by speaking his own louder. Bellowing above the roar of the battered jeep, he pointed out two burned out Soviet armoured troop carriers, casualties of the June offensive, and the engine of a jet in the river bed to our right. He stopped beside a Soviet T-62 tank apparently blown up by a *mujahideen* mine, and, as is the way of guides all over the world, became an instant television director, indicating where to place our cameras, the absence of which seemed in no way to deter him. Beyond photography now, I sought refuge behind a rock.

At the entrance to Khenj (pronounced by us to rhyme with Penge, and as unlike a respectable London suburb as it is possible to imagine) a tree lay across the road, beside a command post of the local *mujahideen*.

Word of our arrival had gone ahead of us, for there to greet us was our new host, like a character from a Dickens' serial turning up again after an absence of several chapters: first we saw the thumbless hands waving in the air in welcome, then the volatile, now beaming, features of old friend Jamir.

Khenj itself proved to be a large village, large enough to have proper side streets running up the mountainside in one direction and across the river in the other. There were half a dozen little shops in the main street that sold cigarettes, grapes and apples; one, a butcher's, was empty, and in another was a barber who would shave you using your own razor and soap.

Jamir lived on the mountainside of Khenj, up a steep climb and above a little orchard, in a house approached by rough steps that led up into a courtyard. It had two rooms: one where Jamir and his family slept and ate, the other ours. It also boasted a rare convenience in the shape of an outhouse, containing a pile of dust beside a hole in the floor.

On the wall of our room, which had a charming view of the village and the valley beyond, was a photograph of Jamir in his younger days, smirking proudly at the camera, and below it a *charpoy*, the nearest thing to a bed we were to come across in Afghanistan. On it I collapsed, and my kind colleagues did not dispute that for the time being my need was greater than theirs.

It is said that human beings cannot remember the sensation of physical pain. (If it were not the case, the argument goes, what woman would give birth to a second child?) I cannot with accuracy recall how acute my pain was during the two days of my illness; only that I thought of seasick passengers who want their ship to sink to end the agony, and found the idea wholly unsurprising. I lay as if run through by a sword, pinned to the bed, while everything in my body that was not bone was turned to liquid; between visits to the fearful little outhouse I mercifully slept.

We never set eyes on Jamir's wife, but from their room next door from time to time children brought a bowl of fatty soup or meat. I tried neither. A packet of chicken powder, which we requested should be cooked in water, came back added to the soup, and that defeated me too.

After thirty-six hours nature, or the antibiotic pills, began to work and I felt better, but still so weak that, despite Sandy's insistence that we should be ready to move out quickly in case of attack, I settled in my mind that had the Russians arrived that day I would have chosen to stay (and indeed such was the fate, after we left, of a French doctor taken ill near Kabul, who was captured and sentenced to eight years' imprisonment for espionage).

After two nights I was strong enough to spend the morning counting the flies on Jamir's photograph. The same afternoon I went into the village to buy a spare pencil: there were none. I sat by the river and three small girls first shouted and then threw stones at me. I moved on, like an unwanted stray dog, and sat in the foundations of what was to have been a theological college, and began to write my diary. An old man greeted me with double handshake and sat staring at my strange Western script.

That evening the Russians did come; but only to bomb, and not to stay; and not to bomb us, but the next village. During the attack we were taken from our room to stand by a wall. It seemed neither more nor less safe than the house, either place being equally vulnerable to a direct hit. Jets whisked by the twin horizons over our heads on either side, cliff to cliff in two seconds, followed much later by their sound. Tony and I photographed mushrooms of dust in the distance and a line of helicopters too far away to register. War-wise children told us to be careful that our lenses did not reflect the sun back in the pilots' eyes and draw their fire – a fragment of expertise that was new to me.

When the raid was over a team of children tore around the village playing a more sophisticated version of the air-raid game that we had seen at Tizeen. As he ran the leader held aloft a carved wooden aeroplane to which was attached some kind of cracker which smoked and belched sparks, followed by the rest of the team squealing with pleasure.

Later we learned that six people, four of them women, and a donkey had been killed in the raid. We had been witnesses to a casual and negligent atrocity of war for which nobody would be called to book. The war in Afghanistan was evidence to support the case that recent American isolationism had achieved not the destruction of war, but the destruction of the balance of power. But all that would be brushed under the carpet: the East had no free press, and the West only limited interest.

I wondered what the war meant to the young Russian pilots. No Russian under fifty-five could have fought in the Second World War, so presumably none of them would have seen action before. Did they really believe the authorized version that they were mopping up bandits? Or was it all simply a video game played from their cockpits with computers and knobs, with map references for enemy and electronic dots for targets, to be completed in the few minutes before the canteen shut at Baghram air base five minutes' flying time away?

The next morning Jamir woke us at six to announce that Massud had advance warning of a Russian landing at Khenj. There would be the usual softening up process first and we would be evacuated in daylight hours up a side valley. To us this meant not just safety but another mountain ridge between ourselves and our television equipment. Adding what appeared to be embroidery of his own, Jamir said that the Russians had probably got wind that he was lodging *ferenghi* journalists in his house.

The whole village was on the move as we began our short journey to a group of caves nearby. As we walked in a long line up one edge of the side valley we could see a second line opposite us on the far side: there was a stretcher bearing a child, and women following.

Massud's intelligence proved astonishingly accurate. We had not been long in our cave when we heard aeroplanes in the cold morning sky; first the propeller engines of the spotter plane, which we recognized as an Antonov, probably carrying the raid commander and the infra-red detection equipment; then jets, three or four of them, wheeling and diving again half a dozen times. In my memory they are as if suspended in mid-air, in slow motion, because of the foreshortening effect as they flew over our heads and away in the direction of the village we had just left. On the terraced hillside black onions suddenly appeared, others from the area where the buildings were. In truth the sequence of sounds eludes me, like a film of which the soundtrack has lost synchronization with the picture. What I do recall is that, although we had learned what to expect, somehow the loudness of the explosions always took me by surprise.

This time we were less frightened than we had been at Tizeen, for we knew we were not the target. The jets were clearly aiming at the village itself, and perhaps the captured Russian machine-gun mounted on a nearby mountainside. The gun, a DShK, known locally as a *dashoka*, was capable of shooting down a jet, and a helicopter if it struck a vulnerable spot such as its rotor blades. But the bombs fell mainly on Khenj itself and the fields around it.

In the evening we accompanied the apprehensive villagers back to their houses to find that the footbridge over the river was untouched. So was the road. But when Tom and I went in search of cigarettes we found knots of shopkeepers wringing their hands as they showed us gutted stores, meagre stocks in chaos, shutters torn off. A house opposite the little commercial stretch where the barber sat had had a direct hit.

Then, with a crowd around him, we saw Jamir, gesticulating extravagantly even for him, wild-eyed and incoherent in his distress. Beckoning to us accusingly, he led us up the little alley where we used to come down to buy grapes. In the orchard the trees had been uprooted, and unnaturally shaped patches of earth seared by fire. Above it was poor Jamir's house.

The neat courtyard was littered with rubble; Jamir's room stood black-eyed where a rocket appeared to have passed through the window. Our own room, to the right, was in turmoil. The window frame was blown in, the solid stone wall fractured: someone had piled the room's belongings on the bed. On top of them the photograph of the young Jamir smirked up at us through a layer of dust. Outside in the courtyard only the thunder-box stood proudly unscathed and still exuding its foul smell.

It was hard to tell whether Jamir blamed the presence of *ferenghis* for the catastrophe that had overtaken him, but the poor man was beside himself with distress, and I think that both Tom and I were content to let him vent his feelings just then on us.

Before leaving I hung his picture in its old place on the wall.

We spent the night in a new hide-out, not in Khenj itself, but just outside and below the hill crest on which the *dashoka* had been mounted. We ate yoghurt and rice and drank *lassi*, a thin and fermented derivative of yoghurt. Massud's light-eyed aide had joined us and through Tony we pressed him about Massud's plan for us: if there were to be an offensive, we explained, we would need to have our television equipment. Once cut off from it by the activities we hoped to record, we would be lost. In our hearts was the fear that our hosts did not distinguish between the television camera and the ones we had with us for taking still photographs. The discussion became heated and all of a sudden the man turned to Sandy:

'Would you like to go and see Massud now? I can take two people.'

'Where is he?'

'Four hours away.' Wrongly, as it turned out, we assumed that he had two places in the jeep, and we agreed at once that Tony and Sandy should go ahead, Sandy as our leader, and Tony because he could speak Farsi. Tom, Charles and I would come on later. The party set off into the night.

The next morning, for the three of us left behind, was identical to the last. As we walked to our cave the rising morning sun cast steep shadows. Only a donkey or a goat moved. Deserted, Khenj sat a mile away in its own dust, partly hidden by the bare brown mountainside awaiting the heat of midday.

The jets came over earlier that evening, as we were sitting down to eat: they seemed to be concentrating now on the *dashoka* on the hill that I suspected was no longer there. At all events it did not shoot back. We were in the direct line of fire as we sat, with dress-circle view of the village. Bombs and rockets shook the earth, and the dust rose once more from the peaceful green terraces of Khenj. Then the silver planes pranced elegantly off stage like ballet dancers. Above the Panjsher River's tumbling water we could tell the different sounds with expert ears now – the Antonov's plodding propeller engines, the flashier roar of the jets – but there was still no sign of the slow purposeful growl of helicopters that would mean troops landing.

Afterwards, when our photographs were inspected, we learned that the jets used that day were new Soviet Su-25s, nicknamed 'Frogfoot' by NATO – fighter-bombers designed for use in mountain areas, capable of flying slower than most jets and therefore of making tighter turns. They had never been seen before in the West, nor for that matter photographed before. The Russians were using Afghanistan, as Hitler had used the Spanish Civil War, as a testing ground for new equipment.

The light-eyed aide came back that evening. Without an interpreter we could not discover how the others had got on in their attempt to find the missing equipment, but by means of sign language we settled that he would take us to them at nightfall.

It was another seven hours' walk, and Tom's turn again to suffer; from time to time he would disappear behind a wall in the moonlit valley. Several times when we went back to look for him he was doubled up in pain. At Do Ab, we recrossed the bridge over the Panjsher and retraced our steps up the Hazara Valley towards

Abdullakhel, where we had entered the Panjsher area. At the entrance to Abdullakhel we turned off to the left, beside the lake where we had seen the village boys bathing. By three o'clock in the morning we came to a roof-top, approached by a plank leading from another roof, where we found Sandy and Tony asleep under the stars.

They woke as we arrived. Sandy told us that Massud had agreed to all our requests and despatched his brother to look after us; that there were 300 tanks massed at Roka together with 12,000 troops ready to advance up the valley; and that we had narrowly escaped being cut off. Massud's forces had already knocked out six tanks with thirty-one officers and men, and he confidently awaited the chance of an early counter-attack.

For our part, we had two weeks left before we were scheduled to leave: we still had no television camera and no idea where it was; we were about to be attacked, and there was nothing left to eat in our back-packs; outside the Panjsher food could only be had for money and all our money, but for small change, was with the equipment.

'How was Massud's morale?' I asked.

'Excellent.'

'And yours?'

'Excellent.'

As I fell asleep I decided that they were all mad.

10. The Soviet Ground Offensive

Massud's brother Yahya was the older of the two, a widower in his late thirties. He had been assigned to look after us partly because of his English, which suddenly enlarged the horizons of our conversation from baby talk. The relief was enormous, even if results were not always to scale.

Next morning, over tea with goat's milk and sugar, we covered again the ground that Sandy had already been over with him. Once we had our equipment, we needed two donkeys to transport it and freedom of movement to make our film. Yahya nodded. 'I find something,' he said.

It turned out that he meant a cave, in which to spend the next two days, waiting. We followed him, up and up once more, thighs heavy with the poison of used energy waiting vainly for the heart to pump new strength into them, but with only goat's milk and two hours of sleep to draw on.

At the top of the first rise the only reward was a lung full of dust, and a preview of another; and then the cave, where we spent the day, as planned, waiting. It was now clear that Massud, who held us all in thrall, made all the decisions himself, and until a message came from him nothing could be done. The logical place for our equipment to be was the next valley of Abdullakhel, where there was the nearest guerrilla headquarters to our entry point: but there was no word from Ghul Bas.

While we were in the cave Yahya told us about the Massud family background. Their father had been a soldier, who had moved to Kabul from the Panjsher as a result of promotions, and had sent his sons to the university. Massud had studied engineering, after learning French at the Lycée. One of the few points on which all Afghans agreed was in their admiration for their distant forbear, Alexander the Great, and Panjsheris liked to compare Massud with him. It seemed that the driving force behind Massud was not the father, but the mother, whom Yahya recalled as a powerful personality. Though not of patrician stock like the weird, half-wild visionary who gave birth to Alexander, she had taught herself to read and write, a remarkable achievement for a woman in her position in Afghanistan at the time. Massud was at Kabul University in the early 1970s during the rise of the Left. He had moved back to his birth-place in the Panjsher, staged the *coup* that failed and fled to Pakistan. After guerrilla training (Yahya professed not to know quite where it took place, but denied that it was with the Palestine Liberation Organization), Massud returned to the Panjsher in 1978. Then in his mid-twenties, and starting out with less than fifty men, he built up a force of 1,000 or so in the Panjsher, taking care that everywhere he went he used locally recruited manpower and local organizations. Paradoxically, the result was to earn him what so few Afghan leaders in the past had earned: adherence in regions outside his own, as well as a nation-wide reputation.

Sitting on a slab of rock outside our cave, we watched the air raids from a safe distance, waiting for news. Instead we had plenty of rumours to discuss. A night watchman who worked in Kabul assured us that Babrak Karmal, the communist leader, had been shot in the shoulder during a cabinet meeting; the evidence being that he had been seen on television without his normal flamboyant gestures. According to several informants Afghan troops were deserting by the score, according to others in hundreds, so that now the Russians would not have enough Afghan army support to launch their ground offensive. We met a farmer with ruddy face and crafty eyes, who claimed to be a defector from the Afghan army. The story he told us was that the Afghan government was desperately rounding up anybody they could find to fill a quota of recruits. He had been visited on his farm in the north by two men while he was bringing in his harvest: they had pressed him into service, and he had been taken first to Kabul, and then flown with 200 other recruits to Jalalabad. There he had been kept for several days, without any training or weapons, until seizing his chance he had defected to join the resistance. Massud's followers had picked him up as he was crossing the Panjsher. Was he a bona fide defector or had he been planted as a government spy? Or did he simply want to get back to his farm? I was inclined to the latter view, but the *mujahideen* seemed ready to accept him as the stuff of guerrillas.

On the second or third day our spirits soared when, without explanation, one of our score of missing cases arrived; then sank again when Yahya asked us whether this was all there was.

The two Frenchmen reappeared. Jean-Phillipe's plans for forward and fall-back medical units had not been advanced, and like us he was still awaiting his equipment with growing impatience. He had spent three hours of the previous night operating on an eight-year-old girl whose intestine had been pierced by splinters from a bomb which had landed behind her. Fortunately he had been carrying an anaesthetic with him (where, I wondered) with which he had been able to inject her. He had treated several other children whose hands or feet had been blown off by plastic booby-traps.

Finally came the news that the gathering storm had broken.

Tony and Charles had decided to make the ascent from our cave early in the afternoon of 30 August to the top of the mountain wall beside us, from where it was possible to see into the main valley several miles away. It took them several hours. Their excited voices woke us from our siesta when they returned. From the top of the mountain they had been able to count 100 Russian lorries, armoured personnel carriers and tanks; some of the tanks were dug in while the other armour was on the move. Overhead they saw helicopters in scores travelling up and down the valley. The ground offensive had begun.

That evening we heard that helicopter-borne troops had been landed on the hilltops at Khenj, as Massud had predicted.

In the night we were woken on our roof-top by a series of crashes coming from the direction of the mountain tops to the north of us that shook the earth in rapid succession. We were now within artillery range. Coming as it did from nowhere, the unseen artillery was more frightening than the jets. (Next morning one of the *mujahideen* bunched all his bare toes and fingers together to indicate a Russian Katusha rocket: a contraption known in the West as a 'Stalin Organ', mounted on the back of a lorry with twenty firing tubes. Tony's textbook reported that its aim was to demoralize the enemy. It certainly rattled me.)

I was awoken a second time in the night by more unripe fruit trouble and, bleary-eyed, I found myself walking the plank, or rather crawling it on hands and toes, across the chasm, when coming towards me in the other direction I encountered Jean-José. The meeting could not have been better timed. At that moment the absurdity of two grown men, facing each other in the middle of the night on all fours, made it impossible to take the situation tragically.

Back in my sleeping bag, I wondered how on earth I had got myself into such a predicament. Before my eyes I could see in the moonlight a sparkling precious stone, then feel the silk of a private inner world of sleep. Awake again, the stone was once again a hard white Afghan stone, the stoniest of all stones, and the silk, the lining of my sleeping bag out of which strong voices would soon call on us to '*Arakat!*'

11. Letting Go of Nurse

The rules of Afghan hospitality bound Yahya to do everything he could to keep his brother's guests alive, an objective which we greatly appreciated. On the other hand we could not make a television programme in a cave without a camera. And so it came about that with the greatest reluctance Yahya was prevailed on to allow us to retrace our steps to the Abdullakhel Valley by which we had entered the Panjsher, in a last attempt to see whether there were any clues to the whereabouts of our missing equipment. Yahya's final proviso was that we should travel everywhere in groups of not more than two at a time to avoid being spotted from the air and mistaken for a convoy. He would follow on later in the day.

We headed back towards the lake which marked the junction of several valleys, the Hazara that led to the main valley, the one we were in, and the Abdullakhel Valley. We cut the corner of the journey by climbing an outcrop of rock high above the lake at the confluence of the valleys, from where we had our first view of the damage done by a raid on the lakeside village which we had watched from our stone slab two days before. The villagers were now huddled in hillside caves. From inside one, clearly for women only, there came shouts of protest as we passed near its entrance. We hurried on, uncomfortably conscious of our inability to establish our nationality, and of the colourful fate that a group of Russian military advisers were said to have suffered after falling into the hands of Afghan women.

A group of *mujahideen* passed us travelling in the opposite direction, evidently coming from the commandeered school building, now a guerrilla headquarters, to which we were heading. They greeted us warmly, seeming to know who we were, and asked for Yahya for whom apparently they had a message.

By noon we had reached the school and found it deserted. It had two floors set around a courtyard. One wall, with a large door by which we entered, had bullet holes in it from an air attack the day before. In the upper rooms we found school-books still on the shelves. The courtyard had running water from a channel flowing along one side beside an oven hollowed out of the ground, and the remains of a fire. We set to work at once on a menu of soup, tea and sugar that we found in one of the rooms, some maize which we unsuccessfully tried to grill, and potatoes that Tom's Irish nose had scented in a field nearby. We had to cook everything in a tea kettle, the only container to hand.

After eating we lay in a patch of purple clover overlooking a village clinging to the slope opposite. Beneath us we could see a wooden footbridge which Yahya would have to cross to reach us, and beyond, in a cleft in the mountains, the wall of the main valley where the Russians were. For the Russian pilots these same charming features, the little school, the village, the river, and the small field bearing the harvest, were no more than a map reference, a target cleared for jets to approach by a gap in the mountains.

A big crater of dried mud scarred the field of maize a few yards from where we sat. Another bomb had fallen short into the river, forming a perfectly round green pool deep enough for us to swim. There was nobody about. Going the whole infidel hog, we took off all our clothes and plunged in.

We emerged feeling human again. As we lay in the evening sun, our time-table shot away from under us, Sandy expressed his full confidence in the imminent arrival of our television equipment and began discussing the oysters he planned for the party he would give on our return to celebrate a successful mission. Charles wrote his diary; Tom slept under a blanket. I think we all felt chemically better; at all events our day's relaxation, without a plane to mar the blue of the sky, seemed just then a great deal more agreeable than our lacklustre cave life with Yahya.

After prolonged discussion we decided to split forces again, and while Tom and I waited in the school for Yahya's news, Sandy and Charles pressed on up the Abdullakhel Valley to look for the equipment. By nightfall there was still no sign of Yahya. Instead a handful of cheerful *mujahideen* arrived after a day in nearby caves, and we gave them potatoes in exchange for some small ripe apples that they had with them.

I thoroughly enjoyed that evening with the young hotheads who shared our meal. After eating they told each other long stories, their strong good features animated in the dancing firelight. One could see that their guiding star was within themselves, each just then a poet warrior in his own mind; and one could sense the lifting of their hearts as the heady tales grew headier, and doubtless feelings replaced facts.

We saw them now without a care for our practical world of plans and schedules. Our pills and plasters and changes of clothes were playthings in a fascinating bazaar but no real part of their philosophy. Theirs was a call to arms, a call from their forefathers to the Moslem conscience within to throw out an infidel invader as others had been thrown out before, including the British; a call from their successful dynamic young leader, who embodied the best in all of them; above all a call to every young Afghan male brought up with a gun in his hand to fulfil, now, the destiny each felt to be his own.

Always seemingly at home with themselves, ready and complete as they stood in their boots and makeshift uniforms with hat and *patou* and gun, ready always to eat or not to eat, to move from deep sleep to marching at a moment's notice, they thrived on this way of life which seemed easy and natural to them. The disruption brought by the Russian invasion, on a scale that would devastate any European, appeared to leave them unscathed. A change of plan, a day or a month in a cave, homes destroyed, made little difference. These young men were as ready to die as any medieval crusaders, confident of their place in the *djennad*, the Moslem garden paradise awaiting the holy warrior.

Among the Afghan qualities we had witnessed were extraordinary generosity, stylish good manners and courage: qualities of the inner spirit in people who had mastered better than most a dependence on material need, who were always ready without the smallest hesitation to share with us what they had. What price such individual virtues in a Soviet world of total planning?

Beside the firelight the harder questions receded into the shadows. How could the Panjsheris survive another winter in caves with their lifeblood flowing out with the refugees? How could Massud, from a minority tribe, hope to unite the resistance? Even if he did succeed in holding the Russians what could he do next? And, always in the back of Western minds: would a state run by fundamentalist Moslems be like Iran next door?

There were two other fruits of this strange fierce culture that the

Russians would have to reckon with, whatever the outcome of the fighting: an anarchical love of individual liberty, and an implacable xenophobia. A British nineteenth-century administrator had once advised London that the less Afghans saw of the English the less they would hate them. Afghanistan had been conquered many times but never subdued. Had the Russians read their history books? In the final analysis, perhaps the best hope for fending off Soviet domination was that so long as they left any Afghans alive they would never govern them, because Afghans were by nature ungovernable.

Tom and I paid for a happy evening in different ways. Tom stunned himself in the night when he hit his head on a beam in the lavatory; I was bitten by a centipede on the upper lip, which seemed to swell to the size of a golf ball.

We left the school at five o'clock in the morning to wait for Yahya beside the little footbridge.

On the far slope of the valley the village looked different again and more beautiful to the morning walker's eye; each house started more clearly now from the rock and dust where it belonged, each bearing its distinct and unique human fingerprint in some small variation of form or height or angle. The surrounding terraces stood out, too; no longer just a haphazard patchwork but a pattern crafted over the centuries in partnership between people and nature.

Even the small footbridge, two poles with cross-planks resting at one end on a heap of stones and at the other on a wall, seemed to span the river more elegantly that morning. We sat beside it in a scarred orchard, where trees had been uprooted in the raid of the previous day, branches snapped off and tossed into mounds of churned up stones and earth.

If we thought ourselves safe from a second strike of lightning in the same place, we should have known better. A line of craters stretching in a straight line from us towards the school indicated that we were now under the direct path of a jet attack. Near the river's edge, we watched a red-tail washing itself busily. It was pleasant to be free of our excitable guides, who walked too fast and shouted incomprehensible orders. I enjoyed the sound of rushing water, and the deep blue of the sky; until all of a sudden the air was filled again with war.

As we waited, with only a fragment of hope now, for Yahya, we heard the first of the Antonovs, and we knew that our turn had come round again on the bombing roster at Baghram. There was a bang and an extra loud jet noise. Tom and I ducked behind a wall. Ahead of us, approximately where we had been bathing the day before, there appeared a huge column of dust. Debris rose perhaps to 60 feet, paused, and slowly began to descend again.

There seemed to be all the time in the world, while the jets wheeled for their second run, to recross the little bridge and take cover in the valley wall on the path up which Sandy and Charles had headed the day before. In fact we probably had less than two minutes before they were bombing again. Over our heads as we ran the Antonov buzzed like an angry hornet. We huddled together by a stone wall under some trees. Anxiously I looked at Tom's face, and was astonished by his expression: I think he was enjoying himself.

Under cover of the copse, we headed along the start of the valley of Abdullakhel. Although our spirits had taken a turn for the better, it was clear to us by now that our fortunes had not. We had broken the rule that says it is best to keep a hold of nurse, for fear of getting something worse. We had lost touch with each other: our equipment appeared to be scattered across Afghanistan, and now we had also lost contact with the last shred of Massud's organization. In addition we appeared to have earned the personal attention of a Soviet spotter plane.

Ahead of us a bomb had hit the irrigation channel along which we were walking, but we suffered nothing more serious than wet feet as we passed its crumbling banks. At the edge of the copse we paused: there was no shelter for several hundred yards. We waited for silence and walked as fast as we could over the open space, until we heard the Antonov again, whereupon we took cover between the built-up sides of a path leading from the next village into some fields. Crouching between the stones we could see the Antonov circling, escorted by two helicopters.

From nowhere a man and a woman joined us. They were clearly terrified out of their wits. Too shocked to veil her face, the woman greeted us with a handshake and offered us not once, but twice, a scrap of bread that she carried in her hand. Despite the danger overhead, I could still find it within myself to be deeply moved by this fine fragment of self-respect. It was as if the act of traditional hospitality dispensed at the roadside under the threat of annihilation held her in touch with her inner self. After a few minutes, the couple left and we never saw them again. Hers was almost the only woman's face I saw in Afghanistan and I could not get her expression out of my head for many months.

The next village was utterly forlorn. Our path took us through its middle, where a building had collapsed on to the little square, half smothering a fine old mulberry tree. There were no inhabitants to be seen, and there seemed to be nowhere left for them to live.

Then we came to Tunkhu, the largest village of the valley. Its main square had been hit, too, and there were piles of dust and rubble in the little crooked streets, but, as our path rounded a corner beside the last of its shuttered and padlocked houses, we found ourselves in an untouched stretch where the pathway made a final sweep round the village. From there we had a view of the smiling valley rising in terraced steps to the skyline on our left. Timeless, the old stone houses looked down on us, with their heavy hand-hewn ladders of seasoned wood placed against them by way of staircase either months or centuries, before. To our right, the stone cliffs rose and rose out of sight, leading eventually to the devil's own work in the shape of the pass over which we had entered the Panjsher only ten days before.

We sat on a stone bench beneath two walnut trees, and again from nowhere, as always seemed to be the way in Afghanistan, an oldish man appeared and greeted us, and conveyed to us what was already apparent: that the other inhabitants had taken to the hills and that he had decided to stay behind. He made a gesture of impatience at the sound of the Antonov directly overhead.

Tom's Farsi was a great deal more advanced than mine and between the two of them a conversation was possible. Tea was, alas, out of the question since there was nobody to make a fire. Would we like some water? We would. The man went off. The Antonov had moved now and was circling a little higher up the valley. In a moment or two our new friend came back with two metal beakers of water.

Would we like some walnuts? We had not eaten that day. We certainly would. As the man shinned up the walnut tree and climbed along a branch, the jets came screeching in directly over our heads towards the upper valley, travelling in the same direction as ourselves but about 500 times as fast. We could see the bombs falling perhaps a mile away among a group of houses. Throughout the raid the man in the tree, though certainly not deaf, took not the smallest notice. Deliberately he collected a handful of nuts and climbed down, while I took pictures with my camera.

'*Hob?* Good?' He meant the nuts, which by now he had cracked and peeled for us, and laid out in my scarf. We ate them under his eye while he stood with his back to the raiders which he quite simply ignored, as a duchess might an uninvited guest, and when I took his photograph with a bomb exploding over his shoulder he did not flinch.

Trudging off again, we had reached what we gauged to be the approximate epicentre of the raid when there was a cheerful shout; under a tree, standing on a hillock not far from a fresh bomb crater, were Sandy and Charles, and beside them a pile of bags.

The fate of Tantalus himself could not have been more cruel: Charles had the perfect position but no television camera to provide unique eye-witness evidence of a bombing policy directed indisputably at civilians. He could not know then that the photographs he took with his own 'still' camera would later be published all over the world; but to any television cameraman, this could only be second best.

The night before Sandy and Charles had struck lucky, staying in the house of a man who, by sheer chance, turned out to have some of the television equipment and who knew the whereabouts of more. They had collected a dozen from a total of twenty missing bags, but unfortunately neither the camera, the bag with our money, nor the food were among them. It appeared that the porters, for want of other instructions, had taken the equipment for safe-keeping to their houses when they returned from Bularen and found that Bazarak, where they were supposed to take it, had been captured.

For lunch Charles produced some Kendal Mint Cake, an astonishingly sweet bar of concentrated calories in the form of mint-flavoured sugar, which we ate with raw maize, following a disappointment in which my untutored eye mistook a vegetable marrow for a melon. Afterwards it was agreed that we would camp out for the night where we were, since we could no longer move without porters; and in any case we needed to wait to question the local cave commuters when they returned for the night. Meanwhile Sandy and I went ahead to continue the search for equipment at the *mujahideen* headquarters at the top of the valley.

On the way up, as we were passing a field in which some black goats were grazing, we came under attack yet again, this time from jets flying in the opposite direction. Sandy and I lay beneath the wall of a terrace where we pressed our faces into the mud as firmly as if we had been modelling for our death masks.

After the first pass of the jets I felt something first treading, and then lying, on top of me. It was a terrified goat. I recall being struck by the astonishing amber of its eyes.

There was a deafening crash as rubble soared into the air, followed by a second explosion and a crimson flash 20 feet or so above the first. The Russians were apparently using cluster bombs that explode above ground to cause the maximum of casualties and scatter thousands of plastic needles that cannot be detected in the body by X-ray. Until then we had felt safe in the belief that only a direct hit could kill. Now we were not so sure.

We picked ourselves up, shaken enough for even Sandy to declare that he felt as if someone had planted a homing device on him that day. We had both come as close as we wanted to being participants rather than mere spectators in the events unfolding in Afghanistan.

Presently we came to another group of farmhouses with ladders reaching to their flat roofs where fruit lay drying in the sun; one ladder was propped against a tree, beside which a man stood, proudly displaying his handiwork – a large nest of straw like a child's tree-house – in a fork some 20 feet above the ground. By his gesticulations we understood that it was his bomb shelter. A more sure way to increase the risk of death would have been hard to devise, but the streak of Afghan eccentricity as ever delighted our hearts, and we bent our footsteps upwards and onwards refreshed in spirit.

It was on this final two-hour stretch to Abdullakhel that I decided gently to prepare Sandy for a possible failure of the mission.

'If we do not find the camera after turning over every stone in Afghanistan, then we will have to face the fact that there is nothing more to be done. We will have run out of the time allowed in our budget in two weeks from now.'

'I remain confident that it will turn up.' The rebuff was implicit. He did not admit the possibility of failure, even to himself. We changed the subject.

At the village where we had spent our first night we drew a hostile blank. Beside the farmhouse with the carved balcony was a crater

6 feet deep in the plot of a smallholder that had flattened his harvest for a further 50 feet around: the area destroyed was enough to represent a family's income for the season. Villagers returning from caves arrived at the same time as ourselves, and if they did not think us Russians they seemed angry with us, as Jamir had been, as though the very presence of foreigners drew havoc from the sky.

A guerrilla who apparently recognized us invited us into the Jamayat house and gave us tea in a room with a portrait of the exiled King Zahir on the wall. We showed him a pencil drawing of our missing luggage made by Charles, but he shook his head. While we waited I made a paper boat for one of his small children, a remembered childhood trick. The child did not seem to understand it, and I wondered whether he had ever seen toys before.

We left again as it was growing dark. An hour later we met a wave of refugees. They were travelling in the opposite direction to us up the valley heading towards Pakistan. They passed like phantoms in the underworld; whole families pausing in the narrow path to let us by, women silent, the men solemnly greeting us. Many had all their worldly goods with them: donkeys half buried under loads of mattresses, veiled women with cooking pots on their heads, or the outlines on their backs of sleeping children wrapped in blankets.

This quiet exodus was the first fruit of the Soviet offensive. From a pre-war population of about 80,000, the Panjsher was now down to half according to Massud himself, the man who best understood that this statistic was the truest barometer of Soviet success.

The moon was not yet up and in the blackness we missed the tree where we had left the others. Instead we came again to Tunkhu, where we found a group of farmers gathering their harvest by the light of a fire, having spent the day in a cave.

Seeing us they stopped work and took us into a house for tea. Unable to communicate by word we showed them Charles's drawings. They stared at them uncomprehendingly and handed them back. In response to our gesticulations, they took their watches from their wrists and laid them on the floor in front of us, eager to know whether they were Swiss (good news) or Russian (bad). Most of them appeared to be Russian, but we prevaricated and said '*Hob!* Good!' With our hands we made boxes and television cameras: with a look of understanding dawning in his face, an old man left the room and came back with a musket which he brandished fiercely, making as if to shoot Russians. Its stock was engraved with the letters 'V.R.' and 'TOWER 1857'. It was loaded. The date indicated that it had missed by one year being used against the Russians before, in the Crimean war. (A military expert in London confirmed later that this was the standard insignia which the Tower of London Armoury put on weapons used by the British army in the nineteenth century.)

It was very late when we found Charles, asleep and alone. It seemed that Yahya had got an urgent message to him and Tom – I never discovered how it found them – that we must all return at once, before daylight. Tom had accompanied the messengers back to Yahya to find porters for our bags; as soon as they came back we would have to set off.

Two hours later Tom was shaking us all awake.

'There is bad news. The Russians have helicoptered troops into the valley to cut off a retreat. They almost captured Massud. They are pushing up the Hazara Valley. One guerrilla commander refused to send troops against them, and Massud went in himself with three men. They've put in the old men to hold the line.' Perhaps our farmer's Crimean musket was going to have its chance. Breathlessly Tom went on:

'Massud has ordered a general evacuation of the Panjsher Valley. We are being sent back to Pakistan and must leave now to reach Yahya outside a cave near the school. The school itself has been badly damaged – except for the toilet.'

Tom had brought with him five guerrillas to act as porters. It was an extraordinary achievement: not only had he repeated the journey of the day before twice in the dark at *mujahideen* speed, but he had conscripted some to carry our bags as well, a role that they normally considered demeaning. Clearly Tom had got his second wind.

12. Beating a Retreat

The moon was up. By its light the stones were diamonds again, and the greenery black velvet. Shamefully I found a certain spring in my step akin to the relief that the condemned prisoner is said to feel when informed that his appeal has been refused and the execution is to go ahead as planned. The agony of hope was over: we were now to be refugees ourselves. We had lost the television camera, our money, supplies, and the documentary programme. The defeat would be complete, in itself an experience. At the end of it there would be at least a hot bath at Dean's. I kept my thoughts to myself as I pressed on behind a youth carrying perhaps three times as much weight as I was.

At four we reached the cave in a side valley somewhere near the school; a few more pieces of our equipment had turned up, but still no camera, food, or money.

We slept for another hour and moved on at daybreak, leaving our bags in the cave. As we did so a knot of *mujahideen* came towards us, heading in the opposite direction. Leading them was Massud.

It was the first time I had ever seen a military commander in the middle of a battle: more significantly, in the middle of a battle that was going against him.

He had not slept for two nights. He had just returned from leading an action. But as he shook hands with each of us in turn, there was no sign of a break in his self-control. I had seen many executives under pressure with their jobs on the line; this was a general with his own and many other lives at stake. He stood the comparison favourably. Here, in the eye of the storm, was not simply calm, but an air of brisk optimism. Massud paused only to tell us that he expected the Russians to press up the valley that we were in and that he intended to hold them approximately at the confluence of the four valleys, past which their tanks would have difficulty in advancing because of the lake. He had been let down by the Hisb-i-Islami forces in one mountain encounter, but had plugged the gap. He was rallying his own forces in preparation for a counter-attack, but he could not exactly predict when this would take place. In the meantime, for our safety we would have to leave. I realized that not for a single moment did he contemplate defeat. The lines of his face betrayed lack of sleep; but they also conveyed concentration and determination.

But if Massud was not contemplating defeat, nor, in our lesser struggle, was Sandy. He explained to Massud that he did not wish to leave until he had made a film to tell the world what was happening, and still less until we had our camera. At once Massud agreed to allow us to stay, and gave orders for us to be lodged in a village further up the valley while the military situation became clear and our camera was found. Turning to his brother Yahya he gave orders that we were to enjoy 'the hospitality of the village'. A moment later he was gone. It was about five o'clock in the morning.

We now had a new guide, a friendly farmer to whose house we were going, who wore Russian riding breeches and carried a Second World War Russian carbine gun with a circular magazine set at right-angles to the barrel, which looked like a prop from an Al Capone film. He led us across another valley wall into the main street of a village which ran straight upwards at what seemed to be an angle of 45 degrees.

A short way beyond the village we came to a clump of trees. Under one of them, unattended, was another find in our bizarre treasure hunt across Asia: three of our bags, one of them my old friend with no handles.

From it I pulled a packet of sweets and chewing mints, and we toiled on. I felt my back muscles knotting against my rucksack as, an hour later, we were installed in yet another first-floor room in a small stone house with an inside staircase at the bottom of which goats and donkeys spent the night.

On this occasion 'the hospitality of the village' meant a lunch of bread with a basin of butter made from goat's milk, unfortunately too rich for our deprived stomachs. After the meal Tony and Sandy went off to make more enquiries about the equipment while I lay in a shameful heap for the best part of the day, unable to find a comfortable position for my damaged back.

Our friendly guide and host offered to take in our washing.

Under blankets, as well as the unblinking stare of the household, we changed our clothes. Having none to change into I accepted the loan of the man's Russian riding breeches and a shirt, in the collar of which was a Harrod's label. To aid the washing we gave him some cold water detergent. He bundled up our clothes together with an unexplained package of film which Yahya told us a previous visitor left for Massud.

A few moments later we heard an altercation with women's voices raised in the rear quarters of the little house to which the family had retired after surrendering their front room to us. Our host returned with the film, which he gave to Yahya; apparently he had mistaken it for a new form of soap.

We were woken by cries in the night: from along the path that ran 100 yards below us, we were conscious of a continuous stream of refugees, growing now in size and travelling mainly before daylight, when they could not be bombed. As they called to each other and to their animals they sounded like lost souls.

We spent several days in the house. The hospitality stretched usually to sugared tea; there was always freshly made bread, but goat's milk was a luxury, and all other food was desperately short. We would drink the tea until the kettle was empty.

We were back in our trap now: every morning Yahya marched us up the hill to our cave like the grand old Duke of York; every evening he marched us down again. Reports of the war reached us like a whispering game, second or third hand and distorted, with outlandish claims of planes shot down, tales of derring-do and dramatic setbacks. Planes and helicopters flew overhead thick and fast, but too high to be interested in us.

Late in the evening, we could see the refugees struggling by with their world on their backs. Tony interviewed a man in his forties who had been driven by the bombing from his little farm. His cows had been killed. He had a child, presumably his son, with him, and two goats, worth the equivalent of £9 each. He was stopping with a brother-in-law on the way to Pakistan where he needed, he reckoned, £100 to start up a new life. He was a fine-looking man with a well-cut face and strong, sure smile.

At home in the evening, everyone shook hands again with everyone who came and went, even residents of the household.

News reached us that the Russians had turned up the Hazara Valley and were now heading towards the confluence (we had come to use the French word Massud coined for the crossing point of the four valleys). Once they reached it we would be cut off from Abdullakhel where we were now sure our camera was. On hearing the news Sandy and Charles decided to find a way through once again.

That afternoon there was a lot of helicopter activity in the direction of Abdullakhel. Before sunset Jean-Phillipe reappeared to confirm that the Russians were indeed pressing up the side valleys, and that he had been ordered back by the guerrillas at the caves where we had last seen Massud. Meanwhile Massud himself was somewhere up at the front, and there was nobody left to countermand his orders.

Jean-Phillipe had been summoned that day to treat a man suffering from a suspected fracture of the skull, after falling from a cliff while hiding his belongings in a cave. The man was unconscious and Jean-Phillipe had no way of knowing whether he would die. His family, however, seemed more concerned that he apparently had a stomach ache and might not be ready to leave for Pakistan at seven o'clock the next morning. After dark Jean-Phillipe left again to tend to another patient.

We were awoken early by a forlorn Charles and a bedraggled but still cheerful Sandy: he had fallen into the river. Their excursion had been abortive, and they had failed to get anyone to take them to Abdullakhel.

'I have a message', said Yahya, 'from Abdul Khay.'

At first we thought he was referring to Abdullakhel, the place; but he meant Abdul Khay, Massud's personal assistant, who, it appeared, was now at a house near the confluence.

'Abdul Khay says we are to go to another valley, further up, in a safer place. There,' – he paused and looked hopelessly at us – 'there are good caves.'

It was probably the mention of caves that clinched the matter. Once again we resolved to slip our leash and make one last desperate *putsch*.

Returning through the near vertical village where we had found the soup bag, we came to a little mosque built on a slope, its wooden outside staircase giving on to a stone irrigation channel. There we were told Abdul Khay would come for prayers at sundown. We slept through the afternoon on its dusty floor and awoke to find ourselves surrounded by twenty *mujahideen* led by a *mullah* wearing a turban, saying prayers around our prone forms. I was struck by the physical exercise to be derived from the performance: hip, stomach and leg muscles must all benefit from the ups and downs. Throughout the ceremony Tom lay groaning on the floor wrestling again with his intestines.

One of the worshippers was identified to us as Abdul Khay. We followed him to another house, approached by a ladder and a door certainly not more than 4 feet high, beyond which was a flat roof with a magnificent view of the valley and mountains around us, and a large room to either side.

Abdul Khay was intelligent, confident, alert, with a slightly shifty look in his eye. He spoke in a high, hard voice, intoning his sentences. His English, though sparse, was florid, learned from old textbooks when he had been a medical student at Kabul University. Most of the time he spoke in Farsi using as interpreter the Afghan apprentice doctor accompanying Jean-Phillipe, who translated his words into French. Next to him sat the *mullah* who had discarded his turban to reveal a bald head above his fine white prophet's beard. The two of them questioned us about the military situation in Beirut, with especial interest to know whether the Palestine Liberation Organization had as good a fighting spirit as the Afghan resistance. It was a reminder of where the natural loyalties of the Afghans lay.

All the while, about forty *mujahideen* sat round the edges of the dusty room on dustier mattresses facing inwards, the elegant pattern of their crossed legs broken every now and then by a Timberland boot projecting into the room from our less flexible European bodies.

Quite suddenly Abdul Khay turned to Sandy and said, in English:

'You want to go to Abdullakhel?'

Sandy explained.

'You want to see Massud?'

'Yes.'

'When do you want to go?'

'As soon as possible.'

'That is all right. Do you want to go now? Tonight? Tomorrow?'

In my weakened state I dreaded the ten-hour walk over the corner of the mountain itself, obligatory now that the confluence was no longer safe. Meanwhile Tom was muttering incoherently to himself. So we settled to leave first thing the next morning. Sandy explained that we would need porters. No problem, we were assured.

Presently dinner came: bowls of flour, fat and sugar mixed to a gruel that made the tongue cling to the roof of the mouth.

We awoke to a customary reverse. A letter sent by Abdul Khay to Massud, who was believed to have been in Abdullakhel, had not been delivered: a messenger bearing it had turned back in the night after seeing a flare that he took for a sign of Russians in the valley. We must wait – a day or two perhaps – to have 'permission', a need that did not appear to exist the night before.

Predictably, Yahya wanted us to go to a cave. We declined. Instead we walked back to our little mosque.

I had the sensation that day of falling apart, needing to take a firmer grip, not only on myself, but on my possessions, which appeared to have been affected as well. My strangely complicated Chinese communist razor had taken itself to pieces. Its amusing grandiose little box had rotted; and the spare blades, wrapped in leaves, were threatening rust. The soap had finally disintegrated into fragments, which had found their way into my hair, nostrils and mouth. My hand mirror had lost the last of its backing and no longer mirrored at all. Toothpaste was squeezed flat as if by a steamroller. My comb's teeth were clotted with dust and soap, and so was my toothbrush. The blue of the wash-bag had dyed my towel in purple patches, disguising its vile condition. Antibiotics were disappearing as fast as the boiled sweets. On the credit side, the folding scissors were holding up well, and there was still plaster for blisters. Socks were frankly repellent, feet Stilton. Over the whole body there hung the sweet sickly smell of putrefaction.

We had the equivalent of £30 left between us in pocket money which meant that there was no question of our leaving Afghanistan without our equipment and our money bag unless Massud gave the order for horses and food to be provided free.

That afternoon while Tom groaned, and Charles and Sandy slept, I lay and thought about death.

At about four the flies came out, dense, sticky and listless, exactly as I felt myself.

There had been aeroplane activity all day, as the Russians backed up their ground offensive. Before each raid there was the busy relentless sound of the Antonov, then the jets wheeling and running in to bomb or strafe, then more Antonovs.

Most of the time it was the next valley. When it was ours, we knew the drill. If caught in the open, one lay flat, but peered out, as one learned the way of jets, to observe their direction and target; once the eye had found them, one could watch the bombs – black objects, usually two at a time, hurtling towards the earth. Then, as the planes veered away, a slash of flame branded the hillside, or there was an oil-black puff of smoke. Always the violence of it surprised me; then, much later, the crude sounds of war, engines and explosions, and finally the shock waves.

Embattled somewhere in the mountains, Massud kept in touch by the system of letters and runners. He moved freely, on foot, and without notice.

All we could do was wait. We had pleaded, demanded, ignored instructions, tramped over the stony mountains – all to no avail. We had buried our noses in mud and watched the floor on which we had just been sleeping rise 60 feet into the air. Until now we had been waiting for something to happen. Now it was as if we were waiting only for the time to pass.

To cheer us up Sandy asked each of his team what we most looked forward to on returning to Peshawar. For me, it was to be liberated from hope; to be indifferent to success or failure; to be always the same whether in adversity or in good times, like the lama of Kipling's Kim; to be free of the Wheel of Things. But I knew that like Kim I wanted something else as well, some of the good things in life as well as the ultimate things; and, like Kim, as we waited we were half menaced and half soothed by blankness.

I had formed a superstitious attachment to the St Christopher medal that Sandy's doctor brother-in-law had given us. I had surrendered the bootlace on which it was attached to a *mujahideen* who needed a spare; and the string replacing it had broken during an air raid so that the medal of this dubious but comforting saint was now attached to my watch.

Doubt, religious or historical, seemed not to trouble the *mujahideen*. Five times a day, they assembled in the mosque, regardless of whether we were there or not, and entered whole-heartedly into their routine, like a PT class. Theirs was a muscular faith, all embracing, certain.

It was our second day in the little mosque. At nightfall we went up the hill to find that Abdul Khay had returned. There was an argument in progress, and we bided our time to broach our own business with him, squatting in place ready to eat. Rice came, bald and dry as only rice can be when you want something different.

Politely Charles said that it was delicious.

'It is not good! It is bad!' cried Abdul Khay vehemently in English. 'This is war. It doesn't matter!'

Nonplussed, we crammed what we could down our throats. Eventually we discovered what was disturbing him. It appeared that the *mujahideen* holding the line of mountains between us and Abdullakhel had not been fed for two days, owing to an oversight, and he was enraged, and not without reason. Slowly the room filled up with men of all ages, some *mujahideen*, others, to judge by their dress, from other parts of Afghanistan. Throughout the evening, Abdul Khay called them one by one to sit in front of him beside an oil lamp on the floor. They brought with them pieces of paper which he studied: like Massud, he gave them written orders in return and, presumably because of the risk of spies listening in, whispered instructions or encouragement into their ears. Next to me an older man in a turban with a fat wad of money in his hand turned to me to ask gravely if I was Chinese. Meat came, for us alone, not thought odd in the room full of hungry *mujahideen*, except by us. We ate it all the same.

Then it was our turn. Beckoning for our attention, Abdul Khay told us that Russian troops were closing in and there was no contact with Massud. He wanted us to go immediately to a place called Astana, higher up yet another valley. If news had not reached us from Massud of a change by morning, then we would have to go on to Pakistan. His manner was final.

'With regret, I cannot get your television camera.'

Through an interpreter we told him that we had no money. At least if we were going back the way we had come, we would not need our warm clothes which were also missing. He said he would give orders for horses to be provided from the edge of the Panjsher to take what equipment we had.

We told him that we would need porters for the first part of the journey. Abdul Khay agreed, but said we should leave at daybreak.

It was ten o'clock at night. One by one, the diners fell asleep, lying where they had eaten, as though there had been a sleeping draught in the tea. Abdul Khay was still writing by the light of his lamp when I lost consciousness, but when I awoke a few hours later he saw me, and shook the interpreter.

'The porters have not come. You must go now, without them. I will look after your cameras. We will send them on to you.' He added in English: 'I regret. This is war.'

We struggled down the hill to our little mosque where Yahya was waiting. He had found some porters willing to help with our bags. Then even Sandy had to admit defeat: there simply was no further choice.

It felt like being sent down for a long stretch for the second time, not less disagreeable as an experience, but different. At least we knew what to expect. For myself there was another difference: I was learning to expect nothing.

Unlike most villages of the Panjsher, Astana had never been bombed, and the villagers were gathering their harvest by the afternoon sun as we arrived, winnowing by hand with the children watching. As the day ended they returned to their houses, the men in turbans and waistcoats, the women in deep scarlet veils, apart.

As in the rest of the Panjsher, there was a critical food shortage, made worse now by the demands of the passing refugees.

Jean-Phillipe's clinic, held in our communal sleeping quarters, was crowded as usual. A woman brought in a baby girl, a little bundle of bone and skin staring upwards with the dulled undernourished look that had become a commonplace to us. The mother thought that her child was suffering from lung trouble. Jean-Phillipe tested her for malaria and worms: she had neither high nor low temperature, no swollen spleen. But she did have chicken pox and a mother who could not give milk, and had been unable to do so since the Soviet bombing began two weeks before. The baby was slowly dying of starvation.

Traumatic complaints, hidden shock, were among the most common that Jean-Phillipe had to contend with: babies with mothers unable to feed them; others who had been in shock and now did not respond to stimuli of any kind, the sort who would suffer again in later life.

At six o'clock next morning a letter came from Abdul Khay. It simply said that the Russians were withdrawing and we should now return at once.

After the relief of despair, the pain of hope again, like feeling returning to numbed limbs. We got under way, down the hill once more. Again we had porter troubles, and relied on Yahya to find us boys whom he conscripted from village to village. They seemed

almost flattened under their huge loads as they heaved them on to
their backs; but then set off at a pace to crack one's thighs, only to
mutiny at the next village leaving us stranded until a replacement
could be drummed up. The journey took all day.

We made our way straight to Abdul Khay, who explained in his
high metallic voice that the Russians and Afghan government forces
had been 'driven out' from the high ground round Abdullakhel,
and were now withdrawing from the side valleys. Twelve thousand
soldiers had taken part in the Soviet offensive, 8,000 reinforcements
and 4,000 already based in or near Roka. There had been 1,000
tanks backed by 100 helicopters. Three hundred Russians had been
killed so far, and 100 wounded. (He brushed aside the disparity
with the normal proportions of war of three wounded to every one
killed.) Twenty-five Soviet tanks had been destroyed; and twenty
mujahideen killed by hand grenades. (We subsequently discovered
that a group had indeed been surprised over a meal and all of them
killed; it was possible that hand grenades had been responsible.)

We had no means of distinguishing between pious aspirations
and clinical accuracy. The statistic most widely used was that the
Russians were suffering casualties at the rate of 3,000 dead and
wounded a year throughout Afghanistan, and within that frame-
work the figures Abdul Khay gave us, though suspiciously precise,
were not impossible.

The most important information that he had affecting our own
fate was that he had now sent a 'strong letter' about our camera.
The danger was that Abdul Khay, a busy man with weightier
matters on his shoulders than ours, might once again bury our
difficulties in elegant but empty assurances. We insisted on returning within twenty-four hours if nothing had happened.

'Of course, my friends,' he said in English, 'I am here.' On that,
he turned to the fine fierce turbaned heads awaiting his attention.
Our interview was at an end.

A new character had appeared among Abdul Khay's entourage
whom I did not recall seeing before. This was a young political
officer, whose task we learned was political indoctrination and
education. We arranged to film him at work as soon as we had a
camera. Like Abdul Khay, he spoke in high ranting tones that
brooked no dissension. With a view to pressing our case concerning
our camera, we engaged him in conversation and told him that
perhaps through television we could help in a small way to bring

pressure through world opinion so that Afghanistan would not be forgotten. We had heard that very morning on the BBC Overseas News that the British Foreign Minister had called in Copenhagen for a negotiated settlement on Afghanistan, and that the United Nations Secretary General was flying with an Afghan expert to Moscow. The sooner we had our camera, the sooner we could present their case.

The reply seemed to take several minutes to deliver. Yahya summarized it for us: the Western powers must work out their anti-colonialist problems for themselves. Afghanistan had learnt not to rely on the West any more. Instead, true resistance must be based on local support and correct orientation. Only self-sufficiency would free Afghanistan and establish the right political policy. It was a set piece answer; wearily I recognized the hollow ring of the interchangeable slogans of extremism, whether of the Left or of the Right.

Our new accommodation was like all the others, a farmhouse, but this time larger, and we had two rooms at our disposal and no family to look after us. Our food came from the local *quororga*, or barracks, the name given to whichever house the *mujahideen* had commandeered. We were soon to learn that it did not pay to be so far from the kitchen. Around our house were hens that clucked but never delivered (rather like Abdul Khay with our camera, we thought). The menu was strictly rice and old boiled goat.

On the first night I was ill. I had developed a cough from lying in dust which I could not shake off. I became aware first of the heat, and then of a cold so intense that, even with all my clothes on inside a sleeping bag guaranteed to withstand sub-zero temperatures, I shivered violently until an aspirin put me to sleep. The following morning, too ashamed to ask Jean-Phillipe who had more serious calls on his time, I looked up the symptoms of malaria in *Pears Encyclopaedia* – imaginatively brought by Charles for light reading – and at once felt proudly better, confident that I could now be taken seriously as an invalid. Strangely, the symptoms never returned.

However, to my shame, I grew hourly weaker. I felt a curious muscular pain in the shoulder blade, and decided that I had not after all contracted malaria but premature old age, and was experiencing the sensation of beginning to die. Just then the chances of emerging from our predicament seemed remote. We were caught like New York's cockroaches in a Cockroach Motel, a cardboard box with an opening at either end and wet glue inside, and on the outside the words: 'They Check In But They Never Check Out.'

A strange and uniquely Afghan sequence of events led to our second experience of hot water. Ever an entrepreneur like all good cameramen, Charles had enquired into the possibility of buying some eggs, since our hens appeared to be sterile. Supposing that he was making headway with the man appointed to look after us, he told him that we would like to have them boiled for five minutes. The final outcome of his initiative was a call at five in the morning to tell us that our hot water for washing was now available.

The bathroom arrangements consisted of a hole in the floor, a hook on the wall and a bucket of hot water. When my turn came I hung up my towel, dirtyish, on the hook; put my clothes on the floor, clear of where the dust turned to mud, and washed in the bucket: first body and hair, then socks and underclothes, followed in order of priority by feet, which may in consequence have emerged less well off than before. I came out feeling a decade younger.

Jean-Phillipe saw patients all that day. A girl with ringworm was brought to him, her head covered with cup-shaped crusts enlarged to form a honeycombed mass. The antibiotics he gave her would cure it up in a matter of days. Without them her head would have to be kept shaved, and if benign the disease would disappear before puberty: if not, it could leave her largely bald for life, a catastrophe for a woman.

On our second day a new group of Frenchmen arrived and occupied the second of the two big rooms. One was a doctor and one a journalist. The third was a young man who spoke near perfect Farsi and whose father had held a post in Kabul, where he had brought up his family. This was Stephane Thiollier. With them they had brought the equivalent of £20,000 in cash, collected by volunteers in France to help the resistance. Once again I felt saddened that the French were so far ahead of my fellow countrymen.

Stephane told us that their group had been delayed on the journey in, which had followed the same route as our own; first by fighting with Hisb-i-Islami and then by an attack from helicopter gunships. Despite their adventures the trio looked quite well and, to our great surprise, used spoons to eat, making us feel like old Afghan hands.

In the afternoon we split forces to press home our quest for the camera. I found myself with Stephane detailed to prod Abdul Khay. He was not in the house where we had seen him the day before. Instead, some farmers indicated a field on the far side of the river. Rather than walking back upstream to the nearest bridge we waded across, sinking to our thighs in the icy water.

We found Abdul Khay squatting in the middle of a field on a large Afghan rug, looking as if he had just arrived by magic carpet. He was surrounded as usual by a waiting delegation of which he took not the smallest notice, and was engrossed in his in-tray, a mass of notes on which he was scribbling replies.

Abdul Khay appeared to be in excellent spirits. He made no mention of the change of rendezvous which had exposed us to the risk of pneumonia or drowning.

'Now that the war is peaceful, we know what scenes you want for your television, and we are arranging them for you.'

'What news of the camera?'

'It will be a trouble for you to go to Abdullakhel to get it. A man has it,' said Abdul Khay. 'He is in Kabul.'

'Kabul?'

'Yes. We will get it. In five or six days.'

Stephane stepped in and the conversation continued in Farsi. It appeared that there was a report that some of the equipment had been left for safety in a cave by a man who had then gone to work in Kabul and who was expected back soon.

Smiling, Abdul Khay then wrote a note for me to take to Sandy. It read:

Dear house of Mr Sandy!
And other gentel companions!
Please accept my greeting. I send again the Mudir Shamsoddin to providing your residual instruments.
By Honour

The signature in Farsi at the foot of the letter resembled a ship in full sail. Beside it was a date: 24-6-1361 (the year being measured from the date that the prophet Mohammed arrived in Medina). It appeared that the Mudir Shamsoddin was the name of the bald *mullah*.

I turned as we left the field. The little party looked as though it was preparing for take-off.

We had by now used up three of the four weeks allocated for filming. We were expected back in London in another three. Desperation was beginning to overwhelm us, swamping thought, just as the swollen torrent of the Afghan winter ahead would, in a few weeks time, swamp the terraces and irrigation canals and close the passes over which our route home lay. Abdul Khay had promised much and delivered only words. He had even promised us food; yet we could not help noticing that he ate chicken and yoghurt while we were held to a diet of old goat and rice, supplemented only by our dwindling supply of soup.

That afternoon we lay surveying the world glumly from our accustomed eye-level of 4 feet above the floor, when quite by chance we noticed three farmers walking by our door bearing huge loads on their backs. Sandy and I recognized one of them immediately as the farmer from Tunkhu with the Crimean model musket. But we all recognized the load on his back. It was the television camera.

13. Massud's War

We were back once again at Do Ab, where the Panjsher's single modern bridge stood miraculously unscathed. Using as our base the doctors' house, as we came to call our recent home after the second French medical group arrived, we had completed two busy days of filming. We were now proposing to set up a new base in the main valley where we hoped to make contact with Massud.

We had said good-bye to Jean-Phillipe who was returning to Bordeaux after handing over to the fresh team.

On the eve of our departure I had found him looking more sombre than usual. That morning he had been summoned to bind the legs of a girl whose feet had been blown off by a bomb dropped from high level for no known reason: perhaps a pilot needing to show that he had delivered his quota of bombs. After performing a three-hour operation he had left her for another patient. When he had returned the father of the girl had invited him to a meal. At the end of the meal the father had thanked him, and without any show of emotion told him that the child was dead.

As we had walked back down the Hazara Valley in the wake of the Soviet withdrawal, we began to understand that, far from being driven out, the Russians had simply completed a mission of destruction.

Above the confluence the damage had been inflicted from the air. As we passed the school we had a chance to survey the Soviet handiwork which Tom and I had so nearly become part of: the school was indeed a mess, and the room where we had slept was no longer there. The little footbridge over which we had scuttled between the bomb runs lay with one end in the water. At the confluence, the lake did indeed appear to have stopped the tank-bound Soviet advance. Tank tracks ran into the water at one end but there they stopped. The infantry seemed not to have ventured beyond without the protection of armour.

Below the confluence the real destruction began. We came to a village in which every house had been almost wholly destroyed. In the context of contemporary history, it was a wholly forgettable sight; to its inhabitants no less a catastrophe than the bombing of Dresden had been in its time.

At one place the river bed was strewn with spent cartridges, empty Russian cigarette packets and cans of Bulgarian baked beans – almost the only litter we were to see during our entire expedition (most Afghans do not belong to the litter-producing economy). Here and there were huge unexploded bombs, carrying 500 or 1,000 pounds of high explosive, with which the guerrillas ingeniously boosted the Chinese mines used against Soviet tanks. Every village we came to was marked by the passing of the Russian army. The houses had been rocketed or simply smashed to make them uninhabitable: some had been bombed, some sacked. Charming old carved doors had been stove in, apparently by gun butts. More blackened houses gaped at us from the mountainside. Some places bore the most literal signs of a scorched earth policy where crops had been systematically burned.

But the pattern was not consistent: the invaders appeared to have concentrated their attention on a surprisingly narrow area. Certainly they had flattened everything in their path and left a terrible wake for us to ponder, but they had not spread out, as if either afraid of attack or else in a hurry. The sturdy stone irrigation canals on which all life depended had stood up well and, in any case, Afghanistan would never be short of replacements for stones and hands to carry them.

Curiously some dwellings had survived where they were hidden by line of sight from the tanks: Soviet T-62 tanks cannot shoot downwards, nor at a steep angle upwards. (Often snipers shooting down at them from mountain tops were invulnerable.) It looked as if infantry had seldom strayed far from the protection of the tanks, and as if the tanks themselves had varied their tactics between reducing everything in sight to rubble, and only shooting where snipers might have lodged with their anti-tank grenades. Helicopters and helicopter-borne commandoes trained in mountain warfare might have done a better job. As it was, the Russians never truly engaged the guerrillas. All they did was to destroy their homes. What we saw looked more like vandalism than war: to a layman's eye it was a brutal but clumsy operation, a product of tank-think.

Just before Do Ab we passed the house of the brothers where we had first met Massud at Tambona. Its windows had been bricked in where a rocket had struck it. The shop where we had bought apples had been smashed for the second time.

We came on a group of brightly robed youths passing through from the north. They gave an account for the television camera of how Soviet troops had burned their houses, together with people left in them. Pressed, a young man in a bright light-blue turban admitted that he had not personally witnessed the atrocity. He had, however, spoken to someone who had buried his family afterwards. Pondering on the quirks of television I wondered whether the young man's evidence would linger as long in the memory of viewers as his fine features and magnificent headgear.

I wondered, too, that the guerrillas appeared to be confident that trained agents posing as travellers or deserters were not being infiltrated into their ranks, then maintaining contact by radio with assassination squads or helicopters that could mount a sudden air strike.

Among Panjsheris themselves, no such need for security existed. In so tight knit a community, loyalty was taken for granted. By virtue of our relationship with Massud, we were accepted as trusted allies. Accordingly, we had no difficulty in learning from a passer-by that Massud had gone to a valley near Khenj where his men had suffered a tragic reverse after being caught in an ambush.

So we found ourselves once again at Do Ab having a breather on the concrete bridge after a long downhill walk. The choice before us was whether to go up to the village where we might reach Massud, or down towards Roka which, we were told, was being evacuated by the Russians. Our informant was a man who had caught us up bearing a sack containing the discarded first half of a paperback edition of *Vanity Fair* (bisected so that Sandy and I could read it at the same time) together with the ever persistent consignment of Massud's film (no use for our video tape camera). We were later to find out that his information was only partly correct, and that in fact the reinforcements sent from Kabul to Roka had been withdrawn, leaving, however, the original garrison of perhaps 4,000 regular Afghan and Russians soldiers behind.

Kabul radio had already announced the victorious return of the troops and their reception by Babrak Karmal.

After a short discussion among ourselves we settled to go up.

We arrived at a little settlement in a cleft in the mountains a short while after Massud had left. But we had our consolation: we found and filmed a carpenter making a butt for a Soviet heavy machine-gun that had been mounted on a tank, to convert it to use by infantry; with a lucky shot, it could even bring down a jet.

It was at this village that we met the *mujahideen* commander whose men had been ambushed and killed by a Soviet patrol, presumably from the unit landed by helicopter on the nearby mountain tops overlooking Khenj. The commander, a middle-aged man, was disconsolate, and it spoke well for Massud that he had found time to visit him. He told us that the neighbouring Hisb-i-Islami forces which should have covered their rear had not done so, and that they had been caught unawares over their evening meal, with no look-out posted. It was one example of where the Soviet forces had shown expertise by not declaring their presence until suspicions were lulled, and then striking in their own time: elementary tactics, not met with elementary precautions. The Panjsheris paid for the lesson with twenty lives.

The next day brought an invitation to lunch. It came from a farmer living, we were told, half an hour away, and the lure of food easily outweighed the knowledge that it would be a three-hour hike.

This time the twist I had not anticipated was the pole walk across the cascading Panjsher River at a point high enough for a fall to break a leg. Free of their television equipment for the morning, the others together with Stephane negotiated it without thought. I survived the experience to dream of it long after I had forgotten the jets. Half-way across I froze, and was only coaxed on by Sandy's threat to come and help, which I felt sure would have fatally rocked the structure and sent me hurtling into the torrent below. At lunch our host told us that the week before he had watched young Soviet troops scampering across it.

The man was a prosperous farmer with five sons, one of whom had been killed in the fighting; two more were with the *mujahideen*, and two worked in Kabul from where they contributed, like all good Panjsheris, 5 per cent of their salary to the resistance. The house, high above the road, was clean and unscathed but for a bullet hole in one wall. It was pleasant to sit in a room without flies.

While we waited for lunch the farmer read us a poem that his son had written:

First I want to speak of God, who has saved us all from water and fire.
I will start with the story of what happened here.
First we were happy with our King.
Like the Tsar, there was nobody like him.
Then came Daoud who gave in to the communists,
Who killed landowners and *mullahs* ...

The poem was translated by Stephane and I had no means of judging its poetic value in the original, but the political message was hard to escape. The mention of the Tsar made me wonder whether, like other Tajiks of the Panjsher, the family had emigrated from Russia at the time of the Revolution: our host was just old enough, but hunger easily outstripped curiosity, and I was deterred by the thought that a question might further delay lunch.

The meal was indeed delicious. Our host watched us, eating nothing himself, as we set about devouring everything before us, beginning with yoghurt, accepting more when offered it, followed by mutton and bowls of salad. We shamelessly consumed not just our own share but probably that of the entire household as well.

Afterwards the farmer, who had betrayed neither surprise nor distaste at our manners, showed us bomb craters pock-marking his fields. He crowned his politeness by providing us with a guide to show us the way back to our rendezvous point with Yahya, by a route bypassing the dreaded pole.

At our meeting point among the blown-up Russian tanks there was a message waiting from Yahya. It was addressed to Stephane, to whom the *mujahideen* had given the Afghan name of Mustafa:

Dear Mustafa,
I got one message from Massud. He has written in his letter that you must go to Roka for taking pictures from fighting and bombing so I am waiting here for you on the brige. Please come quickly. I have brought all of your sleeping bags on the brige. Signed Yahya [*sic*].

We hurried to the bridge to find that he had gone on to Sangana, the place where we had been given hot water on the eve of the Soviet offensive. There we set up our headquarters, and found ourselves assigned to the care of a new nanny figure who was now to take over from Yahya. His name was Ali, known to us as Mr Ali; in an earlier period of his career he had been in charge of room service at the Intercontinental Hotel in Kabul. On our first morning, before we set off, he had showed off his expertise.

'Good morning. What would you like for breakfast?'
'Oh, Mr Ali, we would like eggs. Are there any eggs?'
'I will see. What else would you like?'
'What is there?'
'Tea. I will see if there is bread. Do you like honey?'
'Yes, we like honey.'
'What else would you like for breakfast?'
'Well, that would be fine.'
'How do you like your eggs cooked?'
He returned after half an hour.
'Today for breakfast there is bread and tea.'
'What about the eggs and honey?'
'Unfortunately today, eggs are difficult. And honey is difficult. But there is tea. And there is bread.'

Summer was fading as we made our way down the Panjsher Valley, but it felt like spring, perhaps because of the sudden uplift in our fortunes.

The sun glinted on the river, a narrow torrent in a sea of shingle that would soon become an autumn flood. Curiously during our entire visit we saw no sign of fishermen (other than Jean-José) or of fish in the Panjsher. Apparently some Bulgarian experts, called in during the Daoud regime, had stocked some Afghan rivers with rainbow trout but the habit had not caught on.

To carry our television equipment we now had two donkeys instead of the less reliable *mujahideen*. (Curiously no invading army appeared to have introduced the mule to Afghanistan.) We turned to our right off the main valley road just short of Bazarak, and climbed up the Parende side valley.

Our simple pleasures were as acute that day as any I can recall: the sensation of cold water on the back of the neck falling from an overhanging rock; the flavour of end-of-season apricots, woolly but sweet; and the taste of the few grapes the Russians had left behind.

We paused for a midday meal in a village high in the Parende, in the fortified entrance to a cave where, because of a straighter

stretch of the great gorge to either side of us, there was room for
jets to strafe. Fierce starving cats shamelessly contested with us the
grey bits of boiled goat that we were offered; as shamelessly we
fended them off.

We stopped at a village higher still up the valley and were lodged
in a house, approached by a tiny iron causeway, that overlooked flat
roofs where maize and fruit were laid out. A mountain torrent
tumbled beneath us.

That night the heavens opened, two weeks earlier than predicted.

Thunder claps that I took for artillery echoed against the rock
face like ricocheting shells; then the rain poured through our pane-
less windows and soaked our clothes. Outside, the dust tracks up
which we would have to climb the next day would be turning to
mud slides. But a greater threat still from the gathering clouds was
that they were harbingers of snow that would block the mountain
passes on our route back to Pakistan.

For breakfast the cook, who had served Europeans before, gave
us tea and chips fried in Russian grease sold by the tin in Kabul: we
thought them delicious.

We had one pass to climb to the next valley, the wall of which
overlooked the Russian-occupied zone around Roka. From there
we hoped to film Russian activity. I was heartened by the presence
at breakfast of the only fat man we met in the Panjsher, thinking
that his bulk would slow the pace to suit my failing strength. This
turned out to be Massud's financial controller, who told us that the
biggest single source of Massud's revenue was a tax levied on
emeralds discovered in the Upper Panjsher in the past two decades.
Unfortunately for my hopes he bade us farewell at the edge of the
village.

The start of the walk up to the pass reminded me of my school
days in northern Yorkshire, with green irregular patches and neat
stone walls; but soon our path swept towards the sky, and the
ground grew stonier as we left the fertile valley behind us. We had
no means of measuring altitude, and so we never really knew what
height we had reached: at perhaps 14,000 feet, I was seriously
considering braving a grazing ox that we came across as a possible
ride, reflecting that the worst its horns could do was to put me out
of my misery.

Then we came to a group of migrant shepherds whose animals
fed on high pasture in summer, and who lived in caves or stone huts

in the mountains at this time of year, with fine carpets on their floors. In another minute we were squatting round a bowl of yoghurt.

I arrived last at the top of the pass to find Sandy and the others patiently waiting for me with a prize of Charles's Kendal Mint Cake. On the outside of the packet was an advertisement proclaiming that climbers had nibbled it on the summit of Mount Everest. We devoured it like Alsatians.

On eye-level terms now, we surveyed the lordly view of peaks around us, while a white and brown bearded vulture wheeled over our heads displaying its 8-foot wing span.

It was late afternoon when we threaded our way behind the donkeys to our destination above Roka, set strategically in a mountain cleft in dead ground where artillery shells and bombs could not reach. As the little settlement came into view, a yell echoed down from the mountainside opposite and a man came towards us, half scrambling and half limping. As he arrived I saw that the toe of one of his boots was missing. Out of it protruded a make-shift bandage. Despite his exertions, he was breathing normally.

Through Mr Ali he introduced himself as Gulaidar. We had heard of him. He was once employed in Kabul in a bakery shop crimping the bread to give it a pattern. At the age of twenty-two, he had decided to join the guerrillas. He was now a local commander, one of two in this all-important region near Roka, and Massud was inordinately proud of him. Gulaidar was expecting our visit, and at once said that he would be happy to lead us next afternoon to a spot overlooking the Russian tanks, and shoot at them. This in turn would provoke them to shoot back and we could bring our cameras. We simply did not believe him.

What we did know of him, however, was already Panjsheri legend: one story was that he had been charged to fire a rocket into the house where it was believed a Soviet general was having dinner and had placed his first shot through the dining-room window. He had been wounded four times, the last in the foot, but he jested at his own scars and laughed hugely as he talked of them. He was now twenty-six years old.

It was something of a surprise next morning when we found that far from changing, the plans were advanced, and we were to set off at once on a patrol. Behind Gulaidar we stumbled and scurried along a path that wound its way down the bare mountainside towards Roka. On the way we made a detour to a point that Soviet troops had reached a week before. Here Gulaidar began digging.

Suddenly the centuries yawned once more, as to our dismay he began to unearth the corpse of a Russian that he had killed. For the *mujahideen*, this was infidel trophy of a holy war; for us there was only the stench of death and somehow a sense of sacrilege.

Two hours later we had reached a point where the valley track was almost directly above the Afghan army and Russian forward positions outside Roka. We carried the camera and its electronic trappings down some rocks and on to a ledge from where we could see, a thousand feet below us, a line of Soviet tanks. Their crews, ant-like figures, sauntered between them. On the mountainside opposite us an enemy patrol, looking remarkably like ourselves, was silhouetted for a moment against the skyline.

While we kept our heads down, Charles filmed. Then we withdrew, clambering up the rock face to a cleft, and waited with Gulaidar in a shelter of some overhanging rock, opposite which was a hillside in full view of the Russian tanks below. In a few momentsthere came the rattle of bullets from near where we had been filming: it was Gulaidar's men, shooting at the Soviet position. Gulaidar himself sat smoking a cigarette. As the firing started, he leapt to his feet and vanished. After some more shooting there was a puff of smoke on the hillside opposite, on to which Charles had by now trained his camera. A second explosion followed, a little nearer. We had drawn enemy mortar fire.

In the middle of a salvo, Gulaidar reappeared prancing, leaping and limping by turn, waving his arms and hugging himself with delight as the mortars fell around him, and all the time calling out orders with the shrill eldritch cry of a creature from another world. I have seldom seen a man more happy in his work.

We spent the afternoon back at the little mountain settlement watching the guerrillas training, the gaps in their classical tactical skills made up for by expressions of scowling ferocity. Gulaidar demonstrated a new prize: a captured AGS-17 gun which stood on a tripod and shot grenades any distance up to 200 yards. Like the fighter bombers we saw at Khenj, the AGS-17, a modern Soviet replacement for the heavy machine-gun for use against ground troops, was being tested for the first time in Afghanistan by the Russians. Its tripod was not properly fixed into the ground, and when Gulaidar pulled its trigger it almost kicked him over. Mr Ali was greatly taken with the captured weapon, and referred to it with pride and reverence on every possible occasion.

'Ah,' he would say, when we were discussing a military problem. 'We also have the AGS-17.' He made it sound like the *pièce de résistance* on the room service menu.

That evening we celebrated the best day's filming so far by buying two chickens and, at Sandy's suggestion, decided to ask our cook, himself a *mujahideen*, to roast them. When we returned from the guerrilla training exercise we found that he had cut them up, cooked the pieces in boiling Russian grease, cooled them down and was now boiling them for the evening. The result was warm leather.

'Delicious,' said Sandy, 'although perhaps a trifle overcooked.'

Our return journey to Parende was a happy one: the trip had provided war footage which would be a foundation stone for the programme.

I was exhausted. The huge climb back took most of the day, and this time as I dragged my bones, last again, up the slope, the bearded vulture overhead appeared to be circling a little lower than its predecessor. Doubtless each of us knew what was in the other's mind; even so, I considered the creature's behaviour to be wanting in delicacy.

Once again, beyond and below the top of the pass, hospitable shepherds awaited us. As we sat sipping their tea and hot milk we found we had a new companion for the journey. This was a man who had walked from Kabul with a huge load of cloth on his back and a yard-stick in his hand: he was evidently a travelling salesman-cum-tailor. He was reclining against his load when we arrived with our train of two donkeys and six people, but struggled to his feet to greet each of us, and then insisted on displaying his wares, which included smart grey and blue pinstripe worsteds. He then set off ahead of us at great speed down the mountainside. A few hours later, still last, I came across him lying spreadeagled on his back, looking as if he had turned turtle on top of his load. He seemed to have been waiting for me, and kept me company all the way down to the house at Parende, where saluting politely he took his leave. We never saw him again.

The moment we had crossed the little iron causeway we could sense the air of excitement: Massud was in town. A smart posse of his trusties arrived ahead of him, including a dark bearded commander who had lost a foot when he had stepped on to a mine while

trying to defuse another one. He brandished the stump cheerfully
at us. This was Abdul Wahid. On hearing his story, Sandy at once
suggested that there should be no problem in having a new foot
fitted on in England.

'Apart from the little matter of getting him to London, and
finding the money,' I said.

'Absolutely,' said Sandy airily. 'But these things can be done.'

(And with a lot of help from a lot of people Abdul Wahid was
indeed brought to London and fitted with an artificial foot together
with a spare peg-leg that he made for himself from seasoned walnut
wood, for walking in the mountains. A few months later we heard
with sadness that Gulaidar had lost a foot in exactly the same way,
stepping on a mine.)

Each army has its stock characters, and Massud's was no exception. The demolition expert, Abdul Satar, was now introduced to
us, and from my national service I immediately recognized the
Bomb Happy Joe of legend, the enthusiastic explosives officer
whom everyone expects will shortly blow himself up. For Charles's
camera he demonstrated how to use the contents of an unexploded
bomb to boost a Chinese mine in order to lift a tank 100 feet in the
air. For a fuse he appeared to need only a safety pin and a matchbox.
His first demonstration failed, and the second worked just as he was
approaching it to see what had gone wrong. He was not discon-
certed, but simply brushed the dust from his hair, picked himself
up and laughed.

In the evening Massud arrived, alert, energetic and concentrated
as ever. He agreed at once to all our requests: interview, filming of
a school, visit to the prison. He promised us transport and agreed
to make arrangements for our return to Pakistan.

During our conversations Massud never once referred even to
the possibility of a Soviet victory. He admitted his problems. In
conducting a lonely war he was the focus of Soviet attention, and
risked drawing fire on the Panjsheris. He spoke, though without
disloyalty, of the squabbling political parties in Peshawar and
claimed to be ready to serve under any truly national leader: when
we pointed out that there was none he retreated.

'I am at the service of the Jamayat Party,' was all he would say.

But if we failed to draw Massud out on the subject of his personal
ambitions, two impressions were reinforced in the two days we
were to spend with him. One was of a truly whole-hearted devotion

and trust with which he inspired everyone who came in contact with him. The other was of the quiet confidence that he radiated, seemingly untinged with personal vanity or with religious fanaticism. At the heart of the enigma was a nugget of will-power nourished by unseen resources that defied intellectual analysis.

Massud was guided by a vision of a fundamentalist Moslem state modelled on Iran next door, but there was none of the glint of fanatical fire in his eyes, no foretaste of intolerance that the Ayatollah Khomeini had already displayed in those chilling television interviews given in exile in France before he assumed power.

If Massud did not share the imaginative splendours of an Alexander, he did not show symptoms of despotism or of an unlimited thirst for conquest. But the immediate question was not whether he might become a tyrant, but whether he had the stuff of a Tito in addition to being a talented guerrilla leader. Would his powers of leadership transcend tribal loyalty? Did he possess the talent for devolving authority, all important in a more complex organization where, of necessity, personal contact was not always possible?

Massud had divided his guerrillas into groups: two military and one political. For defending the Panjsher the basic units were the twenty or so *sabets*, which used local volunteers rather than imported fighting units, and this was perhaps the key to their remarkable success, for their soldiers were defending their own homes. In dug-out positions and caves they withstood heavy artillery bombardment and often surprised the attacking forces, first by surviving at all, and then by inflicting heavy casualties on them.

To this basically defensive fighting force Massud had now added his new mobile fighting units, called *motoraks*, which were designed to take the offensive against the Soviet and Afghan armies either in ambushes or at their bases. They were also a part of Massud's plan to extend the war outside the Panjsher. His record of aggression and success had paid off. He had sat up *sabets* and *motoraks* outside as well as inside the Panjsher, in the north and north-east, and these groups, too, were loyal to him.

The *motorak* was organized on classical military lines with companies of about 120 men, divided into platoons and sections, each equipped with a heavy machine-gun. There was a support group for each company of another thirty men armed with mortars, anti-tank weapons, heavy machine-guns and, if available, the AGS-17.

There was even some sort of uniform: black Bulgarian army boots bought in Kabul or taken from the Afghan army, and long-sleeved army tunics of the kind used everywhere from Iran to the United States; commanders wore Soviet breeches, and the prize possession for any *mujahideen* was a fur cap taken from a dead Russian.

Each army unit was accompanied by a political commissar who was part of a propaganda unit reporting directly to Massud himself. It was here that the system was at its most sensitive. Experience of a decade of political commissars from Kabul, with revolutionary plans to collectivize agriculture, had left the deeply conservative landowning Panjsheri farmers implacably opposed to all politicians, let alone new ideas. Moreover Afghans prize fighting skills above all others, and naturally assumed that political commissars had been selected from men who did not pass muster as soldiers. As a result the political commissars tended to attract both hostility and contempt. Above all, their success depended on the support of the influential *mullahs* who had always opposed all changes that reduced their own power. In the minds of moderates, the *mullahs* had a lot to answer for: by turning their backs on modern ideas they had forced progressive elements to turn outside – to the Russians – for help.

But *mullahs* were also the key to the one unifying force of the resistance: religion. Massud had been extremely careful to take them with him at each step of his thinking. More often than not there was a *mullah* beside him when he spoke to us. His political commissars would address the villagers in the presence of the *mullahs*, after prayers. It was vital that they should understand that this was a *jehad*, a holy war. Massud himself was a good speaker, but some of his appointed representatives were not; and always the difficulty he faced was the small but final step that some *mullahs* apparently saw as a danger – allowing Islam to be presented as much as a political ideology as a religion. The prize for Massud was moral as well as political and military authority.

We could see for ourselves that Massud's military skills included human ones of extracting absolute personal loyalty. In return he exacted total obedience and an almost puritanical standard of personal behaviour. In the land which kept a flourishing drug smuggling industry alive across its borders, and where Russian soldiers were reputed to have sold their weapons for hashish, we never once saw even marijuana. Massud only allowed a trusted few of his men to accompany the convoys to Pakistan. As a result his forces, far from being depleted by defections to the flesh pots of Pakistan, were actually growing. It was impossible to trust Afghan statistics, but whatever the actual figures, few would dispute that Massud was the most effective military leader of the resistance.

Repeatedly Massud came back to his theme. In a year or two he hoped to have carried the war outside the Panjsher and to the gates of Kabul. He talked of attacking the Russian-built Salang Tunnel which brought supplies through the mountains from the Soviet Union. His greatest difficulties remained the exodus of the refugees and the shortage of ammunition and the right weapons. Massud was convinced that he was receiving little or no aid from fellow Moslem countries, including Saudi Arabia, or from the West.

'Even the Pakistanis cheat us. When we buy modern weapons we get a top layer in each box of what we ordered, then underneath them the numbers are made up with the old models. We don't get what we paid for. We are fighting the war for the Moslem world, including the Saudis, and they contribute nothing. And even if funds reach Peshawar, they are not reaching the Panjsher. We pay for our own arms from donations from workers in Kabul, and from money from emeralds. The rest we capture ourselves from the Russians.'

It was announced a few months later that Saudi Arabia and the Gulf States had given $35 million to an umbrella organization in Peshawar for the resistance. Isolated in the Panjsher, Massud was probably not in a position to know exactly what Western aid was being channelled through friendly third parties. But he was in a position to deny categorically the repeated Soviet charge that the war was being fought with mercenaries: and certainly we saw none. As Massud pointed out, there was no shortage of manpower and the guerrillas probably had a rough parity of numbers: what he needed was weapons and, above all, ammunition.

Massud needed ground-to-air missiles and heavy machine-guns to deter marauding helicopters and jets and keep them flying too high to do serious damage. Soviet-made heavy machine-guns could be used in portable groups, which could put up a curtain of fire through which jets would have to fly, and then quickly be moved before they could be blasted from their positions. Here again, the problem appeared to be a shortage of ammunition, and perhaps of necessary co-ordination which only training could provide. Massud was very interested in the weaponry of the Falklands war, and especially Britain's 'Blowpipe' missile which had been used against Argentine jet fighters and which Sandy described to him.

He was interested, too, in the possibility of introducing radio communications. Some 'walkie-talkie' radios had been brought in, but left in a cave untouched. It would be hard to persuade the Panjsheris to abandon their efficient and reliable system of couriers with which Massud currently kept in touch with his growing force; but occasions arose when instant communication was vital. Here once again it was a question of training and discipline in restricting use to essential messages, since Soviet monitoring skills were legendary: one of the by-products of six decades of a communist regime heavily dependent on surveillance was the capacity to pin-point on a map in Kabul the source of any but the shortest signal sent by radio.

Massud's political philosophy was simple. He believed that the Soviet Union was expansionist, and that the war constituted a threat to the West. More than once he said to us: 'If we lose this war, you lose it too.' He believed that a self-sufficient Afghanistan, using Western arms (but not Western troops) and united under the banner of Islam, could actually defeat the invader.

A more liberal school held that Soviet invasion of Afghanistan was a manifestation of traditional Russian paranoia about having a *cordon sanitaire* on its borders – more of a reaction than a carefully considered policy, and one which Soviet leaders might even now be regretting. One indication that there was some dissent, at least among middle-ranking officials, came from Ilya Dzirkvelov, a former KGB officer based in Iran who defected to Britain in 1980. He wrote in *The Times*:

> But why Afghanistan? We have enough mountains in the Soviet Union already.... How can you justify to Soviet mothers and fathers the deaths of young Russian lads in Afghanistan? If they were dying for some high political motive that would be another matter, but Afghanistan poses no threat to the Soviet state.

The point, however, was academic: what mattered now was not why the Russians had invaded, but what they would do next. To pull out would be to lose face and authority elsewhere – for a start, in Poland. The price of withdrawal might be too high for the

Russians until they had subdued the resistance and set up a regime acceptable to Moscow. History suggested they were in for a long haul.

Meanwhile the price of remaining was not negligible. Apart from the condemnation of the world, including the Arab world, the assignment cannot have been very pleasant for the Russian soldiers. Told that they were going to Afghanistan to help a friendly power, they found themselves in a civil war with the bulk of the population against them. Their allies were a demoralized and unreliable force. According to the official version, this was not a war but a campaign of pacification against bandits and mercenaries. Thus the Geneva Convention did not apply, and captured bandits were killed. In return they could expect no quarter themselves. Rudimentary efforts to organize an exchange arrangement through the Red Cross produced less than half a dozen Soviet prisoners of war. There was the knowledge that angry Afghans would not forgive atrocities laid at the door of Soviet troops: 105 civilians burned to death while hiding in an underground irrigation system in Logar province, trying to evade the draft; widespread reports, some well substantiated, of Soviet experiments in biological warfare with tales of bodies so infected that they decomposed within hours of death. On the other side, horror stories circulated of acts of revenge of biblical dimensions.

One evening a *mujahideen* showed Tom a letter found on the body of a dead Russian. Translated roughly, the letter read:

Greetings from the Democratic Republic of Afghanistan!

Hello Shura,
Greetings from your soldier friend Yuri! Shura, you promised to write but you forgot, you lazy sod! I suppose you've been living it up where you are, while here we're up to our necks in muck and bullets. We've arrived in a new place, not far from Almaznaya. The worst thing is that they aren't bandits round here, they are mercenaries. They've got DShKs and mortars and sometimes they have us so tightly pinned down that we feel well and truly screwed. Four of our lads have been killed and our commissar, Batueey, was blown up by a mine. There was almost nothing left of him afterwards. As for your battalion, it's being slowly hammered into the ground.

I won't write much, it is impossible to describe everything. We're counting the days till demob. Then it will be home for all, won't it? The three of us will drop in on you, okay? Shura, could I borrow your Parade uniform when we come home? We don't have any. We've got nothing. By the way, the third company has been wiped out. They're all either lying in hospital or in boxes.

Goodbye, we embrace you warmly.

Yuri, Dima, Grigori.

14. Departure Preparations: Theory and Practice

For the few days he was with us Massud came and went without notice. It was natural for him to be secretive. He seemed to have no heir apparent, and nobody in whom to confide. He would appear suddenly and say: 'Go for a walk and we will meet.' A little while later one of his henchmen would approach and give directions to a nearby house where Massud would come separately.

On our last day in Parende, we were introduced to a child spy who we were told was nine years old, but who turned out after all to be eleven. He was remarkably self-possessed, perhaps serene in the knowledge that he was not to be skinned alive or shot, but to be sent to Peshawar for 'correct' indoctrination at Massud's personal wish. His story was that he had been sent, along with several hundred Afghan children, to the Soviet Union to be trained. Quite what his duties were never emerged, but the general impression was that he was to report back, somehow, on the movements of Massud. Kabul radio made no secret of regular holiday visits of children to the Soviet Union. For his part, Massud claimed that this was just one of a number of plots on his life which the loyal inhabitants of the Panjsher had unearthed.

That night the wind rose like fury and barrelled down the narrow Parende Valley; the cold was a foretaste of our journey home over the mountains. Massud had decided that we should leave by the northern route because relations with the Hisb-i-Islami had deteriorated since the recent offensive, and the southern route was no longer safe.

A joint Afghan and Soviet offensive at the top of the Panjsher valley in the Anjuman area meant that we would have to make a large detour through the mountains of Nuristan, emerging at the Pakistani border near Chitral, 100 miles north of Peshawar. The journey would take us over five passes reaching up to 16,000 feet, the height of Mont Blanc, well above the snow-line. We would need eight horses at least for our baggage and for ourselves. Our plan was to leave from Dasht-i-Riwat, the arrival point higher up the valley for a large convoy which Massud was daily expecting. The convoy would provide us with horses and Massud with the ammunition he needed for his counter-attack on Roka, already seriously behind schedule.

It was a blustery, leafy day as Massud led us down the valley towards Bazarak on our way back to our base at Sangana. As usual he walked a few paces ahead of the little posse that formed his immediate circle. The pace was normal by *mujahideen* standards, breakneck by mine. However, our little convoy halted two or three times on the way down the side valley, while Massud disappeared over a wall. Even Afghan stomachs were susceptible to Afghan water.

If the liberation of Bazarak represented a victory for Massud, it was a Pyrrhic one. There was almost no house still standing. Pools of water had formed in shell holes. The road bridge had been blown up, and make-shift iron girders stretched hastily across. Fifty yards away a T-62 tank lay with its barrel blown off, a tribute to the skills of Abdul Satar; if the Russians had not been driven out, at least they had been given a bloody nose.

While we gazed at the ruins, Massud's jeep arrived to ferry us in shifts back to Sangana where, in a house below a mountain as bare as a Welsh mine tip, we found that the French doctors had joined us, together with the final instalment of our baggage with the portable generator, warm clothes and documents.

Tony and Jean-José had long since left the Panjsher to go north. The journalist who had come in with the French party had also left, and Jean-Phillipe's replacement was now ill and lay, as we had done each in our turn, in a heap on the floor.

Life for us became, if not comfortable, at least a little more formal than before. In the ceiling of our room was an electric light socket, placed there purely for prestige only, since there was no question of electricity.

But the real reason for the change was Mr Ali. Morning and evening we danced our routine minuet together.

'Good evening. What would you like to eat for dinner?'

'What is on the menu Mr Ali?'

'This evening there is meat.'

'Mutton or goat, Mr Ali?'

'This evening I hope it is mutton.' So indeed did we, but we knew it would be goat.

On our second morning at Sangana Mr Ali announced triumphantly: 'Today there is honey on the menu.'

'Excellent, Mr Ali. But is there honey to eat?'

It appeared that Massud had instructed him to provide us with some: though since he had willed only the end and not the means, it remained for the time being as stated – on the menu only. However, it did arrive for dinner, more memorable for its excellence than its quantity, in a small tea cup.

On our second morning it was, I think, Charles who called out in jest to Mr Ali at the end of the breakfast litany:

'Send up the hotel barber after breakfast, please.'

Mr Ali was hugely amused and, after the triumph with the honey, determined that we should not get the better of him. In the middle of that afternoon, he came into our room accompanied by a man carrying a carpet-bag from which he produced six cut-throat razor holders. Into one of them he inserted half a safety razor and shaved each of us in turn, using cold water and a cake of Russian washing soap. He set about his task slowly and methodically, with a determined look on his face that made me think of Sweeney Todd. Every now and then a smile revealed a single tooth to match the whiteness of his turban.

A convention of Afghan manners entails refusing anything offered for the first and second times, however empty the stomach or purse, however great the need; and of accepting the third time if pressed. We had fallen so far short ourselves as to have taken virtually to scavenging for food, occasionally even scrumping an apple from someone's orchard, so it was not for us to criticize Mr Ali on this score. Even so, it was hard to avoid observing that Mr Ali seemed to have no difficulty in accepting remunerations the first time round, and even suggesting when he thought one appropriate. As keeper of our purse, I noticed that the advances I gave him to buy food had a habit of turning themselves into tips when, as was usually the case, there was no food available. Not for nothing was he a graduate of the University of Room Service.

As promised, Massud organized for us a day at a school, and the dislikeable political officer whom we had met with Abdul Khay performed for us by chanting questions to a class held in a mulberry

orchard, to which the children intoned the correct answers in unison. It is said that simple minds need authoritarian guidance to
steer them, and perhaps in the more sophisticated schools of Kabul
a more individual approach was taken to teaching. What we witnessed disturbed me. This was the doctrinaire approach, a convey-
ing of dogma to be learned by heart and in no way an encouragement
to thought or individual talent: here were children more anxious to
please than to understand. As they chanted 'Death to Brezhnev' I
wondered how many of them knew who Brezhnev was. (If indeed
it did represent a wish, it was soon to come true.) The exercise
reminded me of catechism at school; but it reminded me even more
forcibly of two of Afghanistan's neighbours – Iran to the west and
the Soviet Union to the north. Over the mulberry orchard there
hung the whiff of intolerance.

We were shaken awake at five o'clock on our last morning by Mr
Ali.

'The singing *mujahideen* are waiting, sir!'

Sandy and Charles had been persuaded that the television programme would be incomplete without some Panjsheri songs. On
the evening before, they had come across the leader of a group and
agreed to record their work first thing in the morning before we
left. The group had taken them at their word.

'They say they are ready. If you do not come at once they will go.'

We were ready in fifteen minutes: there was a drummer, a man
with a *dhamboura*, a sort of banjo made from mulberry wood, and
two others who sang all the time (the two instrumentalists joined in
what I took to be the chorus). To my cloth ear the sound was a low
incomprehensible moan; I wondered how Beethoven would have
sounded to them. I asked Mr Ali what their songs were about.

'All about love,' he said with a huge grin. 'He goes away. She
goes away.'

He listened for a while longer, apparently in rapture.

'I think they are very bad,' he said.

We began the trek home in shifts. Massud's jeep was to take us to
a village short of Khenj for the night: there we were to be picked up
by truck and taken on to Dasht-i-Riwat beyond which the road
became impassable. Massud would be coming with us as far as the
first stop.

Charles and I were in the last shift. While we waited I went to sit beside the river for the last time. There was a foretaste of a chill in the air. In the sun's weaker autumn rays the village seemed to huddle for warmth in the folds of the valley.

Then in the water as it meandered past I saw an old box that I recognized. It was followed by several other familiar objects. I realized that it was the rubbish that we had collected on our journey, which I had put into a sack to be thrown away and left in our room for tidiness. Fifty yards up the river some children were picking through its contents and hurling the rejected items into the river like Bank Holiday picnic makers.

I found Mr Ali and Charles sitting with our bags on the roadside where it passed directly beneath the steep and stony incline of the mountain. As we waited a distant explosion startled some goats grazing above us and they stampeded, dislodging a small avalanche of stones. We moved quickly out of their way, but one boulder struck my bag and delivered the *coup de grâce* to my Chinese mirror. It was our only casualty directly attributable to enemy action.

'In Europe it is considered unlucky to break a looking-glass,' I told Mr Ali.

'In Afghanistan it is considered unlucky if a stone breaks your head,' he replied.

As the moment came nearer I realized that taking leave of Mr Ali would be rather poignant. Through knowing one another's weaknesses, an intimacy had been established that was now to be broken. We had badgered and bullied him for food he could not supply, but he had done his best and his manners were impeccable. In a rush of something like guilt I gave him an enormous tip, which disappeared magically into his pocket.

When finally the jeep arrived and we clambered in, Mr Ali got in too.

'Mr Ali, I thought this was good-bye.'

'I come too,' said Mr Ali.

In my ear Charles said: 'He is counting on a second good-bye tip.'

The jeep broke down twice on the half-hour journey. The first time Mr Ali told us it was the filter. The second time, although the driver peered at a different part of the machinery, Mr Ali blamed the filter again. But each time the driver got us going and we bumped and crashed through the craters to a small village, where we found the rest of the party waiting. By now the replacement

French doctor, who had come with us to see Massud, lay shivering under a blanket: he had diagnosed malaria.

That evening we had supper with Massud in a grand double room together with perhaps fifty *mujahideen* and, using our portable generator to supply the current, Tom rigged up a showing of some of our own material for the company to see. The occasion demonstrated to the greatest possible effect the advantage of video tape, which is ready to view instantly, over film.

The evening had its inauspicious moments. Massud was taken with a fit of hiccups. Ever on the hopeful side, Sandy demonstrated with his glass of tea an infallible cure whereby the sufferer bends forwards and drinks from the far side of a glass. This case followed exactly the pattern of every previous one I had witnessed: the contents of the glass spilled down Massud's shirt front and the hiccups continued unabated throughout the film show.

In order to show Sandy's interview with Massud, Tom had to rewind the reel of tape on which it had been recorded to start at the beginning. In doing so he inadvertently left the switches on, so that the audience, many of whom presumably had never before seen a film, let alone television, watched the picture of their leader speaking and gesturing at high speed backwards, while the sound track resembled two Mickey Mouses conversing in an unknown language.

One part of the showing was a huge success, however, with Mr Ali. When he saw himself standing beside Gulaidar's captured rocket gun, his eyes gleamed.

'The AGS-17,' he said several times to the spectators around him.

In the morning we took our final leave of Massud. Mr Ali saw us off and at the last minute I relented and pressed a parting note into his palm.

We lay in the back of the truck sprawled on our bags, bouncing over the craters, thinking ourselves to be travelling in Pullman comfort. Just after two jets swooped over us, it emitted a cloud of dark blue smoke, like toast burning, and stopped. While Charles filmed oxen crushing corn the driver got it started once more.

At Khenj we paused: the little shops that we last saw after the bombing raid had come back to life, and the ground offensive had added remarkably little to the damage. One shop that had been empty before, was now full of gaily coloured traditional Afghan clothes as well as some Russian ones, sold by departing refugees needing funds for their journey. There were coats of the sort I had seen in my grandfather's cupboard – tough well-cut tweeds sewn to last a lifetime. Stephane bought himself a technicolour outfit of Russian jodhpurs, a fur hat and grandly embroidered waistcoat. Sandy hankered after a pair of tweed plus-fours with a bright green pattern, constructed apparently for a dwarf, which I told him would have got him black-balled at Rye.

There were some familiar faces as well. We had tea with an old man who carried a Second World War Lee Enfield rifle and a bandoleer from which he persisted in pulling rounds of ammunition to show us: every time he could catch an unwary eye he would hold his hands in a posture of shooting Russians and say 'bam'. With his white beard he looked as if he had been got up for the part of a holy warrior by a Hollywood theatrical outfitter. He had pestered us the day before by getting himself into almost every shot that Charles took.

I could not have left Khenj without looking at Jamir's house. It was still standing, as I remembered it, the window black where the rocket had hit it. Then, to my delight as we walked along we came across Jamir himself. As usual, he had a crowd around him. He greeted us with a huge smile and a cheerful thumbless windmilling of the arms. Clearly things were looking up for Jamir, though in quite what way we never did discover. We had seen him fret; now once again we saw him strut. I was pleased in parting to find that the old sound and fury had returned.

At about noon we reached our destination of Dasht-i-Riwat, just beyond which was the end of the road for wheeled traffic. It was here, up a side valley, that the Panjsher's only prison stood. We reached it, travelling as far as we could by lorry and then on foot in the company of Massud's light-eyed aide, whom we had met before in Khenj, and the local guerrilla commander, a good-looking man with a classical Greek profile with forehead and nose forming a fine straight line.

All Panjsheris were convinced that the Russians were using every form of devilish device from experimental conventional weapons to chemical warfare against them, and not without cause. There were persistent stories of their water being poisoned. That day the commander was full of fresh reports that the two jets that had passed over earlier had been seen to drop canisters into the river at the head of the valley, that the river was now bright green and that six cows had already been found dead.

We had to cross the river on the way to the prison and found that indeed the water had turned a bright green colour. We collected a sample which we took back to London with us. Under analysis it showed no trace of abnormality; the green was never explained.

The prison was a stone building like all the others we had visited. Its approach was guarded by a quaint stone sentry-box leading to a plank across the side river. Outside the young guards posed for our cameras as we arrived, and overhead on a shelf of rock two *mujahideen* stood proudly to attention beside a machine-gun. Behind the prison's locked main door was a courtyard lined with rooms that served as cells.

The most striking feature of the prison was the dearth of prisoners: there were perhaps twenty-five in all, including an Afghan government political commissar from Kabul. His replies when he was interviewed for television were heavily prompted and corrected by the local commander and Massud's aide until we stopped them. They seemed unable to grasp that we wanted the man to speak for himself: after all, why ask an enemy, a communist, when they knew the right answers?

The terrorized commissar stood his ground with some dignity, and even contrived a striking feat of syntax in almost non-existent English, managing to praise the *mujahideen* without actually renouncing the Karmal government. I admired his courage. We asked about his future, and were given the impression that he was being kept as a showpiece for visiting journalists or for possible use as a hostage. Even so, I would not have rated him as a good insurance risk.

There was only one Russian, an extremely young deserter who appeared to be treated as half-prisoner, half-convert, hanging about the prison but not living in it. He was one of the Soviet Union's forty-three million Moslems. He claimed that the invasion of Afghanistan had caused great resentment in the Soviet Union: we had no way of telling if this was true, or said to please. I could not help wondering how much Soviet Moslems even knew of the war.

Most of the prisoners were petty criminals. We asked again what had become of the other prisoners of war that the level of casualties suggested. Again we met bland assertions that normal ratios did not apply in Afghanistan. As with the young Russian, there was no means of evaluating the statement. An order to respect the Geneva Convention had been issued from the Jamayat political headquarters in Peshawar in an attempt to reach an agreement for an exchange of prisoners; but when the penalty for capture was death, perhaps preceded by torture, reciprocal treatment could not be considered entirely surprising.

Our lorry was waiting for us near a cemetery, its graves marked by green and white scraps of chiffon fluttering from poles stuck into piles of stones.

The machine refused to start, not surprisingly since it turned out to have an empty tank. A *mujahideen* filled it up, and again it refused to start; again understandably, since he had put in kerosene oil instead of petrol. By the time the tank was drained and petrol discovered from a hidden store our teeth were chattering with cold. Winter, which meant closed mountain passes, was already in the air.

That evening the commander, now our host, presided over our dinner in a fine long silk coat with green and blue stripes which he wore like a cloak, its long ceremonial sleeves hanging empty. We had been joined by a man who spoke excellent English and who introduced himself as Hajji Sefat Mir of Afghan Tours. He explained to us that until the war he had been a guide for foreign tourists, specializing in trips to the Waikan Corridor, a finger of mountainous territory in the north-east of Afghanistan next to the Soviet and Chinese borders, created to separate British India from Tsarist Russia. Until the 1970s rich foreigners used to go there to shoot the strange Marco Polo sheep, remarkable for the great size of the horns of the rams. One of Sefat Mir's regular clients, he told us, was a French Rothschild.

'Now I have changed to another business,' and putting his hand into his pocket he pulled out a leather pouch from which he poured a stream of green stones, 'the emerald business,' he said.

Sefat Mir was now prospecting with a partner in an area near Dasht-i-Riwat. He told us that the business was organized so that a pool purchaser would buy their stones and sell them on the market in Peshawar, taking a percentage of the profits for Massud's campaign funds. Charles picked up an oblong green spike a few centimetres long.

'That one is worth twenty thousand *afghanis* in Pakistan. Not a very good one. It will fetch much more, of course, in Europe or

America.' Even at £200 a stone his pouch contained £10,000's worth.

We soon grew to realize our good fortune in having the young Frenchman Stephane with us. His Farsi was fluent; he was enthusiastic, resourceful and intelligent. His presence had occurred by chance, and he had accepted our offer to hire him as interpreter and guide; it was soon to become essential.

That evening was his first big test. Massud had given us a letter demanding full co-operation from all *mujahideen* of the Jamayat-i-Islami to help us in any way if possible. But the local commander, for all his classical good looks, proved to be no match for the horse dealers who came to bargain with us, and whom Stephane now took on.

These were the peasant farmers who, like their Kazakh counterparts in the Soviet Union, had thwarted attempts by a succession of city bureaucrats to persuade them that collective farming was good for them. They needed no lessons on protecting themselves against exploitation.

Stephane opened negotiations by asking them to rent us horses to go to Pakistan. They had none to spare, but would take us instead to Parian, the main guerrilla trading-post a little further up the valley (a three- or a six-hour journey, according to whether you were selling or buying). At first they wanted the equivalent of £20 a horse for the eight horses needed for the trip. After long negotiations Stephane beat them down to a price that we estimated to be double the going rate, but half what they had originally asked. We settled promptly; although short of Afghan currency, we were even more short of time. We knew our journey to Pakistan might take anything up to three weeks. With October already upon us and signs of rain in the sky, the question mark hanging over our prospects grew daily larger.

Having concluded the deal, Stephane now turned his attention to the commander who had basked silently in his finery throughout the negotiations.

Unknown to us the two had entered into a wager earlier that day when the commander had told us it would take only ten minutes to reach the prison from the river. In a moment of inspiration Stephane had bet the commander a hot meal that it would take longer by his watch. After half an hour the commander conceded defeat; but dinner that night was tea and bread. Fresh from his triumph with the farmers, Stephane now reminded the commander of his commitment. As we bedded down for the night I assumed that that was an end to the matter. But to show that he was a man of his word the commander woke us next morning at five o'clock with a dish of hotly spiced goulash.

I think of our journey home proper as beginning from Dasht-i-Riwat, probably because it marked the start of our personal relationship with Afghan horses. I had never really liked or understood horses. As a child I had learned to ride on a mule. Once in my life a beast of the kind rented to tourists, an iron-mouthed hack noted for dumb sloth, had bolted under me. 'They sense hysteria,' its amazed owner had said. In my mind horses belonged to two categories: stupid and friendly, and stupid and unfriendly.

In Afghanistan I learned to devise a new set of categories for their minders and owners as well. Our first batch were stubborn, unreliable and dishonest. At the outset, they loaded the horses with no regard for our request to have the camera ready for use. This we were used to from the journey in. After we had asked them to stay within calling distance, in case we needed to film, the first two vanished over the horizon ahead of us with their loads. Two others rode the horses that we had designated for ourselves, so that two of us had to walk, while two of the horses never turned up at all. Finally when we arrived at Parian, they all demanded to be paid a second time, thus making up the balance they had lost in bargaining with Stephane. In the absence of the new local commander, due in that evening, the second-in-command at the headquarters took our letter of authority from Massud. He read it carefully and then demanded that not only should we give the horsemen nothing, but that they should repay us part of the extortionate sum already extracted from us. Meanwhile the horsemen had some of our equipment; and thinking we might need their services again we ended up negotiating against our own interests, with the *mujahideen* deputy commander growing increasingly determined to enforce the spirit of Massud's letter.

It was extremely late when the commander arrived and found a furious row still raging in the dark. He studied Massud's letter carefully. Finding that it demanded we should be provided what we needed, but said nothing either way about payment, he finally allowed us to strike a price. It was what the farmers had asked for in the first place.

After a fretful night's sleep we awoke in a charming room with walls 4 feet thick, opening at one end between wooden pillars on to a raised platform where a man who looked like Popeye was baking bread in an oven let into its floor. Another door opened into a room where the commander slept. We joined him for breakfast.

The commander's name was Yacoub. He wore Russian riding breeches to reflect his status as an officer, and a fine fox fur hat from Badakshan.

Through Stephane, Yacoub told us that the big convoy of arms from Pakistan, expected for almost a week, had not yet arrived. Until it did horses would be 'difficult'.

Parian was perhaps the most beautiful hamlet we had yet seen in the Panjsher, a cluster of farms fed by a complicated network of irrigation channels, brimming over now, from which a hollowed tree trunk fed water to a little stone millhouse just below us. It was an oasis of green water meadows where oxen crushed the corn and marauding goats climbed the trees and ate our leather straps. The old trees themselves, the deepest green of all, spread their shade over the meadows. At every level and angle stood houses with hardwood beams similar to ours, and doubtless similar niches in their walls containing hand-made jugs, pots, knives and huge cooking spoons.

There was nothing to do but wait. On our first day the camera crew filmed men winnowing the corn, while women in scarlet robes walked by. Two MiGs whisked overhead in the direction of the top of the valley, and were gone in a flash. We waited, and in twenty minutes they obligingly returned for the camera: they took no notice of us.

By a stroke of good fortune Yacoub took a fancy to Stephane and by the second day the young Frenchman was attired in fox fur hat, Russian boots and new jodhpurs. Yacoub told us that he had recently returned from a mission in the north-east to train guerrilla units along the lines so successfully fashioned by Massud for the Panjsher. The dividends were clearly considerable in extracting commitments of support and broadening Massud's power base. Yacoub told us that there were even resistance groups in Kabul which looked to Massud as their leader. He was a cheerful and intelligent commander who appeared to be a cut above most of the others whom we had seen, in both competence and maturity. He promised to do his best to help us.

Horses began to dribble in. We needed eight. By our second day we had three in view. They could be either rented or bought. Buying was easier, especially at this end of the season, because the responsibility for feeding and reselling animals rested with the owner. Renting was particularly attractive to us because we could pay half the rental in Pakistan where we had more funds. We had come prepared to pay for the horses but not for food – for horses as well as humans – nor for guides. Now we had to finance all three.

Yacoub introduced us to the two horsemen, both guerrillas, who were to accompany us on our journey. One, called Noor, was a charming and open man whom we liked at once. The other, who was to be in charge, was as villainous in appearance and surly in demeanour as Noor was agreeable. His dark face, framed by a black beard, set naturally into a scowl, and he wore his Chitrali beret pulled down over his ears as if expecting them to be boxed at any moment. He spoke in the resentful tone of the unloved. At our first meeting his hand and mine met in a bread bowl, and when he looked up into my face with his untrusting eyes I silently named him Judas. His real name was Rahman. Poor Rahman: Quasimodo would have been more suitable.

Neither Rahman nor Noor knew the route into Pakistan, nor had either of them ever set foot in the province of Nuristan whose reputation for highway robbery and murder seemed to strike terror into their hearts.

Each morning we watched the bread being made in the sunken oven. The cook would knead the flour and water, add salt and leave the dough for about twenty minutes, then place it against the circular sides of the oven. Whatever else might have gone wrong there was always freshly baked bread each day.

Then we would squat round the commander hoping for news. He had sent out his spare men to scour for horses and even prevailed on the *mullah* to make a search. Advance units of the convoy struggled into Parian in twos and threes only, and after two days horses were still 'difficult'. Each evening as the sun slid behind the mountains we saw another precious twenty-four hours slip from our grasp.

We did our best to keep up the commander's interest in our

fortunes. One morning we heard on the BBC that an American congressman was to press for overt government aid to help the resistance in Afghanistan. When we told him, the pleasure on Yacoub's face was genuinely moving. I had not the heart to add how little it meant.

In common with every other Afghan, what Yacoub really liked best of anything we had to offer was having his photograph taken. My Polaroid camera had arrived with the last of our bags as we were leaving Sangana, and it was an immediate success. An instantly developed photograph proved far more valuable, as well as acceptable, to most Afghans than a tip (except in the case of Mr Ali, who liked both). The moment the *mujahideen* caught sight of a camera they would clamour to be photographed, gesturing with fingers circled round their eyes. They would then strike grim heroic poses, weapon in hand. Not once did any of these normally smiling faces smile for a photograph, so that in their pictures they emerged resembling wanted criminals. On seeing themselves, they would then grin from ear to ear with delight.

Yacoub was no exception to the rule. During our stay I photographed him, with his gun, sitting, standing, riding his horse, with his hat, without his hat: anything to keep up his interest in our needs.

If Yacoub could not bring us horses, he brought us the next best thing: food. While we were at Parian we were able to build up some strength with occasional meat, and on one occasion as much yoghurt as we could eat. Our problems with food remained one of quantity and not of quality. We were still voraciously hungry and we stuffed into our mouths all we could get in anticipation of the ordeal ahead, ashamed to be surrounded by Afghans watching politely with stomachs no less empty than our own and only rice to eat. Even then, it was not nearly enough.

The call for horses had by now reached the ears of every ruffian in the neighbourhood. They brought their sick donkeys, horses too lame to walk up a slope, let alone a mountain, one that gasped when it moved at all; some were for rent only if we took the gentler southern route; most of the others were no-rents, no-shows, or no-goes for one reason or another. Between them the two horsemen, together with Yacoub and Stephane, who appeared to enjoy the role of horse-dealer, screened them and fended them off.

After a while we forced ourselves to stop asking for progress reports. To distract myself I tried reading some more torn out pages from Sandy's *Vanity Fair*, watched by a boy with a catapult. At one moment he killed a small red bird. When I remonstrated with him he shot at another.

On the third day we awoke to heavy rain and no sign of the incoming convoy. Worse still, as the peaks to the north and east cleared, we could see that they were covered with snow. The passes normally shut towards the second half of October: it was now the second of the month. If we could not get through soon we would not be able to do so until March, a subject of conversation we avoided by common consent.

At breakfast time the hammer blow fell. Advance reports of the convoy had now reached Parian. Three horses (or twenty-five, according to which version you preferred) had been lost in deep snow. All the passes over 14,000 feet would now be shut. Winter had come early.

We held a council of war. The exercise was more for morale than for taking decisions, for we knew in our hearts and from experience that events would follow an unpredictable course of their own entirely beyond our control.

The southern route was still open, but vulnerable to attacks by the Hisb-i-Islami; moreover there were the difficulties of trying to get transport over the southern wall of the Panjsher, which was too steep for horses to pass. On the other hand, the northern route appeared, quite simply, to be closed. In the end we decided that we should keep what horses we had and try to contact Massud to persuade him to give us porters and armed escorts for the southern route.

Meanwhile another council of war was taking place between Rahman and Yacoub, the commander. It appeared that Rahman, who had been the first to declare the northern route impractical, was now protesting that he could not take us through the southern route either, as it was far too dangerous. Yacoub apparently was explaining that Massud's instructions were for us to be assisted to Pakistan, and that whichever route we took Rahman would be our escort.

For Yacoub the trouble with the southern route was not so much that it was dangerous, but that Massud's orders had specified the other one. If there was to be a change, he would have at the very least to send for new orders. It seemed that he was now beginning to have second thoughts about the northern route.

So was Rahman. All of a sudden the picture had altered, and Rahman told Stephane that the northern route would be all right after all. The dead horses and snow had mysteriously melted away.

'What are our chances?' we asked, through Stephane.

There followed a long speech by Rahman in Farsi. At the end of it Stephane looked at us sheepishly and said:

'He says we are in the hands of Allah.'

After lunch we were treated to a Shakespearian scene, when a traveller came in to the commander's room through the small door set high in the wall, and spoke eloquently of the dangers and treachery attending the southern route. He was closely followed by another traveller, stinking spectacularly, who entered from another door to say that he had completed the journey by the northern route in six days. He then changed it, in fingers, to sixteen.

The sun came out and our spirits rose. For a while at least summer had returned. A lame horse stood down by Rahman that morning, when he was arguing against the northern route, had mysteriously become un-lame; but a donkey had slipped away.

Uncertainty was making us fractious again. Charles had a row with Tom who wanted to abandon some of the television equipment that was not working. Tom argued that it was insured and that it was absurd to carry heavy broken-down equipment when we were short of transport anyway. Charles accused him of vandalism. Sandy quite reasonably suggested that we might have to take what horses we could and go on foot into Pakistan, but then enraged me when he said he would enjoy the walk. I accused him of ascribing some obscure Presbyterian merit to unnecessary suffering. I annoyed Charles by scolding him for taking no notice of my list of provisions before we left, which included a waterproof sheet each against the rain. Now he wanted mine to protect the film.

Then we had confirmation that we would have to make a long detour (in fact by the old butter route, literally once used for carrying butter between Nuristan and present-day Pakistan) because the Russians' presence at Koran Va Monjan in the valley of the Anjuman now blocked the shorter route. On hearing this Charles asked: 'How badly are the Russians at Anjuman?' Since we were all to be unarmed and wished to reach Pakistan alive, I reflected that even a single armed Russian would be the equivalent of making Anjuman 'a little bit pregnant'. I knew what Charles meant, but we were all becoming childishly irritable.

I smoked a cigarette to relieve the tension and watched as an advance unit of the convoy arrived and sat down to count ammunition.

At dinner as we squatted in the dark, the *mullah*, whom we had given up for lost, reappeared with two more horses; a third had been pledged. On the theory that nothing good or bad happened as expected, we tried to control a cautious optimism.

The weather had cleared the next morning, although there was still snow on the mountain visible from our window. The stone on which I usually squatted to wash in the stream was covered by water, and I imagined mountain torrents blocking our path and carrying away our horses.

Of eight horses asked for (five to ride and three for baggage), two were geriatric and one was missing. As expected, the loading went wrong, and we were short of two saddles. We had asked for our personal bags to be placed on the riding horses so that we could get at them. As usual, Rahman and Noor took no notice but distributed the load for balance rather than for convenience, topping the less heavily charged riding horses with the last-minute provisions for us to sit on: sacks of rice, straw for the horses, and, in my case, spare horseshoes, as hard as the nails that went with them.

We set off with everyone in a vile temper.

15. Snowdon Only Higher

As we went on up the valley the vegetation and scenery changed. Already in Parian itself fruit had to be brought in by travellers from the lower Panjsher. Now as we approached Chamar the rivers seemed to swell and stones turned to boulders as the ground rose to meet the mountains ahead.

We stopped once more to film a family of refugees living in a cave, and to pick up an extra horse, so that we had one each to ride. While we waited farmers gave us boiled eggs as hard as billiard balls; and one of the pack-horses took suddenly against its load and charged across a field bucking and rearing, scattering expensive electronic equipment as it went.

As evening came the landscape softened once again. Beside us on our left a stretch of farming land ran up to a group of houses set perfectly to please the eye against the valley wall behind. Far away to the right, a monster awakening, was the start of the long rocky climb into the mountains we were to make the next day; our path would take us over the high Chamar Pass near the 20,000-foot peak of Mir Samir that came into view now, towering above the other mountains on the distant horizon.

Just before nightfall the track we were following fell steeply away. We dismounted and led our horses down through the hairpin bends and across a river that thundered into the Panjsher. Above it on the far side we came to a miniature version of Teremengal, our point of departure in Pakistan. Everywhere horses were tethered, and *mujahideen*, bearing the marks of travel on their faces, stood around. The northern convoy had arrived.

The little horse station, a group of no more than four or five stone houses, was ill-equipped to digest the sudden rush-hour traffic, and we waited outside in the confusion as the bags were unloaded. While Stephane struck a bargain for more saddles, elaborate wooden affairs covered with hide, I watched the light failing on the mountains that lay ahead of us, blue draining to slate grey on the high slopes, gold to hard cold white on the summit of Mir Samir itself.

It was night when we clambered up the stone stairs with our kit-bags to a smoke-filled room packed with *mujahideen* counting ammunition and shouting to each other. The trappings of war were everywhere. In one corner a hat stand was festooned with rifles, muskets, and machine-guns; another corner was piled with parts of rocket grenade launchers, shelves and window sills were stacked with mines. In the distance, above the din of the voices, the river clamoured in our ears.

Taking off our boots, we squatted where we could, hugging our knees, and watched the light from the kerosene lamps dance in the metal of the cartridges as they were counted out into piles on the floor.

The kitbags we leant against now contained a new wardrobe for our new wants. Instead of water bottles and plasters for sore feet we had to think in terms of windproof jackets, heavy oiled sweaters at the ready for the moment the sun went behind a mountain, thermal underwear with long pants that went irreversibly under everything else, so that the price of miscalculation was to boil or freeze.

The fug in the little room was becoming insupportable when all of a sudden, without warning, the *mujahideen* rose to their feet and departed. Evidently because of its vulnerability to air attack by day, the convoy travelled at night. In its place some old men appeared and began talking to us.

There was too little space for all of us to stretch out on the floor of the room. I found a small outhouse and, deciding that the smell of horses was preferable to the smell of humans, spread my sleeping bag on a bed of dung and straw, and for the first time in almost two months enjoyed the luxury of privacy.

We left Chamar at three in the morning. The moon was full and its fierce cold light threw weird shadows on the path that stretched like a grey purgatory ahead of us.

I learned that the Farsi for 'gee-up' was '*shur!*', but nobody appeared to have shared the information with my horse. It took no notice either of the modest switch that I had fashioned into a whip.

A horse cantered past bearing two men on its back.

'*Mandeh nabashi* – May you never grow tired.'

'*Salaam aleikom.*'

Then the moon went down and we lost each other in the dark. Tom's load slipped and he fell off with it: his curses acted as a homing device for his rescuers. My own horse was quite willing to walk, but only at a pace that ensured gradually falling behind the main party. It flatly refused to trot. I estimated that we averaged about half a mile an hour for the first three hours.

At a bend we turned back for our last view of Chamar and for a moment the Panjsher was transfigured in a false dawn; it looked less like a work of nature than a work of art, with unnaturally clear details of the valley we had left standing out in the freak light leaving the surrounding mountains in darkness. Then we turned the corner and it was lost from sight.

Soon we reached a great saucer of stones and snow, tilted upwards, with the face of Mir Samir rising over us in the morning sun. As we laboured on up the endless saucer throughout the morning, Mir Samir appeared to keep pace with us.

At about 14,000 feet we came to the snow-line. We stopped at a miniature Stonehenge: boulders piled on top of each other to make a rough shelter, with stone pens for animals. In one of the pens we found the remnants of a fire left by the tail end of the ammunition convoy. We boiled water and made tea.

The sun came over the mountains, warming us in a flash, and we felt a surge of well-being. As we took off our warm clothes Stephane discovered that there were lice inside the Russian riding breeches which Yacoub had given to him. Then Rahman pointed to the bleak track ahead of us and we put on our clothes again, together with the green waterproof jackets. I traded a Polaroid snapshop of Rahman for the loan of his whip, a kind of wooden truncheon covered in leather. But my poor old mount was past all inducement, carrot or stick. To the cry of *shur!* and a blow on its scrawny flanks, the only response was a trembling of its entire frame, a sort of staggering surge for two paces before it resumed its natural somnambulist's gait. Throughout the trials of riding I was sustained chiefly by the thought of how much more appalling it would be to have to walk.

At the upper edge of the saucer we came to what appeared to be a sheer, clearly impossible cliff. Rahman pointed to it: '*Arakat!*'

The cliff stood on the far side of a mountain lake. As we looked we could just see the start of a zig-zag track that led up its face. It was beginning to snow lightly.

I had already noticed that my horse tended to get its legs crossed on turns, so that regularly we had to stop and start again to avoid falling. At first I thought it was lame; but it seemed to walk, if not trot, more or less normally on the straight. After several near falls, I settled in my mind that the beast was cross-eyed. But now a new phenomenon became apparent. While it seemed reasonably ready to turn to the right, even to face precipices that made me dizzy, it stubbornly halted every time I tried to make it turn to the left. It was when we were about a third of the way up the cliff face leading to the Chamar Pass that I discovered the cause of the trouble. It was blind in one eye.

For the last few hundred yards the track up the pass consisted of a succession of rock slabs separated by hair-pin bends up which we led the horses, dragging them by their bridles. To measure our progress towards the summit I marked a cairn of stones with my eye: when it came nearer I saw, hidden behind it, a second cairn on a higher ledge. At the top of that a bold fresh wind told me that we had indeed reached the highest point of the pass. I turned and saw Mir Samir bathed in sunlight with Charles flogging up behind me, and all at once I forgot the pain of the climb. It was a grand moment.

Ahead of us was a narrow gap, as if a giant had stopped for lunch in the middle of building a rock wall, leaving dozens of loose blocks strewn around. As we squeezed our loads through the gap I was reminded of Eric Newby's account aptly comparing it with the neck of a bottle through which, by dint of pushing and shoving, he and his travelling companion popped their horses like corks.

Facing us was Nuristan. In 1895 King Abdur Rahman of Afghanistan had converted this land with the sword in the name of Allah, changing its name from Kafiristan, the Land of the Infidels, to the Land of Light. Its inhabitants had up to then been fierce pagan worshippers of unknown origin, but bearing strong traces (many have blue eyes and red beards) of Alexander the Great's visit in the fourth century before Christ. After their conversion they had been forced to give up making wine, which they had been famed for drinking in prodigious quantities without getting drunk, and took instead to selling into slavery their women, whose beauty is celebrated in Afghan poetry, in exchange for Afghan cattle. Most

Afghans we had met described Nuristanis as robbers and murderers best left alone.

But the view that met our eyes was not of people. A grey wilderness of rock fell away beneath our feet, then rose again in the distance to a horizon of even greyer crags. There was not a single sign of life, no person, no tree, not even a bird of prey. It was as if the Maker had lost interest on about the fourth day of creation. It was a formidably unfriendly sight.

We led our horses over the slippery slabs of rock that wound down the reverse slope of the Chamar Pass. Every now and then there would be a hair-pin bend with a sudden drop where one person held each horse by the bridle, and another by the tail, for reassurance. My horse stumbled several times and at the end of a two-hour descent its scrawny quarters were sweating and its legs covered in blood. I feared it would never complete the journey.

At the foot of the cliff Rahman led us along another track that my eyes could not pick up, among the stones and down a twisting funnel-shaped defile. Every now and then we came across a horse's carcass.

Tom's Irish temper was fully tried by his horse which had no saddle and had to be coaxed at every step. There was an altercation, the first of many, with Rahman who wanted to hurry him on. I volunteered for a provisional exchange of horses with Tom: for all its other defects mine at least had a saddle.

Then at nightfall there was a cry and Rahman, who had stayed behind with Tom and the three pack-horses, came cantering up to where Sandy and I waited in alarm. High drama illuminated his unlovely features: his eyes rolled, his arms reached menacingly towards us, everything betraying the signs I knew so well from friends who can't wait to tell you the bad news. By his gestures I understood that Tom had fallen from his horse, down a ravine, into a river and was drowned. Rahman's rendering in mime of a compound fracture of the skull was particularly arresting.

I recalled that we had just crossed a shallow river with a bed of loose stones, but I could not remember a precipice. Heart in mouth, I hurried with Sandy back to the spot. There we found Tom, head in hands, supported by Noor. Beside him my purblind geriatric horse was peacefully drinking. It appeared that Tom had indeed fallen from it, and struck his head on a rock. He was certainly half stunned, and we could not tell whether he was concussed; but at least it appeared unlikely that he would be standing upright if he had fractured his skull.

We decided to abandon Rahman's plan to make for the first village, still several hours on. Happily we soon came to two stone bothies beside a stream, and agreed, for once unanimously, to stop for the night.

Tom lay down in one of them and immediately fell into a deep sleep, while the horsemen made a fire and put on a kettle for tea. (Afghans appeared to share with the English an absolute trust in the cup of tea as a sovereign remedy in every crisis.) We were too dispirited to make soup; instead we ate buns made for us in Parian from bread and sugar, and, like a Father Christmas, Charles produced some Kendal Mint Cake.

The mishap had been a reminder of our vulnerability. In this limbo of boulders and precipices we were wholly dependent on the services of Rahman and Noor who were becoming increasingly jumpy. Clearly they had not counted on this combination of unknown hostile territory and puny fractious foreigners unable to load and unload their own horses, unable to understand their orders, and given to shouting at them in incomprehensible English. Our safari was in danger of turning into a rough house.

I consulted Sandy, and through Stephane we told Rahman that from now on we would consider him to be in charge of the convoy, and would follow his instructions. In return we asked to be kept informed of all plans, so that we knew what to expect. We offered peace offerings in the shape of two Swiss army penknives bought in London. Noor had a pair of boots with no socks and no laces. Sandy gave him his own walking shoes – several sizes too large – and I gave both Noor and Rahman a pair of thick English socks. The diplomatic initiative had no effect on the flow of information, which remained non-existent; but it gained a valuable truce.

In the night I lay awake with the smell of dung in my nostrils and the sound of Sandy snoring on one side, and imagined an army of lice advancing from where Stephane lay on the other. We had the equivalent of £160 left in Afghan currency to last for the twelve remaining days of the journey, for humans, horses and emergencies alike. It was simply not enough; but there was nothing to be done. I fell asleep and awoke a few hours later with a wholly unjustified feeling of well-being.

16. Near Catastrophe on the Kantiwar Pass

A minor benefit from the rapprochement of the night before was to come to me in the form of a permanent change of horses: mine now became a pack-horse, and in its place I was given a much stronger animal whose only detectable vagary was a dislike of being mounted. Every time I wanted to get back on to it after dismounting for one of the frequent awkward corners or climbs, it would wait until I had a foot in its rope stirrup and then set off briskly. This issue remained a source of contention between us for the rest of the journey; but at least the animal was a goer.

The night's sleep had restored Tom, who had a large bump on his head as a memento, but no headache. His most serious complaint was that his shaving cream had exploded in his bag, a bearable misfortune since we had long since given up the niceties of toilet.

Our route followed the river all that day down a valley. We saw only a few travellers, stray *mujahideen* for the most part on their way to the Panjsher or Badakshan, but not the colourful robbers of which we had heard so much.

In the evening we came to the destination that Rahman had hoped to reach the night before: this was what Stephane called the 'restaurant', in fact a glorified *chaie khana*. A party of *mujahideen* with donkeys was also passing through on their way from Pakistan and we waited on the hillside while they ate.

It was quite large, a split-level affair of stones and mud with several flat roofs stacked high, with a covering of straw and grain as much to keep the rats away from the harvest as to keep in the heat in the winter. On a flat pole outside there fluttered the green and white colours of the Jamayat-i-Islami.

Eventually the owner came up to us. He was a wild-looking man with a long nose, disturbing grey eyes, and a pistol in his belt. The moment I saw him I recognized in his features what Eric Newby had meant when he wrote of 'the air of scarcely controlled violence' about the first Nuristanis he met.

Negotiations were conducted by Stephane, who asked for meat. Speaking in a high nasal whine, the man told us that we could buy a goat for 900 *afghanis*, which meant that dinner would cost us the equivalent of £1.50 a head. Indeed, he added, he had the very goat; we accepted the offer, and a moment later, producing a knife from where it was lodged beside the pistol, he cut the animal's throat.

Inside the restaurant we climbed a ladder to a platform supported on tree trunks overlooking the cooking area. The room had no chimney and the smoke had nowhere to go except into our eyes. Tom, sitting below beside the cook, shifted his feet and accidentally kicked over a pot of unidentified liquid, at which the owner flew into a rage and yelling at the top of his voice turned us all out. Retiring to our sleeping quarters, a room at the back of the house, we resigned ourselves, now that Tom had so literally put his foot in it, to another night without food.

Then, as we were getting into our sleeping bags, the goat arrived. It had been divided not among the seven of us, but among double our number, to include some new arrivals; and as a result was more of an appetizer than a meal. When Stephane complained, the owner launched into another tirade: he had a brother in the next valley who, we would find, charged exactly the same rates. Nobody, he assured us, had ever complained before (perhaps, because like us, they had been unarmed).

There were two disturbances in the night. It began to rain, and we moved my waterproof sheet, which was fastened to the door, to cover the precious camera gear and cans of videotape outside. The second awakening was to a fearful rumpus, and for one moment I thought our landlord was on the loose again, perhaps going over the bill with an early departing guest. Stephane went out to investigate, and a few minutes later the row ceased. In our physically weakened state the last thoughts to enter our minds while we were in Afghanistan were erotic ones. Not so the donkeys. When Stephane returned he told us that one had broken loose and had tried to mount one of our horses, which had taken violent exception to this ambitious project.

I fell asleep again and dreamed that I was recommending Stephane for canonization.

In the morning Stephane began bargaining again with the owner who wanted to charge us the full rate for our dinners. Stephane argued rightly that we had paid for a whole goat and only been given part of a goat. To the price of our dinner an outrageous sum had now been added for straw for the horses. Despite our financial difficulties I told Stephane that we had better pay and go: the man was clearly insane, and if he had a brother in the next valley, he probably had several cousins who were freelance highwaymen on the road between.

Stephane, however, was made of sterner stuff. He flatly refused to give in. After half an hour he suggested that I should give the man what we had offered. I did so. This was by now a total of 2,000 *afghanis*, or 350 less than he was asking. He counted it and gave it back to me.

'Not enough.'

'That's all you get,' Stephane said. For a fearful moment I thought Stephane meant us to turn our backs on this armed and now angry psychopath and walk away.

'Couldn't we offer a little more, and a Polaroid snap as well?'

Stephane snorted. But so it came about. In the end the man accepted the equivalent of fifty pence less than he had asked and three Polaroid photographs of himself, more costly in the long run, but a saving of face all round and vital ready cash. I meant to keep one, but when he took all three I was not disposed to argue.

The man may have been a terrible restaurateur, but at least we had found our colourful robber.

The *chaie khana* stood at the T-junction formed by the bottom of the valley down which we had come, and a cross valley that led down to the village of Pushal, the main town of the Siah Posh people, celebrated for being the last of the Kafirs to yield to the invading armies of Abdur Rahman.

Our route took us uphill in the opposite direction. It seemed that the Siah Posh used the upper reaches of the valleys for summer pastures, so that the stone huts and little patches of green that we came upon were deserted at this time of year.

The weather grew more ominous as we advanced up the valley to the Kantiwar Pass. Now that his worst fears concerning Nuristan had been confirmed, Rahman was in a panic, and when we came to the only open *chaie khana* he severely bypassed it. Stephane stayed behind with Tom to have tea; the rest of us jolted on up the valley which grew stonier and blacker by the hour.

Towards evening Rahman called a halt. We were now told that what lay ahead of us was not a single but a double pass, with no shelter in between. Rahman's idea was that we should start early, by moonlight, travel throughout the next day and complete the double pass before the following nightfall.

The only shelter where we had stopped, high up the valley near the foot of the pass, was a huge rock on one side of which we built a fire. Some nomads had left another nearby: we added its remnants to put on top of ours, made up of armfuls of gorse-like shrub that Noor collected. We watched as a blue-black storm cloud drew a curtain of rain across the mountain wall ahead of us, blotting out the setting sun.

I masterminded a menu of lentil soup followed by Jackson's Earl Grey tea. Rain had got into our sugar bag and we literally had lump sugar with it.

As it grew dark it also grew bitterly cold: the gorse burned hot but fast. While Noor collected more, Rahman astonished us all by singing love songs in a deep baritone voice a great deal more melodious to our Western ears than the sounds we had recorded for our television programme. The moon failed to appear on time, probably because of the high mountains which shortened the horizons around us.

When the gorse ran out, we set off in the freezing dark.

We got lost almost immediately, putting everyone in a bad temper, particularly myself since Rahman had my torch. After a spell in pitch darkness up ever steeper slopes, Rahman told us to dismount and walk so as not to tire the horses for the ordeal ahead. This turned out to be a second Chamar, but this time by night, twice the distance and under a layer of ice.

The final series of zig-zags to the summit began well enough; at first there was only the familiar problem of exhaustion to contend with. Two-thirds of the way up, Sandy gave me a glucose tablet for which at that moment I would readily have mortgaged my future. It was my first bonus; but there was to be a second. By dint of hanging on to my horse's tail I found for myself the next best thing to a ski-lift. Thus I made excellent progress.

Then, at midnight by my watch, the moon appeared. At almost the same moment we reached the ice line.

On the stone slabs that made up our path there now formed a thin slippery layer, as hard as tungsten, so that we were climbing the equivalent of giant black ice cubes. I led my horse, slithering and skating on his metal hooves, but somehow, thanks to sheer physical strength, it managed not to fall to its death. We clambered to the top where, in a cold that gripped the soul, I stopped and beheld a spectacle unlike anything I had ever seen before.

If Chamar looked like the beginning of the world, the view from the top of the Kantiwar Pass, in the middle of the night, resembled its end.

Standing on the ice beside my horse, not daring to move for fear of falling, I looked at the dreadful beauty of the mountain. All round us was dark desolation with, in the distance, the beginning of another morning, revealing another horizon of mountain tops as savagely bare as the one we were on. It was the sort of view best enjoyed through the window of a Boeing.

Then there was a cry in the dark, and I recognized the clarion call of catastrophe. Ahead of me Rahman stirred from where he was waiting, as I was, for the others to arrive. In a moment he passed me and disappeared over the ledge up which we had come. A few minutes after that Tom appeared carrying in his arms what looked like a dead body wrapped in silver foil. It was the silver camera box we had bought in Pakistan, now crushed into a scarcely recognizable shape.

Tom told me that two of the pack-horses had fallen on the ice. One, carrying the camera, had fallen 10 feet on to a ledge hanging over space. There it lay on its back on top of the camera box, kicking its legs in the air. With incredible strength, the two horsemen held its legs and gradually coaxed it to its feet. The other horse had rolled over three times with its load, and was now caught by one leg in a crack between two slabs of rock: Noor was even now prizing the rocks apart.

It was two o'clock in the morning. We had been close to the brink of tragedy: waiting on the ice in a sea of black boulders at 15,000 feet I felt the grip of physical fear.

One by one the convoy assembled at the summit. Last came the two horses that had fallen. Rahman immediately unloaded and fed the terrified beasts. Noor followed, having been kicked by the horse he had rescued. The pair set off ahead of us almost at once.

It was deathly cold. We moved on down the reverse side of the mountain, mercifully less steep, but horrifyingly slippery. I fell once and bruised leg and face, but hardly felt the pain. My horse skidded but stayed upright as I held on to its bridle. After half an hour we caught up with our two horsemen: they had stopped to sleep to allow Noor to recover. The two of them were stretched out on a bare rock with nothing to protect them apart from an army anorak and shirt. The five Europeans huddled together for warmth.

I dozed for a few moments and then woke up, conscious that my body was losing heat. I was afraid that we would fall asleep and freeze to death where we were, trapped on the far side of the moon.

I shook the others awake, and shook the guides as well. We struggled off again, down across the swooping moonscape. Gradually the terrain improved and we turned down into a funnel-shaped defile at the bottom of which, in the early daylight, we came quite unexpectedly across a camp of nomads. There were perhaps fifty of them in several groups: they were striking camp as we arrived. A woman in a red cotton veil with her mobile kitchen on her head and three children at her skirts sailed off like a galleon scolding them as she went. They left not a single scrap of litter behind them.

Some extra source of energy seemed to galvanize us. As I dismounted, a barking mastiff startled my horse, which began to run blindly up the hillside in the direction of its tormentor. Seeing the brute it hesitated. With one hand I caught the horse by the bridle, and with the other hurled a sizeable stone at the dog. To my intense satisfaction the missile struck home, and it ran off howling.

Charles, always greatly addicted to yoghurt, asked Stephane to see if the nomads would sell us their *most*: Stephane came back with *lassi*, the thinner derivative, but under the circumstances a triumph.

We made up a fire and cooked some rice bought in Parian, made more interesting with Sainsbury's raisins, and used up the last of our Russian oil to cook potatoes. The result was a memorable fry-up.

Afterwards we lay on a bank in the morning sun. I slept for half an hour and dreamed of a Laurel & Hardy film I had seen as a child about transporting a piano over the Rocky Mountains. I cannot recall how it ended, but I think there was a gorilla.

We awoke to another bonus: the information about the double pass was wrong. From here it would be all downhill to our next destination of Kantiwar village.

On the debit side, we had already lost one day and according to Rahman we were in danger of losing another. On the long descent from the Kantiwar Pass he continually pressed us to hurry as if our lives depended on it – as, for all we knew, they did. Somehow he managed to keep well ahead of us with two of the three pack-horses which from time to time he rode himself, squatting in a perch on top of its load like a camel driver, while Noor drove the other on foot. Usually one of the Europeans brought up the rear.

The next two days followed a sequence that in memory seems like endlessly sitting through the same film, so that the passage of time is lost. Our path would follow down, or up, the valley; always there was the urgent meaningless message of rushing water in our ears as we rode with our eyes fastened to the track ahead to detect where it was worn to mark the way. Every half-mile or so, we came to a bluff where we would dismount and lead our horses; our path would fall now, and follow along the river bed itself, or else rise suddenly in giant steps over the corner of a valley wall, often over a precipice offering a grand panorama of a waterfall or, according to one's point of view, the prospect of a sudden death drop. Then mounting again we would jog and jolt to the next obstacle.

We encountered only a handful of travellers, mostly returning from Pakistan, and to pass the time on the route to Kantiwar I counted the dead horses. We had reached the sixth when I caught up with Rahman and Stephane in animated conversation. Stephane explained that Rahman was refusing to take us over another pass without extra hands to help with the horses. There were three more to go including the highest, Papruk; moreover the weather was uncertain. He was anxious to press ahead to the nearest stopping place, where there was a Jamayat-i-Islami house just short of Kantiwar. There he meant to press some *mujahideen* into service, using Massud's letter as authority. But our slow progress meant that we might arrive after the *mujahideen* convoy just ahead of us had left. (It was a continuing source of wonder to me that travellers, crossing in opposite directions, provided an up-to-date and reasonably reliable information service throughout Afghanistan.)

Not only did Rahman's plan seem sensible, but clearly it would be irresponsible to risk a repetition of the previous night. It was agreed that Stephane and Rahman would go on ahead. Afghans make progress twice as fast on foot, and the pair set off at *mujahideen* speed, feet scarcely touching the stones as they vanished over the horizon ahead of us.

We were now left with one driver, three pack-horses and Stephane's horse between the five of us: Tom, Charles, Sandy, Noor and myself.

Late in the evening we came across a man heading in the opposite direction. We had been misled too often to place our trust in statistical information of any kind in this land. But this traveller sported a large black digital diver's wristwatch. In the absence of Stephane we were dependent on a combination of Tom's rudimentary Farsi together with sign language for enquiring the distance to the Jamayat house. The difficulty with digital clocks is that while they display *the* time they cannot convey Time: it was therefore impossible to point to the numbers on the dial, our normal practice. Instead Tom held up his fingers.

'One hour? Two hours? Five hours?'

The man said something. Tom tried again. The man repeated the identical answer. Tom checked with Noor. 'He says it is two hours and ten minutes. He won't change his story.'

It was of course the fatal precision of the ten minutes that we could not ignore. Applying our normal conversion table we doubled the figure for ourselves to four and a half hours. It took seven.

At the end of the valley as night fell Sandy and I paused at the top of a steep dusty incline down to the junction of two side valleys below us. Then taking our horses by the bridle we half ran, half skied down its side. Like falling drunks, we reached the bottom unharmed, but my bridle broke. There we found Charles, Tom and Noor waiting for us. They appeared to have joined up with some other travellers, and so at least they knew which way to turn at the junction.

We had now been on the move with only short pauses, one for half an hour of sleep, for almost thirty-six hours. I was scarcely able to keep my eyes open.

'They say it's another hour,' said Tom. We knew only too well what this meant; but at least we had our horses.

As we headed along a side valley, going uphill again now, I occupied my mind with the business of forcing myself to stay awake. Without my torch and with my bridle broken, I had no means of steering other than placing my horse behind Sandy's and hoping for the best.

Then an old trouble returned: I began to have hallucinations again.

The first extraordinary vision was of Sandy in front of me walking his horse under a fly-over. I had no idea that there was a four-lane highway in Nuristan; but here it was. It seemed incredible, but then many incredible things had happened, so I settled with myself that it must be true. Then, to my left, there was the long flat roof of a shopping precinct, with a barrier of the kind that lifts electronically, leading into a multi-storey car park. But the barrier did not lift. Instead my horse kept going, while the barrier, turning into the bough of a tree, pressed against my chest. I yelled to Sandy.

'Are you all right?' he enquired.

'Wonderful! Except that I'm being bisected.'

'Hold on, old man!'

Under the circumstances it may have been unsound advice. However, at that moment there was a rending sound which I at first took to be my rib cage; but by great fortune the bough had broken first. At least the shock kept me awake. In the darkness ahead, waving torches marked our way. I reflected that we would surely never have found it had it not been for the chance encounter with the other travellers. Only later did I learn that Stephane had sent them to meet us.

We came to a camp into which my horse, mistaking it for our destination, trotted out of control through the middle of a group of nomads having dinner.

We reached the Jamayat house an hour later, and were greeted by friendly strangers who showed us to a room where Stephane was asleep; we lay down and were unconscious in a moment, only to be woken for some boiled chicken – all but Sandy, who could not be roused. Then, climbing back into our sleeping bags, we fell dead asleep once more.

The friendly faces of the night before were still there in the morning. They belonged to a Panjsheri family that had settled in Nuristan but were moving out. Through Stephane we asked why. A young man with two magnificent hand-wrought daggers in his belt told us that two members of the family had been murdered the week before. They knew who the killer was, because he had come back the next day and told them that if they did not move out he would kill the rest of the family as well. There was nothing they could do. There was no question of law.

Using Massud's letter Rahman had already drafted two *mujahideen* to help us over the next pass. We decided to get going as quickly as possible.

As I waited for the loading to be completed I listed in my head the dangers facing us. There had been four, in an order that changed daily: injury to horses; injury to humans; weather, and starvation. I now added a fifth: murder.

17. A Journey through the Middle Ages

We went at a more gentle pace next day, and arrived at Kantiwar village early in the afternoon.

At first I thought I was still suffering from hallucinations. Astride the valley in front of us was what looked like a fine medieval village on a hill of its own. The houses, supported on wooden stilts, ran piggy-back one above the other up the hillside: at the summit was a crumbling building that could once have been a castle. We might have been in Tuscany.

We tied up our horses in a little square, charmingly shaded with trees. At one edge stood the *chaie khana* under a flat roof of reeds supported by upright wooden poles. In it we dumped our bags and eagerly set out to explore the town and, more particularly, its inhabitants. There were two of these, sitting on a stone bench, observing us as we unloaded. They were dressed like other Afghans that we had seen, with Chitrali hats (Chitral, now in Pakistan, was once a part of Nuristan) and they were wrapped in *patous*. They appeared neither friendly nor shy: we were foreigners, perhaps the first they had seen, but we were on their ground, without arms and at their mercy; and we felt it.

The most striking aspect of them was their facial structure. Fine bones and long aquiline noses gave them an air of aristocratic distinction, to which watchful light blue or grey eyes added the sharp look of birds of prey. There was something degenerate about them, as if generations of inbreeding had taken its toll. The sinister impression of incest grew on us as we looked around and saw that the inhabitants all looked strikingly alike, with the same pointed predatory faces. Over this Shangri-la there hung a small smell of evil.

By now Stephane had entered negotiations for our dinner with a blind man who had a piping voice. While he was talking, another inhabitant came up to tell us that the headman wanted to see our credentials. To this we readily agreed, thinking to ingratiate ourselves to the point of an invitation to eat. Sandy elected to wait with the bags while Charles, Stephane and I followed the blind man. Without assistance he led us across a narrow bridge formed by a double tree trunk to a house with a ladder propped against it.

We climbed the ladder and were shown into a small room with a desk and chair. We sat on the floor. Presently three men came in. They might have been brothers. The oldest sat at the desk, and the other two on the floor opposite us. The one nearest to me opened his mouth, in which position it remained throughout the interview, as if he were about to speak.

The old man began with a longish opening speech, to which Stephane replied. I asked what had been said.

'He says he is extremely important.'

Another speech followed. Stephane turned to me:

'Have you got Massud's letter?'

The man read it with care, turning it round to study the signature. He spoke again. Stephane translated.

'He says it is not properly authenticated and should be addressed to him. We are illegal visitors.'

'What does he want?'

'He wants proof that we are not Russians.'

We had left our passports in Pakistan on the advice, clearly questionable, of Es Haq. However, I knew that Charles had a cameraman's Scotland Yard pass which would have the word 'London' written on it, so I asked him to show it. Charles looked worried.

'They won't issue a new pass if I lose it.'

'They won't issue a new body if you lose that.'

Reluctantly he handed it over to the headman, who was now writing furiously on Massud's letter. The man opposite continued to gape.

There was a further exchange with Stephane. The headman then delivered his summing up, apparently directed to his companions, a judge addressing the jury. Stephane paraphrased it for us.

There was the possibility of having us shot at once as Russian spies; then there was the alternative of locking us in the room below the house until confirmation of our credentials arrived from the Panjsher. There was also a third possibility, opened up by

Stephane's case for the defence: although we had illegally entered Kantiwar, there was nowhere other than Kantiwar itself where legal permission could be sought. At this point there was a diversion, as, somewhat to our relief, a small boy arrived: even in this sinister place it seemed unlikely that we would be subjected to physical violence in the presence of a child. All at once the old man seemed to lose interest. He took the boy by the hand and left.

Night was falling. We followed the gaping man who stopped outside a mosque and began to chant. It was only then that I realized that he was the local *mullah* and that he was calling the faithful to prayer. Only ninety years earlier the grandparents of these people would have been worshipping Imra the Creator, Moni the Prophet and Gish the God of War.

Dinner was a meagre and expensive affair, divided between nine of us including the two extra *mujahideen*, who looked as unhappy as everyone else. Afterwards the blind man produced a set of cups from an attaché case and we drank sweet tea. For breakfast we requested eggs. Asked how we would like them cooked, I hit on the brainwave of having them raw. In this way we could make a quicker getaway, we would lose no nourishment from them, and the villagers would not have the opportunity of poisoning us.

I dreamed of the blind man stealing our belongings in the dark. We left early with Rahman, like the Duke of Plazatoro, leading the retreat from the fore. He had refused to address a word to anyone since we entered Kantiwar and I do not believe he slept a wink all night.

That morning the evil spirits of Kantiwar possessed all of us: all manner of quarrels broke out over issues of no consequence.

The children were one of the village's many redeeming visual features. As we were waiting to leave I saw what I thought at first was an exotic bird moving along a wall: it turned out to be a child wearing a cloche hat made of bright patchwork quilting with a tassle. As we left we came across some more. Charles became enraged with me because I refused to dig into my bag, tightly roped to my horse, to get out my camera. Instead he photographed them himself with far better results than I could ever have achieved.

We were well clear of Kantiwar when we discovered that Stephane had vanished together with the horse carrying our completed film. Apart from being the main fruit of our expedition it now represented a financial value greater than all the rest of our equipment. We imagined that he had been murdered or arrested until, half an hour later, he appeared and said with dreamy nonchalance that he had been shopping: he had some walnuts. Reproved, he retreated into silence.

Then Sandy flew at Tom for allowing a pack-horse under his care to bolt up a blind gully from which it had to be retrieved. When we caught up with the main body of the convoy we found that the two extra *mujahideen* had deserted, taking with them a supply of our flour and rice. Charles began an argument with Rahman, and half in jest Rahman raised his whip at him. The half that was jest was bad enough: but it was the other half that was more disturbing. To placate Rahman I offered to pay for a replacement for the two *mujahideen*; and from nowhere a fine-looking, powerfully built man appeared and offered to take us over the next pass for 1,500 *afghanis*, the equivalent of £15. Over Stephane's walnuts, which we cracked on stones, a deal was struck. Trusting no one I offered to pay half in advance, but the man was adamant that I should pay the entire sum. Some atavistic instinct stirred in me: I found myself insisting that he give his word that he would stay with us until we had safely cleared the obstacle, which I now learned was called Mum Pass, and made him shake hands on the deal. Seldom has an advance payment been made against more slender collateral.

The man, however, was as good as his word. The issue before us was whether to make a direct assault on the pass, which was more steep than high, or to take a longer route round it by the river that might by now be in spate. After discussions with Rahman, stretching over much of the day, leaning first this way and then that, it was agreed that we would tackle Mum direct. The news was a relief to me: we had now less than 10,000 *afghanis* left to feed eight people for approximately eight days, and the shorter the route the less money we would need. Already we had no provision for any contingency: one closed pass, and we were done for.

The only thing that seemed to smile that day was the scenery. We were walking along a gorge of pines on a slowly rising pass in autumn sunlight. Ahead of us and to our left was the pass, a steep sandy wooded climb, its summit guarded by rocky teeth set in a now familiar grimace. At its foot we came to a group of stone and wooden houses. One of them was a *chaie khana*, and it appeared to be open. I turned to consult Sandy.

'Everyone is in a filthy temper. We're all tired and hungry, but if we stop to eat we'll use up valuable time and money.'

'Quite. I appreciate the financial situation. On the other hand I'd love some chicken.'

'We have to decide what to do.'

'Absolutely.'

'What do you think?'

'Well, on the one hand . . .'

Suddenly, and unpardonably, I lost my temper, and accused him of facing both ways to avoid difficult decisions. I regretted my outburst immediately.

By now the others had arrived, all of them down at heel. At once Sandy rose to the occasion and gave us all a pep talk. He was going to eat. Everyone was to settle down. We were going to rest and recover and proceed in the morning, whatever the consequences. It was his finest hour, and it did the trick. The expedition leader had rallied his men.

Adding to our problems, and confirming the wisdom of his decision, the horses were also in a bad state. No sooner had it arrived than my own had lain down fully laden and fallen asleep like a human. Two others had developed sores on their backs. Stephane suggested antibiotic powder; but we had too little to cover the affected areas. Rummaging in my plastic medicine bag I came across a jar of cream that had been puzzling me ever since we left London: on one side was written in capital letters FOR NAPPY RASH and on the other KEEP OUT OF REACH OF CHILDREN. We applied it to the horses together with two tins of Athlete's Foot Powder, and hoped for the best.

For 600 *afghanis* we bought a chicken and had it cooked with the last of our own potatoes, on top of which we crammed in as much rice as we could eat.

We had a fellow guest at the *chaie khana* who turned out to be travelling in our direction. This was an oldish man with one stiff leg who carried with him a bird that he claimed was a falcon, but which Stephane thought was a species of buzzard. The man said he had paid £500 for it and planned to sell it for a profit in Pakistan. According to Stephane, himself a bird fancier, even at a tenth of the price a buzzard dressed as a falcon was hardly a bargain. The bird had a restraint on its wings and an uncertain looking tether round its feet to limit its arc of movement. I did not like its Nuristani look. That night I lay awake with indigestion and listened to the scrabbling sound as it struggled with its bonds.

Mum turned out to be the least trying of the five passes we had to cross. Despite what felt like a few pounds of rice in my stomach it was a particularly easy one for me. Lurking behind the others to avoid being spotted, I once again hung on to my horse's tail at the steepest patches.

The view from the top was Switzerland; and the drop down the other side devastating, chiefly for the horses. At one point we stopped while the prodigiously strong Noor dug a slab of rock from our path; at another he pulled my horse from where it had become wedged in a tree.

At the bottom of the gorge it was a relief to find ourselves in lush vegetation again after a week of bare rock. We waded a river on horseback and spent the day making leisurely progress down the defile beside its far bank.

We came to a wood where the sun shone through huge lemon- and lime-coloured leaves. In another all the trees stood dead, as if struck by lightning a thousand years before. Sandy spotted a falcon stooping on its prey. I stared for several minutes at what looked at first like a man in a tree on the other side of the river, trying to decide whether it was a brown bear. The more I stared the less sure I became.

Unexpectedly that night we were invited to dinner by a local farmer for no reason other than that we were strangers. His son arrived to collect us at a village mosque where we had settled in, bearing a brazier in his hand; and as he led us up some steep steps cut into the rock the light of its burning cedar resin turned the scene into a grand opera stairway.

We ate in a strange house at the edge of the village marred by one of the few ugly crafted objects I saw in all our wanderings. It was a cream-coloured wooden ceiling decoration, a self-conscious attempt to be modern that would have looked more in place in a trendy dentist's waiting-room. In fact it came from Kabul, which to our amazement we learned was only three days' journey away by horse and bus in normal times.

Rahman had refused to join us for the meal, probably because he was afraid of being poisoned. When we came back down the grand opera stairway we found him greatly agitated, and muttering darkly. He told Stephane that one of the horses, a mare, had disappeared and, since it had been tightly tethered, he was clear in his mind that it had been stolen. He had, however, retrieved it after a search of the neighbourhood, from another house.

'Then all is well,' I said.

'No,' said Stephane. 'Rahman says it has been used for purposes.'

'What purposes?'

'Bestial purposes.'

Our imaginations reeled. 'Is it all right? Can it still walk?'

'Rahman says that there is a lot of bestiality in Nuristan but the animal is all right.'

At this point I injudiciously commented:

'Thank heavens it's nothing serious.'

I was to pay for this last remark, which unfortunately Stephane translated for Rahman, who now wagged his finger in my face, while Stephane translated his words:

'He says that you, too, are maltreating the horse by holding on to its tail.'

I had been found out; but not only had I broken the eleventh commandment: somehow my crime was linked with obscure unmentionable practices. Clearly I would have to abandon my private ski-lift.

Already determined not to exchange an unnecessary word with any Nuristani, Rahman now grew steadily more ill-disposed towards us as well. The following night we stayed in a farming village that was the poorest of any we saw. There was nothing to eat: the little mosque, where traditional hospitality required the villagers to let us stay, had no outlet for our cooking fire and, blinded by smoke, we brewed what was almost the last of our soup. Ahead of us was the redoubtable Papruk Pass, the highest and by all accounts the most difficult of all. Just before dark a storm crossed its face.

The ever resourceful Stephane eventually scavenged some cheese from an outlying house which we ate melted into a fondue with bread. Rahman and Noor, both good Moslems, were making a concession by eating out of the same bowl as infidels. Inadvertently, while helping himself, Charles let some melted cheese drop from his lips back into the pot. At once Rahman rose to his feet in disgust and stalked out of the mosque.

Stephane now presented us with an unwelcome surprise. Suddenly he gave us the news that the only way to cross the Papruk Pass was by unloading all the gear at the snow-line and carrying it by hand to the top. We might even need extra blankets to put on the snow for the horses to walk on. He had learned of this in the farmer's house the night before, but forgetting that we did not understand Farsi had omitted to mention it.

Our arrangements were now at sixes and sevens again.

There was little point in asking our guides for plans when even straight information was hard enough to come by. We knew that our entry point in Pakistan was the border nearest to Chitral, 100 miles north of Peshawar, but we could not establish whether we had another five or six days to go: somewhere we kept gaining or losing a day, according to the fluctuations in Rahman's mood and Stephane's zest for translating questions that he knew nobody could answer.

There was talk of taking on an extra porter for Papruk and of paying him off with one of our fading horses; but when the potential candidate saw our animal he understandably insisted on cash instead. Stephane hinted that Rahman carried some money with him which I could repay in Pakistan, but it was a question of picking the moment to approach him.

By the strange telepathy that we had now grown to take for granted we knew that there was yet another group of *mujahideen* waiting ahead of us at the foot of the pass for the morning light, so it made sense to start early to try to catch them up and recruit assistance.

Alone of us all, Sandy remained unruffled. As we set off for the Papruk Pass, now in darkness, it was as if the sun had never ceased to shine on his prospects.

Inside the stone hut at the foot of the pass where we sat squashed together, there were no less than five separate fires and no chimney, so that the smoke made us weep – a small price, however, for the breakfast of melted cheese in oil followed by sweet tea.

It had been a four-hour walk. We left at three, got lost at four, threaded our way in the dark up the rising slope and through a divide in the hills leading up the big path.

Our fellow travellers in the hut were *mujahideen* and dealers in lapis lazuli from the mines of Badakshan, which Marco Polo wrote about in the thirteenth century. The Badakshanis were small smiling men with oriental faces, fur hats and pointed moccasins: not one of them looked more than twenty years old. We had observed their strange method of progress, skimming in a line across the rocks at great speed for half a mile or so at a time in a half run, and then pausing for a five-minute breather before the next spurt. They had travelled exactly twice the distance that we had in the same time, although without horses. Crucially for us, four of them agreed to help us over the pass ahead.

It was eight o'clock in the morning by the time we set off for the serious part of the day's work. Our four Badakshanis led the way. At a resting place we noticed that one of the horses, with the worst of the sores, was no longer in the convoy. Looking back, we saw it far below us, grazing on a slope of the mountain where the last green pin cushions of coarse grass yielded to unbroken rock. Stephane told us that Noor and Rahman had decided that it would not survive the pass, and had cut it loose. There was a chance that travellers in the opposite direction would find and sell it; more probably it would die of exposure. Circling overhead, other eyes were watching too.

We lost the doomed beast from view as we rounded a shoulder to our left: above us now was the final slope of the pass, rising clear in the snow. Just below the top, against the white, we could see the convoy in front of us, a column of ants winding slowly upwards. Behind us, always hard on our heels, the Long John Silver figure of the bird man limped in our wake.

At the snow-line, we found that the *mujahideen* had unloaded the gear from our horses and, one holding the tail and one the bridle, they were manhandling each in turn across the last traverses to the top; once there, they returned for the baggage, carrying on their shoulders loads that I had only been able to drag across the floor of our hotel.

The weather was perfect: had it not been we would never have managed the last part of the climb. As it was one horse came close to falling to its death on the final near-vertical slide, smoothed to a toboggan run by the other horses. For once there was no false crest to the mountain. At the top of the pass, seated on a rock, I found Sandy, Tom and Charles eating a slab of Kendal Mint Cake. It was the end of Charles's supply.

After the elation of the summit the four-hour walk down the far side seemed nothing; and a new delicacy for our evening meal cheered us further – fresh goat cheese dipped in salt and eaten, bite for bite, with *nan* dipped in hot oil. Perhaps the meal was responsible; perhaps the feeling that after Papruk we had broken the back of the journey.

There were only three or four days to go now to Chitral.

Rahman, however, became steadily more agitated: after Papruk it became clear that he was working himself up for a big scene.

It began with an obscure incident. While we were enjoying green tea in a stopping place, Rahman asked Stephane to order black tea, which he preferred. Apparently Stephane omitted to do so. This for Rahman was a *casus belli*. By way of revenge, he prepared another of his medieval jokes.

Our convoy had once again become spread out, with Tom and myself held up at the back on a narrow path behind a man carrying what appeared to be a front door on his back. Rahman had gone ahead of the main party and, overcoming his terror of all Nuristanis, had taken a villager to one side and persuaded him to bar our way and demand a huge ransom for each horse.

When Stephane, dauntless, sat down to negotiate, the man sprang to his feet and said he could not sit with an evil-smelling infidel. This, it transpired later, was the point of Rahman's joke. Tom and I arrived and Stephane told us what had happened, while Charles, waiting idly by, had taken the opportunity to steal a pomegranate from a nearby orchard.

Tom, already in a rage because he reckoned we had taken a wrong turning and missed a stop for food, shook his fist at Rahman. Rahman shook his fist back. The two squared up for a fight.

Recollections differ on what happened next. Conscious that with one pass still to go, whatever else we needed, we needed Rahman, I stood in front of Tom and said: 'You'll have to hit me first.' By great good fortune he declined the offer.

Meanwhile Sandy appeared on the scene. Informed of events, he stood between the would-be protagonists and told Rahman in a loud voice in English that the incident would be reported; then, drawing himself to his full height, he directed quelling glances about him.

At this point the drama was interrupted. Charles, who had been caught in the act of scrumping, was led on by an enraged farmer;

and through the middle of the group, heading for his unknown destination in central Asia, came the man carrying his front door.

In the few vital moments gained by the diversions, tempers cooled. Still waving his arms, Tom said he was going off to find food. Rahman made a speech which Stephane did not trouble to translate. Tom changed his mind. Charles returned his pomegranate, and the late mid-summer madness left us all.

Later I asked Sandy: 'What did you make of all that? Do you think Rahman was trying to punish us for something?'

'Oh, I don't think so,' said Sandy, 'although it's true that he did seem to be in rather a bad mood.'

By now I was as much preoccupied with money as with hunger. There was no *mujahideen* organization here, like the one in Tere-mengal, to smuggle us over the border into Pakistan, and we had no passports. By the time we had eked out our remaining cash to cover our bare needs on this side of the border, there would be nothing left to offer as bribes to frontier guards except travellers' cheques, which hardly seemed suitable for the purpose. However, I consoled myself the next morning by selling a pair of Sandy's waterproof trousers to a man for the equivalent of £1. Sandy was indignant, but though it represented a large book loss, it might also mean a meal.

Following along a tumbling river we came to a small town called Nik-Muk, which we entered through a triumphal trellis-work arch. A double cantilever bridge of wood and stone spanned the river at its centre. Traditional Nuristani houses with complicated carving stretched up the hillside beyond.

In the middle of the little town we were stopped by an armed sentry outside a small military-looking headquarters with a flag and a covered cannon, which could well have been a veteran of the war of 1895. We were shown into a room where we waited for the *malik*. Nothing happened. We were then ushered into a nearby tea-house, the only one we visited in Afghanistan that had chairs and tables. A line of local inhabitants sat against the opposite wall looking at us. An old man spat into his hands and rolled the spittle on to the floor.

Over tea we learned that we were in the administrative centre of the region. It seemed that the system of government in the area leaned towards socialism, presumably partly as a result of a decade of Marxist rule in Kabul; but also, according to one informant, as a result of contacts made with French socialists in previous decades. If we waited, the *malik* could issue us with letters entitling us to free food and accommodation in a people's rest house.

But the *malik* never appeared, and after a while the townsfolk seemed to lose interest in us. When I went to settle our bill the cook, who doubled as cashier, told us that if we would stay for lunch as his guests we could have our tea as well without payment.

Stephane was every bit as curious as I to become further acquainted with this strange system – all the more if it was to entail a meal. But Rahman argued forcefully that it could cost us a day. If we pressed on we might reach the village of Peshawarak, at the foot of the last pass into Pakistan, by nightfall. If not we would have to wait another day to cross it. His reasoning prevailed.

Pausing to buy some round cheeses, Pakistani toffees that tasted of soap, and cigarettes (an expensive luxury under the circumstances, but both Tom and Stephane were chain-smokers), we hurried on towards the Bigosht Pass.

We were making excellent progress, and had paused in a clearing of birch trees to wait for the pack-horses. When they did not arrive Tom went back to investigate. A long time later he returned with Stephane bearing the video camera, this time without its crumpled silver box, but with water dripping from it. One of the pack-horses, it seemed, had decided to have a drink in the river; in a hurry to reach Peshawarak, Rahman had gone into the water to drive it out. Rahman had a way of clouting the horses between the ears using the wooden heel of his whip as though to stun rather than goad. Most of the horses did not seem to mind; but this one apparently did. Instead of making for the bank, it had plunged deeper into the fast flowing river. In a moment the water was up to its withers; in another it had closed over our precious camera.

For the second time, the two horsemen had pulled the poor brute to safety. They now appeared in the clearing, looking none the worse for wear, Rahman riding the camera horse which he coshed from time to time to keep it moving. But the episode had cost us another day.

It was too late by now to reach Pesharawak. We made our way instead to a rest house just short of it, taking turns to experience the extraordinary discomfort of trotting while hugging a heavy television camera.

We slept in a first-floor room with weirdly carved upright wooden supports. With dwindling funds and growing appetites, we had reason to regret that we had not stayed for a free meal in Nik-Muk. After a meal of boiled mutton, we were almost broke.

Before he went to bed Tom took the camera to pieces with a view to drying it to prevent further damage. It appeared to consist of a thousand tiny electronic objects now strewn among the stray wisps of straw on tables, floor and shelves. As a child I once irreversibly took to pieces my grandmother's carriage clock and I thought Tom would never even find the bits, let alone reassemble them. 'Oh, no problem,' he said. Nor was there.

During the night I thought I heard the blowing and munching sound of a horse eating straw in the room. My watch read a quarter past nine, or a quarter to three, I could not be sure which. Then I realized we were on the first floor which was approached by a wooden stairway. Looking again, I saw that the source of the sound I heard was Sandy squirting himself with flea powder.

We reached Peshawarak late next morning: like Nik-Muk it was a charming village set in a fertile valley. Its little main square was lined like a stage set on three sides with carved doorways, and open on the fourth. Such was the curiosity of its inhabitants that when we settled into our ground-floor rest-house room they leant through the open windows to stare at us, and when we closed the shutters they came and sat inside.

In the afternoon there was a diversion.

For some hours the place had been humming in anticipation. There was to be a game of *buzkashi*, a cross between polo and American football with a few variations: in place of goalposts there was a single circle in the ground, and in place of a ball, a headless goat. *Buzkashi* means 'goat grabbing', but it is said to have originated in Mongolia in a darker age when prisoners of war were used instead of animals.

We watched the game from a flat roof covered with drying maize.

The horses glistened with the oil rubbed on their flanks to prevent their opponents getting a grip. As they came into the little arena, a roughly round area with a rock in the middle, they pawed the ground. There was an air of excitement in the crowd to match any cup final.

It started with the two teams, about twenty in all, galloping off into the distance, and then, a moment later, galloping back again.

There then ensued what looked like a wrestling match on horse-back, with blocking moves, cries to curdle blood, and somewhere in the middle of it all a rider hugging the dead goat, which he had to manipulate into the circle. The game was played with skill and unparalleled ferocity. To my hungry eyes it seemed nothing more nor less than an outrageous way to treat the Sunday joint.

The Bigosht Pass was by no means the worst. It was not the steepest, nor the longest; nor was there snow, although the weather was foul. It was simply one pass too many. Symptoms of dysentery had returned to attack intestines and weaken climbing muscles. I trudged up the slopes feeling like a very old man, thighs fast failing to respond to the task of lifting the weight of my body again and again. Ahead of me, labouring too, I could see Sandy and Charles. Youthful strength and stamina carried Stephane and Tom ahead of the rest of us.

I was back to counting TIMBERLANDs backwards in the dust ahead of me, hoping for a miracle. At a corner I sat ignominiously down to watch a line of Badakshanis prance up the mountainside towards me. As they reached me their leader paused, and signalled me to join them. Too tired to laugh, I found myself staggering to my feet. Far from resuming their Badakshani pace, the leader actually took my hand and, like a nanny, pulled me up the next 100 yards. Then, after a short rest, we walked on at a pace I was just able to sustain unaided, if only from shame, until we came to another stone bothy where our party was making tea. We all sat down; I gave my benefactor all I had in my pocket, a squashed hard-boiled egg. I wished it had been made of solid gold.

It was the last pass. At its top, as ever, the human capacity to banish pain wiped everything from our minds except the pleasure of gazing at the view in front of us – the mountains of Pakistan.

18. A Red Tape Welcome

If our wanderings through Afghanistan had their moments of glory, leaving it was not one of them.

At the foot of the Bigosht Pass we halted to consider the choice before us. We could either lie up until nightfall in some nearby bothies and then steal our way past the little frontier post, said to be unattended after dark; or we could try to slip through unnoticed with the crowd of Badakshani travellers to whom the frontier guards turned a blind eye: this would be the higher risk, but the more immediate reward.

The choice was taken from us. While we were talking, Rahman set off at full tilt with the horses, riding mine. By the time we had caught up with him the frontier post was in sight, and we could not turn back without drawing attention to ourselves. We wrapped ourselves in our *patous* to hide our bright green wind jackets, and covered our heads with *mujahideen* scarves or whatever else we could lay our hands on. In Sandy's case this appeared to be a bath towel.

The frontier post was no more than a stone hut in the narrow neck of the valley down which our path had led us. The way was jammed with *mujahideen* when we got there. A single official not in uniform was standing against a wall, letting the arrivals past.

A party of *mujahideen* was waiting to come through in the other direction. One of its numbers wore an ear-ring, another had a flower in the barrel of his gun and a third wore a pair of dark glasses with the price still stuck on to one lens.

The crowd would have been more of a help to us had we not been taller by head and shoulders than our travelling companions; but even this was a minor difficulty compared with the problem of slipping eight fully laden horses across a frontier known to be one of the world's most notorious for drug smuggling. Trying to banish from my mind the simile of the camel and the eye of a needle, I looked back at Afghanistan. A great rain cloud blackened the sky behind us. The storm that we had dreaded ever since leaving the Panjsher had broken. By morning Papruk would be impassable. As I watched, a barrier of rain came down and blocked Bigosht from our view, the final curtain ringing down on Afghanistan.

Not, however, on our troubles. At the little frontier post the inevitable happened.

From the back of the scrummage I saw the frontier guard's eye pick out Tom, Sandy and Charles. Then it met mine, and I knew the game was up.

Ahead of us Noor and Rahman had passed the scrutiny, taking with them two of the horses. Somehow in the confusion, I found myself in charge of my own horse as well as the pack-horse carrying the film, behind and separate from the others who were now being led off.

Thinking somehow still to retrieve the irretrievable, I spurred the two animals on in the general direction of Pakistan, imagining that I might at least prevent the film from being impounded.

Infected by the drama, the two horses charged through the little frontier hut, pursued by myself on foot. Veering to the left, they careered into a farmyard where men were feeding chickens. The birds panicked, whereupon the horses followed suit and, wheeling in a circle, cantered out again. In its excitement one of them became wedged between two trees, failing to grasp that while there was room for its head to pass, its body together with the load of camera equipment stood no chance. It kept pressing forward in a series of ineffectual lunges. Out of the tail of my eye I could see the frontier guard approaching. In desperation I went round to the front of the horse and punched it hard on the nose. It did the trick. Apparently none the worse for wear the beast retreated and stood about looking for something to eat.

But it was too late to escape. A moment later I was being led to the house of the local policeman where Sandy and the others were waiting, staring blankly at a man with an extraordinarily high-pitched excitable voice.

Somehow the man's hysteria made us all calm down. Even Rahman appeared subdued. We had by now resigned ourselves to the further delay of an encounter with the Pakistani authorities. We argued that we had not exactly broken the law, since we had valid

passports and were entitled to be in Pakistan, although our passports were in Peshawar; but we had certainly left the country
illegally and were now in a restricted area. All this added up to a
prima facie case beyond the competence of the local policeman,
who decided to accompany us to Garm Shishma, a frontier town
and terminus for the horses, where there was a police station. The
thought of being in the company of a man whose uniform level of
speech was a scream was not an agreeable one, but it was preferable
to his first notion of holding us at the frontier while he went off to
consult higher authorities.

On the ride to the one-time spa of Garm Shishma ('Hot Springs'
in Urdu), our policeman stopped to hold a conversation with a man
on the other side of the valley, his emasculated voice carrying clear
across the intervening space; after several minutes the second man
ambled in our direction, paused at the river to take his boots off,
waded over, donned his boots and joined us. He turned out to be
the second-in-command of the local constabulary, a pleasant
enough individual who took a fancy to Tom, to whom he presented
a handful of marijuana.

As spas go, Garm Shishma was not in the de luxe category. We
slept in a hotel, half a dozen to a single back room with no window,
and a door that fell open by gravity, where we were given tea with
condensed milk. Sanitation meant the river bank. In the morning
we were called by the second-in-command who announced in a
voice of awe that the Commissioner of Police in Chitral had summoned us. Happily his screaming superior had gone home.

Sadly we said good-bye to the patient and friendly Noor, and the
horses: I was glad to see that the half-blind one seemed well when
we left him. Then with all our luggage we climbed into a small
pick-up truck, together with Rahman, the policeman, Stephane
and a new young acquaintance of his, who was ready to lend us
some money until we reached Peshawar provided he had his father's
approval.

It was like coming in from the Middle Ages.

On the drive to Chitral we blinked at the football fields, and the
irrigation channels made of cement instead of stone. Disbelievingly
I looked at the familiar colonial-style police uniforms and cap
badges, and the line of white-washed stones outside the police

barracks. There was even something reassuring about the familiar after-taste of condensed milk.

The Commissioner of Police in Chitral explained to us that matters were not so simple as we had supposed. There would have to be routine investigations, but the telephone line to Peshawar was out of order for the day. It would require a magistrate to determine whether there was a case for us to answer; we could, however, be provided with legal assistance. Meanwhile, we would take tea together.

Legal assistance proved to consist of a young man with a great command of legal jargon and a passion for detail. He told us that he was anxious to secure a place at the London School of Economics.

'The question at the heart of the case is this: you have entered Pakistan by an unfrequented route. There is a precedent here.' He stretched out his hand for a heavy bound volume of the Criminal Code of Pakistan. 'We must face this issue fairly and squarely. It is a criminal case. Don't worry about a thing. I will take care of you and in due course justice will be done. The procedure is clear. We have to determine whether a distinction exists in law between the concept of "unfrequented" and the further concept of "unauthenticated".'

I asked him whether he meant perhaps 'unauthorized'. The young lawyer hugged himself with delight at the prospect of the extra nicety.

'Now that', he said, 'would be a more serious matter.'

Our hotel was a dingy and sinister establishment: the sun had long since set on its day with the Raj. Its grimy basins had no plugs and only cold water. On the mirror above mine, an American tourist had left a despairing message traced in the dust: 'GET ME BACK TO BOSTON DAD.' In spite of its shortcomings I shaved, blunting two new blades on my beard.

Over supper we were joined by a black-bearded man who introduced himself in the grand manner, as Khallilullah Nuristani, Political Leader and Foreign Minister of the Islamic Revolutionary State of Afghanistan; he had a visiting card to match. Stephane had found him somewhere as a replacement for the young man from Garm Shishma whose father evidently did not consider us a sound business investment. However, Khallilullah Nuristani assured us in excellent English that he could solve any problem we might have.

He began with a short political lecture. Massud, he made clear, was small beer. The revolution had begun in Nuristan, and growing from there had reached five million people. The super-powers were now looking for a truly national leader. Massud was an unsophisticated peasant, famous only because the Russians were attacking him. Take the limelight from the Panjsher and Massud would be eclipsed. Already he was outmanœuvred in Peshawar. Foreign aid coming in was diverted from the Jamayat-i-Islami to the rival Hisb-i-Islami because of their links with Pakistani Pathans: the Pakistani commissioner of refugees, a Pathan himself, controlled the funds.

The lecture started impressively enough. In the middle of it he paused to roll a cigarette which he lit, inhaled deeply, and passed to his bodyguard. There was the sweet smell of marijuana. The bodyguard offered it to Sandy, who declined on the grounds that he only smoked cigars. After several deep puffs the bodyguard returned it to his leader, who resumed his discourse.

'We do not need small beer. What is needed here is a truly major personality and leader.'

It was by now clear whom he had in mind.

As the evening wore on the bodyguard became more and more sleepy. At one point his gun fell to the floor.

'And now', concluded our new friend 'I will write a letter instructing members of the Islamic Revolutionary State to clear the path for you with the authorities.'

He did so. Signing it he handed the envelope to a messenger who went off somewhere. Then he turned back to us.

'Meanwhile, I can show you some excellent carpets that I have in my shop. If you would like to see them I can arrange for some extraordinary prices. I am well known, all over the world, in the business. I have friends in New York. Ring this number when you next go there and mention my name.' He took his visiting card and wrote the number on the the back. It was 666-6666.

By the time we rose to go to bed, the bodyguard appeared to have passed out.

A new and polite young police officer had been assigned to take us to Peshawar. To our delight we found ourselves in reserved seats the following morning on the regular internal airline flight to Peshawar. This reduced the journey from two days' drive to one hour. As the plane flew, we covered approximately the same distance that we had travelled in the two weeks since leaving the Panjsher.

So far the bureaucracy had been working for us, drawing us through its mysterious web towards our intended destination. But once in Peshawar it soon became clear that we were back in the administrative trap, like the soup bag, in a system from which nobody seemed to have the power to release us.

We were not exactly under arrest, but our passports were impounded. By happy foresight Charles had brought two, and he slipped out of the country that night with the film.

For the rest of us, a bizarre sequence of interviews now got under way.

The police officer returned to Chitral and was replaced by yet another, who drove us at high speed to the police headquarters. At full tilt we passed a sign in its gateway which read ACCIDENTS ARE CAUSED. As if to prove the point a sleeping policeman set in the road caused the car to lurch, throwing us from our seats and cracking our heads against its metal roof. Outside the headquarters building another sign proclaimed JUSTICE THROUGH SCIENCE. We were received by a fierce-looking officer who asked:

'Are you pure British?'

There was a discussion on the meaning of the term 'true blue'. Then he asked:

'Have you been in Hendon? I attended a police course there. The British police receive a handsome salary.'

'They don't think so.'

'It costs two hundred dollars for me to go to Karachi and back for a visit. How can I expect to pay two hundred dollars?'

From here we were sent to Crime Branch. There we were told that we must proceed to 'another cell'. This, we discovered to our relief, meant Special Branch, where a major questioned us about our trip, first separately and then together.

On the second occasion as I entered the room, I recognized two figures from the past: Ghul Bas and Akha Ghul. The two were sitting on a bench, looking distressingly reduced by the Kafka setting. With a stab of guilt I wondered if we had got them into trouble: afterwards Sandy told me he had spotted them walking by in the street, waiting to take another convoy of arms into the

Panjsher and, with their unfailing sense of Afghan hospitality, they had volunteered to come and help secure our release.

There was a break for lunch. Afterwards we resumed, this time a step higher up the ladder. Our appointment was with the Deputy Commissioner of Police.

'So you footed it in, I hear?' It was clear from the outset that he was a kindly man; but it was equally clear that he was unable to influence the slow grinding mills of the judiciary. After all, however exalted, he was only a policeman. What was needed now was political clout.

In one of his absences from his office, the young police officer who had been responsible for almost fracturing our skulls turned to me and whispered:

'Sir, I wish to speak to you, but not in front of my Chief. He will not permit it. This affair is censored.'

'Which affair?' I enquired.

'We must stop speaking of this matter when he returns. We should meet later.'

'By all means.'

At that moment the Deputy Commissioner returned.

'Alas it is not possible today for me to give you back your passports. The Minister is being consulted.'

The young assistant drove us back to Dean's hotel. We were now consumed with curiosity. It was he who brought the mystery subject up on the way home, although indirectly:

'I have studied your passports.'

'Do you think you could help us get them back?'

'They say you are important people in television.'

Strangely, this was untrue. We had carefully avoided any reference to television against the entry 'Profession'; but sensing an approach, we said nothing.

'I wish to have your help in presenting a very important matter on television. I would like to discuss it with you.'

His English was imperfect, but the general drift was familiar. He went on earnestly:

'It is extremely important. I wish to establish on world television that Einstein's theory of relativity is incorrect according to the Koran. There is one difficulty. My Chief does not permit me to discuss it. It is censored. But I will meet you at the hotel this afternoon.'

As he spoke, he looked extraordinarily young, but no less single-minded. I began to see what his Chief meant.

There now seemed only one thing left that we could do. At Dean's the telephone in my room was not working so I went to the reception desk and put in a call to the British Embassy in Islamabad.

Then I went to have my first bath for more than two months. Undressing I found myself looking in the glass at what appeared to be a total stranger. Never overweight, I was now confronted with the spectacle of a skeleton with hunted eyes and a pot belly. I looked like the survivor of a concentration camp with a nasty go of *kwashiorkor*.

With indescribable pleasure I bathed not once but twice: once for the body, which turned the water black enough to lose the soap; the second time for the hair. I was dressing when there was a knock at my door.

'Your man at the Embassy is on the telephone, sir.'

The instrument stood where I remembered it, in the reception beside the photograph of the polo players in colonial topees. I picked up the receiver. The voice at the other end said: 'You fellows seem to have got into a fine mess. I think I had better come and sort things out. We know the Minister quite well. He's a decent enough chap.'

As I looked up at the photograph, I wondered whether it was against the rules to invoke help from outside. Then I remembered that in the Great Game our man at the Embassy always played a central role. It may have been my imagination, but I fancied I saw one of the topees nodding to me in approval.